We at Diamond of California, the world leader in culinary and in-the-shell nuts, proudly present NUTS: Sweet and Savory Recipes from Diamond of California. Our company is owned by two thousand farming families who grow half of all the walnuts produced in the United States. Our orchards are located in the vast interior valleys of California, where nature has created ideal growing conditions for Diamond walnuts, the world's favorite.

We will soon celebrate Diamond's 90th anniversary, which will mark our historical commitment to building positive relationships with consumers everywhere. Through the decades, the company has pioneered innovative technology and growing practices to ensure the highest standards of quality and provide superior products, time after time.

We want to help you discover new ways to enjoy culinary nuts — and most especially walnuts — in every meal, and in that spirit we are delighted to offer our collection of delicious recipes and ideas. You will find all-time favorites as well as creative, contemporary dishes from some of America's leading chefs. We hope this blend of tradition and innovation adds to your enjoyment of Diamond nuts for years to come.

Sincerely,

Michael J. Mendes
President/CEO

We at Diamond of California, the world leader in culinary and in-the-shell nuts, proudly present *NUTS: Sweet and Savory Recipes from Diamond of California*. Our company is owned by two thousand farming families who grow half of all the walnuts produced in the United States. Our orchards are located in the vast interior valleys of California, where nature has created ideal growing conditions for Diamond walnuts, the world's favorite.

We will soon celebrate Diamond's 90th anniversary, which will mark our historical commitment to building positive relationships with consumers everywhere. Through the decades, the company has pioneered innovative technology and growing practices to ensure the highest standards of quality and provide superior products, time after time.

We want to help you discover new ways to enjoy culinary nuts — and most especially walnuts — in every meal, and in that spirit we are delighted to offer our collection of delicious recipes and ideas. You will find all-time favorites as well as creative, contemporary dishes from some of America's leading chefs. We hope this blend of tradition and innovation adds to your enjoyment of Diamond nuts for years to come.

Sincerely,

Michael J. Mendes
President/CEO

Nuts

SWEET *and* SAVORY RECIPES *from*
DIAMOND *of* CALIFORNIA

Nuts

SWEET and SAVORY RECIPES from DIAMOND of CALIFORNIA

TINA SALTER

WITH STEVE SIEGELMAN

Food Photography by Holly Stewart

Location Photography by Robert Holmes

TEN SPEED PRESS

BERKELEY   TORONTO

TEN SPEED PRESS

Ten Speed Press/Post Office Box 7123/Berkeley, California 94707/www.tenspeed.com

Distributed in Australia by Simon and Schuster Australia, in Canada by Ten Speed Press Canada,
in New Zealand by Southern Publishers Group, in South Africa by Real Books,
in Southeast Asia by Berkeley Books, and in the United Kingdom and
Europe by Airlift Book Company.

Concept, recipe development, creative and editorial direction by Tina Salter
Written by Steve Siegelman
Art direction and design by Madeleine Corson Design, San Francisco
Food styling by Sandra Cook
Prop styling by Sara Slavin

The trademark "Diamond of California" and the Diamond Design
are registered trademarks of Diamond Walnut Growers, Inc.

The Walnut-Stuffed Artichokes recipe (page 110) reprinted from *The New Enchanted Broccoli Forest* by Mollie Katzen
(Ten Speed Press, 2000); the Country Walnut Mashed Potatoes (page 113) reprinted from *The Olives Table* by
Todd English and Sally Sampson (Simon & Schuster, 1997); the Hazelnut-Cranberry Rugalach (page 174)
reprinted from *The Olives Dessert Table* by Todd English, Paige Retus, and Sally Sampson (Simon & Schuster, 2000).

Library of Congress Cataloging-in-Publication Data
Salter, Tina.
  Nuts : sweet and savory recipes from Diamond of California / Tina
Salter.
      p. cm.
Includes index.
  ISBN 1-58008-347-1
  1. Cookery (Nuts) I. Title.
  TX814 .S25 2001
  641.6'45--dc21
                                              2001002475

First printing, 2001 Printed in China 1 2 3 4 5 6 7 8 9 10 — 05 04 03 02 01

FOREWORD

(BETTY FUSSELL)

I can't imagine childhood without walnuts, because I was a California child. In California, even in the Depression, our Christmas stockings bulged—not with wrapped toys, but with large and small globes of winter fruit. The large globes were navel oranges, each wrapped in its own bright skin. The smaller ones were walnuts, each in its own sealed container. We tore open the wrappings of our few toys quickly in order to spend sun-kissed hours outside, on the front porch, peeling oranges and cracking walnuts—that task of young and patient children—removing the meat within, nugget by nugget, as if we were mining diamonds.

Nor can I imagine adulthood without walnuts, or without nuts of every kind. I've traveled most of the world by now and have never found a country in which nuts of some kind did not complete the most delicious and most nourishing of native dishes: pistachios in Pakistan and Greece, almonds in Sicily and China, peanuts in Africa and Indonesia, cashews in Guatemala, macadamias in Hawaii, Brazil nuts in Brazil. Where would the world be without nuts? Quite apart from their essential life-giving nourishment, I can no more imagine a world without the particular texture, richness, and flavor of nuts than a squirrel can.

Neither could early humans, who first roasted nuts in the ashes of campfires to make their unmistakable taste even tastier. Later, people learned to coat nuts with honey, spice them with salt, mix them with figs and dates or with olives and herbs, grind them into pastes or "butter," press them into oils, and liquefy them into "milk" and "cream." As cooking skills evolved, cooks began to tuck nuts into breads and cakes and cookies and pies, stuff birds with them, coat fish with them, sauce meats with them, heighten vegetables, enliven salads, and glorify chocolate with them. There is nothing so good that nuts won't make it better. A brownie without nuts is like a sky without stars.

But in California's blessed kingdom of nuts, surely the walnut is king. Ancient Greeks thought so too, calling it the kingly nut. The Romans called it brain food, because the convoluted kernel in its shell resembles a human brain within its skull. Spreading from Persia to Babylon to Europe to England and ultimately to America, the most ancient and noble of the world's many kinds of walnuts is still called Persian.

To me, however, the walnut—wherever it came from and wherever it goes—will always be as Californian as I am, since through my long lifetime California has supplied the world with Diamond walnuts. When I moved from the West to the East Coast a half century ago, I discovered America's indigenous black walnut, with its dark, earthy flavor and formidable husk, but it was not my nut. Its shell was not wrinkly brown like wrapping paper. Delicious it was, and is, but it did not speak to the kernel of my life, or to the seed of my childhood.

In my kitchen drawer today, I still have the metal nutpicks and the old-fashioned hinged metal nutcrackers that my grandfather showed me how to work when my hands were too small to hold them. Now, when my grown children come to my New York apartment at Christmastime, on the table I always have a large bowl of walnuts in their shells, which we can crack at leisure as we crack jokes, pick one another's brains, and mine the nuggets of our past. So how can I not embrace a book so full of nut lore and of enticing recipes for the whole world of nuts, from walnuts and black walnuts to hazelnuts, almonds, pecans, macadamias, pine nuts, and Brazil nuts, reflecting culinary cultures from around the world?

NUTS: A RECIPE FOR BETTER HEALTH

(GENE A. SPILLER, PH.D., CNS)

In ancient times, before the era of agriculture, people went into forests to gather foods that would give them sustenance. Nuts were one of the most important foods they found. They grew in virtually all regions of the earth, and, with their hard shells, they could be stored for long periods of time, while many other foods from plants or animals would quickly spoil. Today, science tells us that our ancestors' instincts were right. Nuts still have an important place in a good diet, just as they did in ancient times.

Let's look into a nut—the seed from which a new plant will grow. We find proteins high in arginine, an amino acid that current research has shown to protect blood vessels and help lower blood cholesterol. Arginine is found only in low levels in most animal proteins.

Nuts also contain vitamin E and some of its lesser-known relatives, like gamma tocopherol—all powerful antioxidants—as well as important minerals like potassium, magnesium, copper, zinc, and calcium that play a key role in heart health. Just as critical, nuts contain the dietary fiber that is so sorely lacking in most modern diets.

Common tree nuts, such as walnuts, pecans, almonds, hazelnuts, macadamias, pine nuts, and Brazil nuts, all contain good fats—the unsaturated fats, mono- and polyunsaturated—while they are extremely low in saturated fats. When we replace some of the saturated fats that are the main fat in most meats and dairy products with the unsaturated fats found in nuts, we take a major step toward more healthful eating. It is well known that the substitution of unsaturated fats for saturated ones results in a drop in high blood cholesterol. The southern Mediterranean diet, in which olive oil, an unsaturated fat, is so important, is a perfect example of this. Heart disease is significantly lower in this region than in parts of the world where saturated fat is consumed in higher quantities. Furthermore, the fats of nuts contain plant sterols that help to control blood cholesterol.

Each nut has its own "health personality" and has something nutritionally unique to offer. The examples are too numerous to cite here. But consider the case of walnuts: They are high in gamma and delta tocopherols and are an excellent source of polyunsaturated fats, including omega-3 fats, related to the beneficial fats found in fish like salmon. These fats have been shown to reduce the risk of heart disease by helping lower cholesterol and by aiding in the prevention of blood clots, which may also lead to strokes. Almonds and hazelnuts are high in monounsaturated fats and alpha tocopherol. And nuts in general are a good source of folic acid, a vitamin that has, in recent years, been found to play an important role in the nutrition of the brain. Could it have been folic acid and omega-3 fats that made our ancestors consider walnuts a "brain food"?

In recent years, several studies from a broad spectrum of respected institutions have confirmed the health benefit of nuts. Prominent among them is a six-year study at Loma Linda University, with more than thirty-one thousand subjects, which showed that people who ate a handful of nuts a few times a week regularly over many years had a lower risk of both fatal and nonfatal heart attacks. In two other major epidemiological studies that followed participants for several years—the Iowa Women's Study, with about thirty-four thousand women, and the Harvard Nurses Study, with about eighty-six thousand nurses—the results were similar to those of the Loma Linda study: regular consumption of nuts meant less risk of heart disease.

While these studies did not intervene in any way with the subjects' dietary habits, in other studies subjects were placed on a good diet and fed a reasonable amount of nuts each day. These studies also confirm the health benefit of nuts. Walnuts, almonds, macadamias, pistachios, and pecans were all shown to lower blood cholesterol.

At the Health Research and Studies Center in Northern California, we carried out two studies in which people with high cholesterol were given three ounces of almonds a day. After just three or four weeks, their "bad" blood cholesterol (LDL) went down, while their good cholesterol (HDL) did not change. And while many subjects were concerned that eating three ounces of nuts every day would make them gain weight, they quickly found that this was not the case, and that nuts gave them that magic feeling of satiety (satisfaction and "fullness").

A second major study at Loma Linda University that followed the long-term study I mentioned earlier found that two to three ounces of walnuts in the daily diet led to lower total cholesterol and a reduction in bad cholesterol. In two other studies, one at the Commonwealth Scientific and Industrial Research Organization (CSIRO) Division of Human Nutrition in Australia and the other at the Hebrew University of Jerusalem, both walnuts and almonds were again found to be very effective in lowering blood cholesterol. Most recently, researchers at the Hospital Clinic of Barcelona found that eating walnuts lessens the risk of heart disease by 11 percent by lowering cholesterol.

Macadamia nuts were also shown to lower blood cholesterol in a study at the University of Queensland in Australia. Recent studies have shown that both pecans and pistachios lower blood cholesterol as well. In another study conducted at our research center, a diet of mixed nuts combined with lots of vegetables, fruits, whole grains, and beans was shown to reduce total cholesterol.

A handful of nuts can help satisfy your hunger while supplying healthful energy along with a variety of important nutrients. Studies are now underway to document the effect of nuts on satiety. These results will help to develop more effective methods of weight control. It is already widely recognized that the feeling of satiety that results from a nut snack at the right time can help prevent excessive cravings for foods that can lead to overeating.

The more we study nuts, the more we realize that they are more than just an acceptable food and more than a mere "indulgence." They are truly one of our superfoods. Today the question is not, Should I give myself permission to eat a few nuts a day? but rather, Am I eating enough nuts for good health?

The good news is that nuts are ideal both as snacks and in a wide variety of recipes, like the ones you'll find in this book. However you enjoy them, remember that a handful of nuts a few times a week—along with a diet that includes plenty of vegetables, fresh and dried fruits, whole grains, and beans—is itself a recipe for better health.

ENGLISH (PERSIAN) WALNUT

Juglans regia

Walnuts, the world's oldest tree food, were a treasured delicacy in ancient cuisines and cultures throughout Europe and Asia. They were brought to California with the Spanish padres in the 1700s. Today, 95 percent of the U.S. walnut crop is grown in California's Central Valley, the very best by Diamond's family of grower-owners.

ALMOND

Prunus dulcis (P. amygdalus)

Believed to have originated in China and Central Asia, the almond was later introduced to the Middle East and the Mediterranean, where it has been prized since ancient times. Virtually all of the U.S. almond crop is now grown in California's Central Valley.

PECAN

Carya illinoinensis

The pecan is native to North America and is related to the walnut and hickory. Native Americans called it paccan, *which loosely translates as "nut so hard it must be cracked with a stone." Pecan trees can grow up to one hundred feet tall and live more than a thousand years. Most pecans are grown in the Southeast and Southwest.*

HAZELNUT OR FILBERT

Corylus avellana, C. maxima

Hazelnuts, also known as filberts, were revered in ancient China, where they have been cultivated for more than forty-five hundred years. The first North American hazelnut tree was planted in the Pacific Northwest in 1851, and today Oregon and Washington produce more than 98 percent of all commercially grown hazelnuts in the United States.

PINE NUT

Pinus cembroides, P. edulis, P. koraiensis, P. monophylla, P. pinea

The tiny pine nut, or piñon, is the seed found inside certain kinds of pinecones. It has a long pedigree: savored from the time of the ancient Greeks and Romans, in North America it has long been a significant part of the diets of the Hopi, Navajo, and other Native American tribes. Today, many pine nuts come from China. The pine nut is one of the best sources of protein of all nuts.

MACADAMIA NUT

Macadamia integrifolia, M. ternifolia, M. tetraphylla

Although it has become known as a Hawaiian nut, the macadamia is native to Australia, where it was first eaten by nomadic Aborigines. It is now grown commercially in Hawaii, Australia, and South Africa. Because of its rock-hard shell, the nut is almost always sold shelled in vacuum-packed jars or cans.

BLACK WALNUT

Juglans nigra

American black walnuts are known for their rich, full-bodied flavor, which makes them ideal for adding to baked goods and ice cream. Unlike their English (Persian) kin, black walnuts are not cultivated. They instead grow wild throughout the middle and eastern United States, where they are gathered by hand.

BRAZIL NUT

Bertholletia excelsa

Brazil nuts are grown exclusively in South America, along the tributaries of the Amazon River. They grow wild on trees that often reach 150 feet tall and produce from five hundred to one thousand pounds of nuts a year. The nuts grow in a pod, segmented like an orange, which accounts for their triangular shape.

THE WAY *of the* WALNUT:
A TALE *of* GODS, GROVES, *and* GROWERS

The ancient Greeks and Romans spoke of a long-past time of simplicity and harmony— a golden age when humble mortals lived on acorns while up above, on the lofty peaks of Mount Olympus, the gods feasted on something a bit more fitting to their station: *juglans,* the "acorn of Jupiter."

Our first publication, circa 1923

What was this heavenly food? Here's a hint: it's something you can find in any supermarket. You've probably even got a few sitting on that lofty top shelf of your kitchen cabinet. The acorn of Jupiter was nothing more, and nothing less, than a walnut.

If you've ever stopped to really consider a walnut—how a hard-shelled work of art etched with creases and folds like a finely carved ornament emerges from a soft green husk; how cracking open that brittle shell reveals two hemispheres as intricately formed as tiny brains; how toasting the meat of the nut releases an encitingly rich aroma, a buttery flavor, and a texture somehow both crunchy and creamy—that shouldn't come as a surprise.

Eaten right out of the shell or tossed in with other ingredients in sweet and savory recipes like the ones in this book, the gods' favorite food has a way of making just about anything taste, well, divine.

But how did walnuts and their cousins—almonds, Brazil nuts, hazelnuts, macadamias, pecans, and pine nuts—find their way from being foods of the gods all the way to your grocer's shelf and into that batch of brownies on your kitchen counter? That's a whole story unto itself. Our story.

THE VERY WORLDLY WALNUT

The English or, more properly, Persian walnut *(Juglans regia)* is believed to have originated in Asia and southeastern Europe and has been cultivated for more than two-thousand five hundred years. There are other species, the best known of which is the black walnut *(Juglans nigra),* but the Persian walnut is by far the most frequently grown worldwide. When people say *walnut,* more often than not this is the nut they're talking about.

Now here's the amazing part. Over the centuries, the Persian walnut has thrived under vastly different conditions and climates, from the frigid heights of the Caucasus Mountains through Persia into India and China, and in the sun-baked hills and valleys of Greece, Italy, France, Spain, and South America. Trees often live for hundreds of years, outlasting many human generations. And throughout the ages, walnuts and the rich oil they produce have found their way into all of those cuisines and cultures.

The Greeks and Romans believed that, because walnuts were shaped like two halves of the brain, they would cure headaches. The Romans also believed walnuts brought good health and fertility. At Roman weddings, the lucky couple was pelted not with handfuls of rice, but with fistfuls of walnuts. In China, where walnuts arrived as early as the first century B.C., their elaborately carved shells were used as cages to carry lucky crickets trained to sing on cue. In medieval Europe, the nuts were used to ward off everything from lightning and evil spirits to fits of epilepsy. And in Romania, a bride would stow a roasted walnut under her bodice for each year she wished to postpone childbearing.

All over the world walnuts have been toasted, chopped, and ground to enhance, enrich, and thicken sauces, soups, salads, and stews, from garlicky tarator sauce and creamy Circassian chicken in the Middle East to pesto in Italy and succulent walnut prawns in Hong Kong. They're the essential toasty crunch in Greek baklava, the seductive flavor of a rich gelato in Genoa, the "flour" in a flourless French chocolate cake, and the familiar, indispensable flavor accent in a slice of old-fashioned American banana bread.

In some countries, such as France and Italy, in fact, they've become such culinary staples that the generic word for *nut* (*noix* in France, *noce* in Italian) is simply used as the word for walnut.

Yes, walnuts have helped shape culinary history, even in the most far-flung corners of the world. But our story begins a little closer to home, just a little over a hundred years ago. It's the story of how the rich cultural and culinary tradition of Persian walnuts grew into a modern industry and a remarkable company that now brings Jupiter's acorn full circle—and brings California walnuts to markets and homes all over the world.

THE JOURNEY TO THE WEST

The very first Persian walnuts probably came to America with the early settlers in New England. And while native species of walnut existed in California long before settlers ever set foot there, it was the Old World species, first cultivated in earnest in California in the 19th century, that turned out to be the best suited to commercial production and the most adaptable to the climate of the New World.

Historians believe the Franciscan priests who established California's missions were the first to plant walnut trees of the Juglans regia *species.*

It's almost certain that these walnuts came with the Spanish Franciscan priests who established the California missions in the late 1700s. By the mid-1800s, landowners in San Diego, Los Angeles, the San Gabriel Valley, Carpinteria, and as far north as the Napa Valley had begun to plant them. Although these initial plantings were mostly for decorative use or personal consumption, knowledge of walnut culture was increasing, and a California walnut industry had quietly begun to take root.

The elements were all in place: a region blessed with an ideal climate, walnuts brought over from Europe, and a growing interest in planting and cultivating them. Now the most important ingredient could be added to the mix: people.

People like Joseph Sexton, who settled in the Santa Barbara area in 1867 and established a nursery where he began growing walnuts from a bag he had bought in San Francisco. Some of his seedlings would turn out to be the soft-shelled variety on which the entire Southern California walnut industry would be based.

People like Felix Gillet, who introduced harder-shelled walnuts from his native France to Northern California, where the softer-shelled varieties proved too delicate for the colder winters and late frosts. Or Russell Heath of Carpinteria, who experimented with transplanting and cultural practices and, by the 1880s, was growing an amazing six thousand orchard trees.

People like Harriet W. R. Strong, the 39-year-old widow of a California silver prospector, who saw, in the 20 acres of semiarid land she had inherited, the opportunity to extract wealth of a different kind. Studying local crops and climate, she planted walnut trees and would eventually invent and patent an irrigation system based on flood-control and storage dams that would be adopted as far away as Central America.

It was people like these, along with hundreds of other hardworking entrepreneurs and experimenters, whose shared vision would give rise to a commercial walnut industry that is still a model worldwide.

By 1885, these pioneering horticulturalists and growers were already producing well over a million pounds of walnuts a year, and their efforts had created a commercially viable orchard crop for the state's farmers. In the decades that followed, advances in irrigation, pest management, and horticulture helped walnut growers improve the yield and quality of their crops.

But that wasn't all the fledgling industry needed. As supplies increased, it needed to find new markets and better business systems. Not everyone agreed on the best way to achieve these goals. But California's growers did agree on one thing. The task before them was too great to tackle as individuals. The time had come to band together.

A GATHERING IN THE GROVE

Initially, individual nut growers had been dependent on brokers to sell their crops throughout the United States. But these brokers often handled many other commodities as well and had little incentive to push for higher returns for growers.

A Toast to Better Flavor

You won't find a single raw nut in any recipe in this book. That's because we believe that toasting nuts—either before you use them in a recipe or during the cooking process—is absolutely essential to bringing out their best qualities.

Of course, you can eat nuts raw. But toasting them, especially using dry heat, enhances their sweetness, depresses bitter notes, and releases rich, savory aromas and flavors. Suddenly that nut really tastes like a nut.

The toasting process also causes some of the water in the nut to evaporate, drying and crisping the tissue. In other words, it makes nuts nice and crunchy.

Whenever a recipe calls for pretoasting, specific directions are given in the method. We recommend using a timer and setting it for a minute or two less than the directions indicate. That way, you can start checking the nuts early and pull them out the minute they look and smell lightly toasted.

In 1887, in an effort to negotiate better prices, about 20 walnut growers in Los Angeles County formed the state's first walnut growers' association. That initial gathering marked the beginning of a groundswell. By 1892, the association was more than a hundred members strong, and it was shipping almost half of the state's crop—as well as the first trainload of walnuts ever to be sold outside California—to markets in the East. A plan soon emerged to organize a centralized Southern California Walnut Growers Association (SCWGA).

Above: *In 1917, CWGA moved to a two-story building in downtown Los Angeles.*

Opposite: *As demand for walnuts grew, new plantings spread throughout California.*

The collective marketing quickly brought substantially higher prices, and more local associations joined the ranks of the SCWGA. But as the number of growers increased, so did competition for buyers. By 1909, prices had fallen, and growers had begun to undercut one another.

In that year, a 23-year-old manager from the Santa Paula association decided to do business a little differently. He would bypass brokers altogether and sell directly to the wholesale grocers and jobbers. Sending out high-grade nuts under local brands and making extraordinary efforts to build strong customer relationships, he reasoned, would attract loyal customers who would pay more for quality on which they could depend. His name was Carlyle Thorpe, and he was right. That year, the growers he represented enjoyed returns much higher than those who were still selling through brokers. Thorpe's vision and leadership would help shape the growth of the California walnut industry for more than 35 years.

1912: A LANDMARK YEAR

In 1912, the SCWGA evolved into the California Walnut Growers Association (CWGA), under its first president, Charles Teague. The following year, Carlyle Thorpe was appointed general manager. Among the early actions taken by the new group was the creation of the Diamond brand for premium walnuts. Nuts of inferior size or quality would be sold under other brand

names. In 1913, Thorpe set out on a sales tour, visiting walnut buyers all across America. By September of that year, his campaign had already brought in more orders than the CWGA could fill. Direct selling was working, and the commodity-based broker system had been replaced for good.

Within just five years, the association could list among its achievements the standardization of grading, inspection, and shell-bleaching methods; the development of packaging and national advertising for the Diamond brand; and, perhaps most importantly, the establishment of good-will and a positive reputation among both grower members and buyers.

But that was just the beginning. With the CWGA now a reality, it was time to take on a new challenge: making the Diamond brand a trusted symbol for consumers nationwide.

The new association's achievements attracted growers, and membership continued to swell.

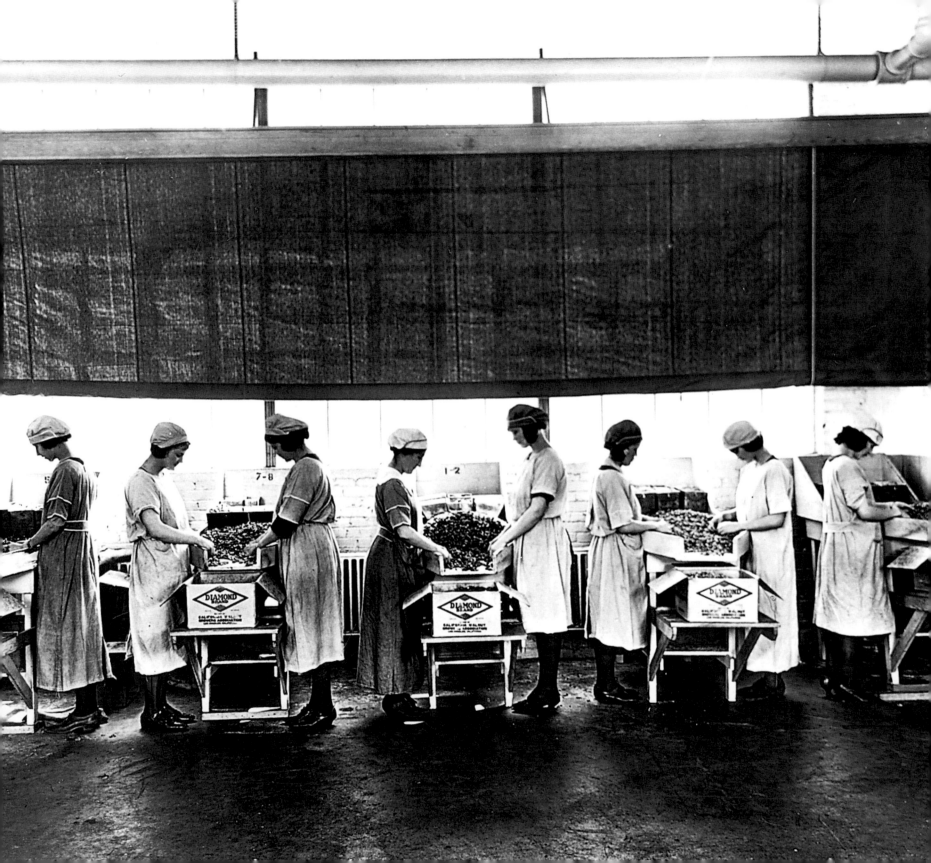

An early walnut branding machine, circa 1926

A BRAND NEW DAY FOR CALIFORNIA WALNUTS

"We are going to make our Diamond Brand on walnuts stand for the same thing as the sterling mark does on silver," wrote Carlyle Thorpe in 1914. And by 1919, he had found an ingenious way to do just that. In the face of increasing foreign competition, CWGA wanted to emphasize its premium nuts in a way that would ensure that neither wholesalers nor retailers could mix lower-priced foreign nuts with them. But since most walnuts were traded in easily opened 100-pound bags, the only guaranteed way to do this was literally to "brand" each individual nut with the Diamond logo.

The CWGA put out the word. It offered a ten-thousand-dollar prize for the invention of a machine that could stamp the logo on each premium walnut. By fall, 127 entries had been received, and by the next year, the first-ever branded walnuts were shipped to market. That branding process has continued ever since, a visible guarantee of quality and commitment.

To build consumer demand, Thorpe's strategy also included extensive—and expensive—national advertising, designed to stimulate nut consumption not only during the holidays, but throughout the year. Campaigns reached readers of the *Saturday Evening Post, Ladies' Home Journal, Good Housekeeping,* and other national magazines. A CWGA recipe booklet gave recipes for "100 new and exquisite goodies"; a glossy 98-page booklet, *The California Walnut Industry,* proudly touted the value and benefits of the Diamond brand; and in 1918, a Pathé Weekly newsreel on California's booming walnut industry played in theaters across the nation.

If you think all of that sounds like typical marketing tactics used by any modern food company, well, you're right. But remember, the year was 1918. Thorpe, Teague, and their colleagues weren't just doing food marketing; they were helping to invent it—and elevating food production standards to new levels of consistency in taste, appearance, and product integrity.

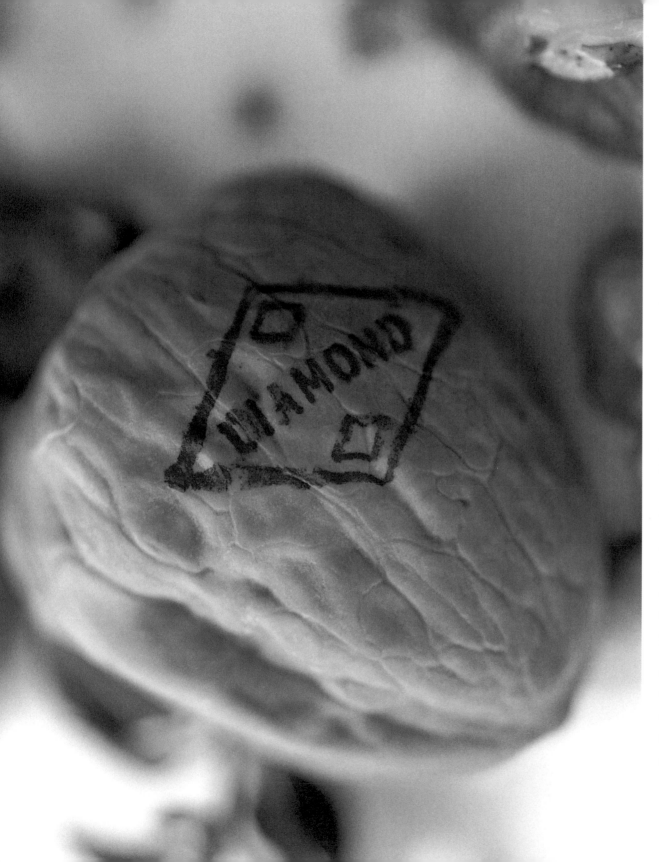

Freshness Is Everything

Treat nuts as you would a fine olive oil. Their enemies are light, heat, and moisture, all of which can cause rancidity and off-flavors. Nuts in their natural package—the shell—keep even longer than shelled ones.

Store nuts in an airtight container in a cool, dry place, such as a cupboard or the refrigerator. Or better yet, place them in a resealable plastic freezer bag, place the bag in a second bag for extra protection (make sure to add a date label), and freeze them. Most nuts will keep for up to two years in the freezer.

If not used within a few days, toasted nuts should be frozen to maintain their quality. However, it's best to store them raw and roast just what you need when you're ready to prepare a recipe.

Before using nuts in a recipe, always taste a few of them. If they have any hint of rancidity, throw them out; no technique or cooking process can fully mask this flavor.

"If you think it's a long, long way to Tipperary, just try tracking the Chinese walnut to its lair. It's bad enough to ride for days on a burro, worse to travel in a rickety, bouncing sedan chair for days over mountain trails and barren, rocky wastes, but riding a camel bareback over sizzling desert sands is my idea of the height of discomfort." —Carlyle Thorpe, writing about his 1921 fact-finding mission to China, where he discovered growing, harvesting, and drying techniques that would greatly improve the agricultural practices of California's walnut growers.

More innovations quickly followed. Seeing the potential for shelled walnuts as a product that would offer both convenience for the consumer and a better return on in-shell walnut "culls" (nuts rejected because of blemished shells but still containing perfectly good kernels) for the grower, CWGA built a new cracking plant in Los Angeles and instructed its growers to send all culls there. Shelled walnuts gradually became more popular, and in 1918 CWGA introduced an eight-ounce Thermokept vacuum-packed can to ensure freshness, placing shelled walnut meats in the hands of the consumer for the first time in history.

By the late 1920s, through advertising and in-store promotion, Diamond had become a trusted and familiar brand nationwide. And throughout the 1930s and 1940s, CWGA took a leadership role in piloting the industry through the often stormy seas of depression, war, surpluses, labor conflicts, technological innovation, and gradual but steady growth.

For decades, walnuts were gathered by hand—hard, dirty, time-consuming work.

THE NORTHWARD PASSAGE AND THE NEW ECONOMY

In the years following World War II, the landscape of Southern California began to change rapidly. Real estate development gobbled up orchards and farmland, and the walnut industry began a gradual shift northward. After a period of difficult soul-searching and evaluation, CWGA embarked on an era of streamlining, modernization, and restructuring that in 1956 would culminate in the relocation of its operations to the Northern California town of Stockton, in the heart of the state's booming northern growing region. The organization also got a new name. It would be known henceforth as Diamond Walnut Growers.

Tractors and other innovations revolutionized fieldwork.

Meanwhile, a new consumer trend was sweeping the nation: the supermarket. As more women entered the workplace, the demand for efficient shopping and convenient food products was taking off. Diamond responded with new products (some of which, like walnuts with rainbow-colored shells, were short-lived) and new packaging solutions.

By 1962, Diamond was selling 6 different in-the-shell products and 13 shelled walnut products, and had introduced pecans, peanuts, cashews, and mixed nuts in test markets. To boost sales and interest, the company's home economists developed hundreds of recipes for home cooks and distributed more than 4 million cookbooks and leaflets to consumers, schools, bakeries, candy manufacturers, and restaurants. Efforts to market to food manufacturers who would use Diamond nuts as ingredients in consumer food products also began in earnest at this time.

BRANCHING OUT

Throughout the 1970s and 1980s, Diamond led the way in building a worldwide market for California walnuts. From an almost nonexistent market share, Germany thus became California's number-one destination for in-the-shell walnuts, while Japan, where the company spearheaded the introduction of shelled walnuts, grew to become the leading export market for walnut kernels.

Today, the Diamond brand can be found in more than 45 countries. Building on its roots as a single-commodity company, Diamond has transformed itself into the leading marketer of

McCall's *magazine, November 1928*

culinary nuts worldwide, bringing consumers a full range of products, including almonds, Brazil nuts, hazelnuts, macadamias, pecans, and pine nuts. And along with these and other innovations have come a new look, logo, and packaging—and a new name: Diamond of California.

BRINGING IT ALL TOGETHER

Our Stockton nut-processing facility is now the most modern in the world, receiving shipments of some 8 million pounds of nuts every day during the peak harvest season. (For a perspective, compare that to the 1-million-pound annual output of the earliest California walnut growers back in 1885.)

And although much has changed since Joseph Sexton planted those first walnut seedlings over a century ago, one thing has remained constant. Diamond is more than a brand, more than a company, and more than an industry leader. Diamond is people: people coming together as individuals to make a greater, stronger whole. Carlyle Thorpe and Charles Teague believed in that simple idea right from the start. The five generations of California walnut growers who followed them believed it, too. And today, the more than one-thousand nine hundred farming families who own Diamond believe it more than ever. They're owners of a company, yes. But they're also growers: men and women whose lives are bound up in the promise of living trees, fertile soil, and hands and hearts to tend them.

"Quality from our orchards to your table through grower ownership"—that's our philosophy in a nutshell.

In that spirit, we offer you this collection of recipes, tips, and simple, good ideas with nuts. They come from the kitchens of our growers, from our own archives, from our friends and families, and from some of America's favorite chefs and food writers. They are tried-and-true favorites, fresh takes on much-loved classics, and new ideas that will surprise and delight you. Taken all together, they tell a story. It's the story of how all over the world, as well as right here at home, nuts are a part of the foods we love to eat. Diamond is proud to be a part of that story, and prouder still to be a part of your life and the foods you and your loved ones treasure.

APPETIZERS & SALADS

Who will eat
the kernel of a nut
must break the shell.

JOHN GRANGE
"THE GOLDEN APHRODITIS"
1577

MAPLE-GLAZED WALNUTS 20

CINNAMON-SPICE NUT MIX 21

TERIYAKI WALNUTS 22

SWEET-SALTY ROASTED NUTS 24

MAHOGANY ALMONDS 25

TURKISH TOASTED WALNUTS 26

CHIPOTLE-HONEY NUT MIX 27

GRAPES *with* GORGONZOLA
and PECANS 30

TERRINE *of* ROQUEFORT
and GRAPES *by Roland Passot* 32

ENDIVE *with* BRANDIED
CHEESE *and* WALNUTS 33

CROSTINI *with* CAMBOZOLA,
CARAMELIZED ONIONS,
and WALNUTS 34

BRUSCHETTA CAPRESE 35

CRAB CAKES *with* ALMONDS
and ROMESCO SAUCE 36

SPICY CHICKEN-WALNUT
TRIANGLES 39

WALNUT-PEPERONATA
WONTONS 40

PAPILLOTE *of* FOIE GRAS *and*
LANGOUSTINES *by Hubert Keller* 42

ROASTED BEET SALAD
with APPLE, DANDELION LEAVES,
and ALMONDS *by Charlie Trotter* 44

ASPARAGUS SALAD
with SESAME-GLAZED
WALNUTS *by Martin Yan* 46

SPINACH SALAD *with* BACON,
ALMONDS, *and* WARM
GOAT CHEESE 47

PAN-SEARED SEA SCALLOPS
with GRAPEFRUIT, ENDIVE,
and WALNUTS *by Mark Franz* 48

BABY LIMA BEAN SALAD *with*
SHRIMP *and* ALMONDS 50

CAESAR SALAD *with* GREEN
ONIONS *and* WALNUTS 52

APPLE *and* RADICCHIO
SALAD *by Bradley Ogden* 54

ROASTED SWEET CORN SALAD 56

DIAMOND WALDORF SALAD 57

MAPLE-GLAZED WALNUTS

1 CUP PACKED LIGHT BROWN SUGAR

½ CUP GRANULATED SUGAR

½ CUP SOUR CREAM OR PLAIN YOGURT, DRAINED OF ANY EXCESS LIQUID

⅛ TEASPOON SALT

4 CUPS WALNUT HALVES

2 TEASPOONS MAPLE FLAVORING

These easy candied nuts make a fine addition to a cheese platter or a holiday cookie assortment. You can find maple flavoring in the spice section of most supermarkets, along with the vanilla and other extracts. For an equally tasty variation, substitute pure vanilla extract for the maple.

LINE a large baking sheet with foil or parchment paper, coat with vegetable oil spray. In a heavy, medium saucepan, mix together brown sugar, granulated sugar, sour cream, and salt. Cook over medium heat, stirring frequently, until mixture is smooth and comes to a boil. Continue cooking, stirring, until mixture reaches 236° to 240° on a candy thermometer. (A small spoonful of the mixture dropped into ice water will form a soft ball when rubbed between your index finger and thumb.)

QUICKLY stir in walnuts and maple flavoring; cook, stirring, until nuts are coated completely, 2 to 3 minutes. Working carefully, spread walnuts in a single layer on the prepared baking sheet, separating nuts with a fork. Let cool completely.

STORE airtight at room temperature up to 1 week.

YIELDS 4 CUPS

CINNAMON-SPICE NUT MIX

Make a batch of these easy candied nuts, and you'll find all kinds of ways to serve them. You can set them out by the bowlful at a party, use them to top a salad containing apples and goat cheese, or sprinkle them over ice cream. And what could be sweeter as a homemade hostess gift?

IF using hazelnuts, preheat oven to 350°. Spread hazelnuts in a single layer on a baking sheet or pan. Bake, shaking the pan once or twice, until nuts are lightly browned and fragrant, 10 to 12 minutes. Wrap warm hazelnuts in a clean dish towel and let cool 10 minutes. With the towel, rub off as much of the papery skins as possible. Add to bowl with other assorted nuts. (You can omit this step if not using hazelnuts.)

REDUCE oven temperature to 225°. Line a large baking sheet with foil or parchment paper; coat with vegetable oil spray.

IN a large bowl, whisk egg whites until foamy. Add nuts, tossing to coat well.

IN another large bowl, combine sugar, cinnamon, salt, ginger, allspice, cloves, and nutmeg. Blend well. Add nuts, tossing until evenly coated with sugar mixture.

SPREAD nuts in a single layer on the prepared baking sheet, separating with a fork. Bake until coating is dry and crunchy, about 2 hours. Let cool.

STORE airtight at room temperature up to 1 week.

YIELDS 4 CUPS

A Cup of Kindness

Fill a coffee mug with any of the glazed nuts in this chapter. Set the mug in the center of two pieces of transparent plastic gift wrap or floral wrap. Gather the wrap around the mug and tie it with a wire ribbon; add a gift card with a message on one side and the recipe on the back. (For extra credit, use a personalized photo mug.)

4 CUPS ASSORTED WHOLE NUTS
(such as walnuts, hazelnuts, pecans, almonds, and macadamias)

2 EGG WHITES

1 CUP SUGAR

2 TEASPOONS GROUND CINNAMON

½ TEASPOON SALT

¼ TEASPOON GROUND GINGER

⅛ TEASPOON GROUND ALLSPICE

⅛ TEASPOON GROUND CLOVES

⅛ TEASPOON FRESHLY GRATED NUTMEG

TERIYAKI WALNUTS

4 CUPS WALNUT HALVES

3 TABLESPOONS SESAME SEEDS

¼ CUP FROZEN ORANGE JUICE
CONCENTRATE, THAWED

¼ CUP SOY SAUCE

2 TABLESPOONS ASIAN
SESAME OIL

2 TABLESPOONS LIGHT
BROWN SUGAR

2 TEASPOONS GRATED
FRESH GINGER

2 CLOVES GARLIC, MINCED

½ TEASPOON CRUSHED
DRIED RED CHILES

Food scientists tell us that the reason we love teriyaki flavor is that it's a perfect balance of the four basic tastes: sweet, salty, bitter, and sour. We discovered that adding a fifth—the toasted, buttery flavor of walnuts—makes teriyaki even more irresistible. Let the teri-snacking begin.

PREHEAT oven to 350°. Line a large baking sheet with foil or parchment paper; spread walnuts in an even layer. Bake, stirring once or twice, until lightly browned and fragrant, 10 to 12 minutes. Set aside baking sheet for later; reduce oven temperature to 300°.

IN a large frying pan over medium heat, toast sesame seeds until pale golden brown, 3 to 5 minutes. Scrape sesame seeds onto a plate and set aside. In the same pan, combine the orange juice concentrate, soy sauce, sesame oil, sugar, ginger, garlic, and chiles. Bring to a boil. Add walnuts and cook, stirring, until liquid has evaporated. Add sesame seeds, stirring to coat evenly.

ON the baking sheet, spread walnut mixture in a single layer. Bake until nuts are glazed and dry, 8 to 10 minutes. Let cool.

STORE airtight at room temperature up to 1 week.

YIELDS 4 CUPS

Opposite *Top left: Mahogany Almonds*
Top right: Maple-Glazed Walnuts
Bottom left: Cinnamon-Spice Nut Mix
Bottom right: Teriyaki Walnuts

SWEET-SALTY ROASTED NUTS

4 CUPS ASSORTED NUTS *(such as walnuts, hazelnuts, pecans, almonds, macadamias, and pine nuts)*

2 EGG WHITES

1 TABLESPOON COARSE-GRAINED SALT

1 TABLESPOON SUGAR

There are all kinds of tricky recipes for glazed nuts that involve deep-frying. We've come up with a super-easy way to make them in the oven. The secret is the egg white, which helps the sugar and salt adhere and adds an attractive glazed finish. Serve these as a cocktail snack, or use just one kind of nut (such as pecans or walnuts) and toss in salads.

IF using hazelnuts, preheat oven to 350°. Spread hazelnuts in a single layer on a baking sheet or pan. Bake, shaking the pan once or twice, until nuts are lightly browned and fragrant, 10 to 12 minutes. Wrap warm hazelnuts in a clean dish towel and let cool 10 minutes. With the towel, rub off as much of the papery skins as possible. Add to bowl with other assorted nuts. (You can omit this step if not using hazelnuts.)

REDUCE oven temperature to 300°. Line a large baking sheet with foil or parchment paper; coat with vegetable oil spray.

IN a large bowl, whisk egg whites until foamy. Add nuts, salt, and sugar, tossing to coat evenly. Spread nuts in a single layer on the baking sheet. Bake, stirring once or twice, until nuts are crisp and fragrant, about 20 minutes. Let cool.

SERVE slightly warm or at room temperature. Store airtight at room temperature up to 1 week.

YIELDS 4 CUPS

MAHOGANY ALMONDS

It's difficult to believe that the flavor, texture, and lustrous lacquered sheen of these nuts could be the product of just four ingredients. Well, eight, actually, if you count the star anise, Sichuan peppercorns, cinnamon, cloves, and other spices that go into the Chinese five-spice (which you can find in the spice section of most supermarkets). But who's counting? As in any really simple recipe, it's important to use the best ingredients you can find, especially when it comes to the pure maple syrup. The imitation kind will cook up sticky and flavorless.

⅔ CUP PURE MAPLE SYRUP

2 TEASPOONS CHINESE FIVE-SPICE

1 TEASPOON SALT

4 CUPS WHOLE ALMONDS

PREHEAT oven to 300°. Line 2 large baking sheets with foil or parchment paper; coat with vegetable oil spray. In a large bowl, combine syrup, five-spice, and salt; stir until well blended. Add almonds, stirring to coat evenly.

SPREAD mixture in an even layer on 1 prepared baking sheet. Bake, stirring once or twice, until nuts are glazed and deep golden brown, 50 to 60 minutes. Working quickly and carefully, immediately spread almonds on the other baking sheet, separating with a fork. Let cool completely.

STORE airtight at room temperature up to 1 week.

YIELDS 4 CUPS

TURKISH TOASTED WALNUTS

4 CUPS WALNUT HALVES

3 TABLESPOONS WALNUT OIL,
ROASTED GARLIC WALNUT OIL,
OR VEGETABLE OIL

½ CUP MINCED GREEN ONION

2 TABLESPOONS GROUND
CUMIN

1 TABLESPOON GROUND
CINNAMON

1 TABLESPOON SUGAR

1 TEASPOON SALT

1 CLOVE GARLIC, MINCED

½ TEASPOON GROUND ALLSPICE

½ TEASPOON FRESHLY
GROUND BLACK PEPPER

½ TEASPOON CAYENNE PEPPER

¼ CUP WATER

Walnuts were first cultivated in Persia and Asia Minor, and they still figure prominently in the cuisines of those regions. These wonderfully perfumed spiced nuts would be right at home there. Serve them as a snack, toss them in salads, or try them as a crunchy topping for Asian noodle dishes.

PREHEAT oven to 350°. Line a large baking sheet with foil or parchment paper. Spread walnuts in an even layer. Bake, stirring once or twice, until lightly browned and fragrant, 10 to 12 minutes. Set aside baking sheet for later; reduce oven temperature to 300°.

IN a large frying pan, warm oil over medium heat. Stir in onion, cumin, cinnamon, sugar, salt, garlic, allspice, black pepper, and cayenne. Cook, stirring, until fragrant, 1 to 2 minutes.

ADD water and bring to a boil; immediately stir in the walnuts. Cook, stirring occasionally, until all the liquid has evaporated. Spread walnuts in a single layer on the reserved baking sheet. Bake until nuts are browned and dry, 10 to 12 minutes. Let cool.

SERVE slightly warm or at room temperature. Store airtight at room temperature up to 1 week.

YIELDS 4 CUPS

CHIPOTLE-HONEY NUT MIX

If you wanted to create the perfect nibble, you'd make it salty, sweet, spicy, and nutty. In that spirit, this easy glazed nut mix is our little gift to nibblers everywhere. The chipotle chiles add just the right amount of heat, plus a hint of earthy smokiness.

4 CUPS ASSORTED NUTS *(such as walnuts, hazelnuts, pecans, almonds, macadamias, and pine nuts)*

⅓ CUP HONEY

3 TABLESPOONS SUGAR

3 TABLESPOONS WALNUT OIL OR VEGETABLE OIL

1 TABLESPOON MASHED CANNED CHIPOTLE CHILES IN ADOBO SAUCE

1¼ TEASPOONS SALT

IF using hazelnuts, preheat oven to 350°. Spread hazelnuts in a single layer on a baking sheet or pan. Bake, shaking the pan once or twice, until nuts are lightly browned and fragrant, 10 to 12 minutes. Wrap warm hazelnuts in a clean dish towel and let cool 10 minutes. With the towel, rub off as much of the papery skins as possible. Add to bowl with other assorted nuts. (You can omit this step if not using hazelnuts.)

REDUCE oven temperature to 300°. Line a large baking sheet with foil or parchment paper; coat with vegetable oil spray. In a large bowl, combine honey, sugar, oil, chiles, and salt. Add nuts, stirring to coat evenly.

SPREAD mixture in an even layer on prepared baking sheet. Bake, stirring once or twice, until nuts are glazed and golden brown, about 30 minutes. Let cool. Break nuts apart, if needed.

STORE airtight at room temperature up to 1 week.

YIELDS 4 CUPS

Chipotle Chic

Chipotles (chee-poht-lays) are all the rage these days. But what exactly are they? Well, for starters, their name refers to a process, rather than a botanical variety of chile. Chipotles are actually jalapeños that have been slowly dried over a smoldering fire, so that they take on a smoky flavor. They're often canned in a spicy vinegar sauce called adobo. You can find this magical stuff, sold as chipotles en adobo, in Latino markets or in the Mexican section of many supermarkets. Mash the chiles and sauce, or purée them in a blender or food processor, and you've got a rich, complex seasoning paste that adds spice, depth, and smoky flavor to sauces, marinades, dressings, soups, and salsas. And wait until you taste what chipotles do to nuts.

Chopping Spree

To chop nuts, use a sharp chef's knife, and remember: warm nuts chop more easily than cool ones. If you're using a food processor, pulse the motor frequently, and stir the nuts occasionally to avoid creating nut butter. Or save yourself the trouble and buy nuts that are already chopped, ground, or sliced.

How to Pick a Nut

If you can't judge a book by its cover, how can you tell a good nut when the shell is still on? For starters, look for an unblemished exterior, free of cracks and holes. The nut should feel heavy for its size. Give it a shake. If it rattles, throw it back—that's a sign that the meat may have dried and shriveled. Shelled nuts are an easier matter. They should be firm and not shriveled and should snap, not bend, when you break them.

GRAPES *with* GORGONZOLA *and* PECANS

2 CUPS PECAN CHIPS

8 OUNCES CREAM CHEESE, AT ROOM TEMPERATURE

4 OUNCES GORGONZOLA OR OTHER BLUE CHEESE, AT ROOM TEMPERATURE

2 TABLESPOONS WHIPPING CREAM, HALF-AND-HALF, OR MILK

½ POUND *(about 1¼ cups)* SMALL SEEDLESS RED OR GREEN GRAPES, RINSED AND DRIED WELL

Fruit, cheese, and nuts, all rolled into one! You can serve these elegant little bites as an hors d'oeuvre, as an appetizer, or as part of a cheese course. They're particularly appealing when arranged in a cluster and garnished with a grape or fig leaf. You can substitute any chopped toasted nut for the pecans, and if you're not partial to Gorgonzola, try a mild goat cheese.

PREHEAT oven to 350°. Spread pecan chips on a baking sheet or in a shallow pan. Bake, stirring once or twice, until lightly browned and fragrant, 5 to 10 minutes. Let cool.

IN a medium bowl, beat cream cheese, Gorgonzola, and cream with an electric mixer until smooth, 2 to 3 minutes. Completely cover each grape with about 1 teaspoon cheese mixture; repeat with remaining cheese and grapes.

(If making in advance, refrigerate airtight up to 3 days.) Roll each grape-cheese ball in pecan chips until well coated.

YIELDS ABOUT 48 BALLS

TERRINE *of* ROQUEFORT *and* GRAPES

(ROLAND PASSOT)

2 CUPS CHOPPED WALNUTS

½ CUP SAUTERNES OR OTHER
SWEET WHITE WINE

1 TABLESPOON UNFLAVORED
GELATIN

4 CUPS *(about 1 pound)* CRUMBLED
ROQUEFORT OR BLUE CHEESE

1 CUP WHIPPING CREAM

½ POUND SEEDLESS RED OR
GREEN GRAPES, HALVED
IF LARGE

½ CUP FINELY CHOPPED
FRESH CHIVES

Chef Roland Passot recommends serving this dense, creamy terrine as a first course accompanied with a small green salad and a slice of toasted walnut bread (such as Toasted Walnut and Olive Yeast Bread, page 212). It can also be unmolded and served as a party spread with crackers or baguette slices. If you find the flavor of Roquefort too robust, substitute a milder blue cheese.

PREHEAT oven to 350°. Generously coat a 6-cup terrine or loaf pan with vegetable oil spray and set aside. On a large baking sheet, spread walnuts in an even layer. Bake, stirring once or twice, until light golden brown and fragrant, 8 to 10 minutes. Let cool.

IN a large heatproof bowl, soften gelatin in ¼ cup of the Sauternes; let stand 1 minute. Bring a saucepan filled with 2 inches water to

a boil over high heat. Place bowl with gelatin securely over the saucepan to form a double boiler. Reduce heat to medium and cook until gelatin has dissolved, 3 to 5 minutes. Stir in the cheese and the remaining ¼ cup Sauternes; stir until cheese has softened and mixture is almost smooth, 3 to 5 minutes. Place bowl with cheese mixture into a larger bowl filled with ice. Let cool, stirring occasionally, until mixture is cool and begins to thicken, 15 to 20 minutes.

IN a large bowl, beat cream with an electric mixer until stiff. Fold about one-third of whipped cream into the cheese mixture, then fold in the remaining cream until no streaks show. Fold in the walnuts, grapes, and chives. Scrape mixture into the prepared terrine; level the top with a spatula. Tap the terrine on a firm surface several times to remove air bubbles. Cover with plastic wrap and refrigerate until firm, at least 2 hours or up to 2 days.

TO loosen mixture, run a metal spatula or knife around the edge of the terrine. Unmold onto a flat plate; cut into ½-inch slices.

SERVES 10 TO 12

ENDIVE *with* BRANDIED CHEESE *and* WALNUTS

The crisp texture and clean, pleasantly bitter flavor of Belgian endive work beautifully with the richness of cheese and nuts. For a fancier presentation, use a pastry bag fitted with a wide star tip to pipe the cheese mixture onto the endive leaves. Or go casual and simply serve the cheese as a spread in a crock with crackers or croutons of toasted walnut bread on the side.

½ CUP CHOPPED WALNUTS

1 CUP *(about 4 ounces)* CRUMBLED BLUE CHEESE OR GOAT CHEESE, AT ROOM TEMPERATURE

3 OUNCES CREAM CHEESE, AT ROOM TEMPERATURE

2 TEASPOONS BRANDY

5 MEDIUM HEADS *(about 10 ounces total)* BELGIAN ENDIVE

PREHEAT oven to 350°. Spread walnuts on a baking sheet or in a shallow pan. Bake, stirring once or twice, until lightly browned and fragrant, 8 to 10 minutes. Let cool slightly.

IN a medium bowl, combine blue cheese, cream cheese, and brandy. Stir in half the walnuts.

CUT root end from endive heads to separate leaves. (Save the endive hearts for another use; add thin slices to a green salad.) Place 1 heaping teaspoon of the cheese mixture on the base of each leaf. Top with remaining walnuts. On a serving platter, arrange leaves in concentric circles, with tips facing out.

YIELDS ABOUT 24 PIECES
SERVES 8 TO 10

VARIATIONS ON A CHEESE BALL

For decades it reigned supreme at cocktail parties from coast to coast: that little ball of cheese encrusted with chopped nuts and ringed with crackers. And for good reason: cheese and nuts are a natural combination, made even better by a hint of sweetness from port wine and fresh or dried fruit. In that spirit, allow us to offer a few updated variations on this classic theme:

• At the end of a meal, serve individual plates with a small wedge of cheese, such as sweet Gorgonzola or robiola, toasted walnuts, figs, and slices of apple, pear, or persimmon.

• Press a dab of soft, spreadable cheese—or the cheese mixture from either this recipe or Grapes with Gorgonzola and Pecans (page 30)—between the flat sides of toasted pecan or walnut halves to make miniature nut sandwich hors d'oeuvres.

• Cut a small wheel of Brie in half horizontally. Spread the bottom half with a layer of Walnut Pesto (page 126) and replace the top half. Press warm, freshly toasted pine nuts or chopped walnuts into the top of the cheese. Let the cheese sit at room temperature for 1 to 2 hours; serve with crackers or baguette slices.

CROSTINI *with* CAMBOZOLA, CARAMELIZED ONIONS, *and* WALNUTS

½ CUP CHOPPED WALNUTS

24 SLICES BAGUETTE, CUT
¼ TO ⅜ INCH THICK

4½ TABLESPOONS EXTRA-VIRGIN
OLIVE OIL

2 LARGE RED ONIONS
(about 1 pound total),
THINLY SLICED

2 TABLESPOONS CHOPPED
FRESH SAGE

1 TEASPOON BALSAMIC VINEGAR

¼ TEASPOON SALT

⅛ TEASPOON SUGAR

FRESHLY GROUND PEPPER

4 OUNCES CAMBOZOLA,
BAVARIAN BLUE, OR OTHER
SOFT-RIPE BLUE CHEESE,
AT ROOM TEMPERATURE

The next time you're reaching for a box of crackers in the grocery store, put it back and pick up a baguette. Crostini, thin slices of bread crisped in the oven, are an easy homemade alternative to crackers; they are somehow both rustic and sophisticated—especially when you top them with sweet caramelized onions, toasted walnuts, and that creamy blend of Camembert and Gorgonzola called Cambozola.

PREHEAT oven to 350°. Spread walnuts on a baking sheet or in a shallow pan. Bake, stirring once or twice, until lightly browned and fragrant, 8 to 10 minutes. Let cool.

INCREASE oven temperature to 400°. Arrange bread slices on a baking sheet; brush tops with 3 tablespoons of the oil. Bake until lightly toasted and golden brown, 5 to 7 minutes. Let cool. (If making in advance, store airtight.)

IN a large, heavy saucepan or flameproof casserole, heat the remaining 1½ tablespoons oil over medium heat. Stir in onions, sage, vinegar, salt, and sugar. Cover and cook, stirring occasionally, until onions are very tender and browned at the edges, 20 to 25 minutes. Season to taste with pepper. Stir in walnuts.

SPREAD each crostini with about 1 teaspoon cheese; then mound onion-walnut mixture on top. Serve slightly warm or at room temperature.

YIELDS 24 CROSTINI

BRUSCHETTA CAPRESE

Italians love to make a simple *insalata caprese* of ripe tomatoes, fresh mozzarella, basil, and good olive oil. And we love to combine that idea with another Italian favorite, bruschetta—grilled crusty bread rubbed with a clove of garlic. More than an appetizer, this is a perfect way to get a party going: you grill the bread, and the guests top it to their liking. Meanwhile, crack open a bottle of Sangiovese and take an informal poll to see if anyone actually knows how to pronounce bruschetta (it's broo-*sket*-a).

PREHEAT oven to 325°. Place the pine nuts in a small pan and bake, shaking once or twice, until just golden, 5 to 7 minutes. Let cool.

IN a medium bowl, combine the tomatoes, mozzarella, olive oil, and salt and pepper to taste. Toss gently to mix. (If making ahead, cover and leave at room temperature up to 2 hours.)

PREPARE a medium-hot charcoal fire, or preheat an oven broiler. Position the grill rack or broiler pan 4 to 6 inches from the heat source. Grill or broil bread slices until golden brown, turning once. Immediately rub each slice with garlic, pressing the garlic against the rough surface of toast to distribute the flavor. Cut each slice into halves or thirds.

STIR pine nuts and basil into tomato mixture, then spoon onto each piece of warm garlic toast. Serve at once.

YIELDS 16 TO 24 PIECES

½ CUP PINE NUTS

1 POUND RED AND/OR YELLOW VINE-RIPENED TOMATOES, CUT INTO ½-INCH CHUNKS

2 SMALL BALLS *(about 3 ounces total)* FRESH WHOLE-MILK MOZZARELLA CHEESE, WELL DRAINED AND CUT INTO ½-INCH CUBES

2 TABLESPOONS EXTRA-VIRGIN OLIVE OIL

ABOUT ¼ TEASPOON SALT

FRESHLY GROUND PEPPER

8 SLICES RUSTIC ITALIAN OR COUNTRY-STYLE BREAD, CUT ¾ INCH THICK

1 LARGE CLOVE GARLIC, HALVED

3 TABLESPOONS COARSELY CHOPPED FRESH BASIL

CRAB CAKES *with* ALMONDS *and* ROMESCO SAUCE

Romesco Sauce

½ CUP SLIVERED ALMONDS

1 SMALL RED TOMATO
(about 4 ounces), QUARTERED

¾ CUP COARSELY CHOPPED
ROASTED RED BELL PEPPER

1 TABLESPOON RED
WINE VINEGAR

2 OR 3 CLOVES GARLIC

½ TEASPOON SALT

½ TEASPOON CAYENNE PEPPER

½ CUP EXTRA-VIRGIN
OLIVE OIL

⅓ CUP LOOSELY PACKED FRESH
FLAT-LEAF PARSLEY

1 STALK CELERY, CUT INTO
1-INCH PIECES

2 GREEN ONIONS, CUT INTO
1-INCH PIECES

¾ POUND CRABMEAT, PICKED
OVER TO REMOVE ANY BITS
OF SHELL OR CARTILAGE

½ CUP FRESH BREAD CRUMBS

1 EGG

3 TABLESPOONS MAYONNAISE

2 TEASPOONS FRESH LEMON
JUICE

¼ TEASPOON SALT

⅛ TEASPOON CAYENNE PEPPER

1 CUP SLIVERED ALMONDS,
CHOPPED

Miniature crab cakes with a golden coating of chopped almonds and an exclamation point of bright red romesco sauce make an elegant hors d'oeuvre. These crab cakes are lighter and easier than most because they're baked, not fried. (If you prefer to fry them, see "Fearless Frying" on page 38.) To serve these as a light brunch entrée, divide the mixture into 12 larger cakes and cook a bit longer. Place each cake at the center of a large plate, top it with a poached egg and a drizzle of romesco sauce, and surround it with a salad of baby greens and halved cherry tomatoes tossed in vinaigrette. People will say you should open a restaurant. ❦ The pesto of Spain, romesco is a zippy red pepper sauce that is every bit as versatile and colorful as its Italian counterpart. You can use the leftover sauce on grilled chicken, fish, or vegetables; spread it on sandwiches; or serve it as a dip with crudités. To save time, use jarred roasted bell peppers. Look for peppers preserved in olive oil or water, rather than ones pickled in vinegar, and be sure to drain them well.

TO make the sauce: Preheat oven to 350°. Spread almonds in a single layer on a baking sheet or in a shallow pan. Bake, stirring once or twice, until lightly browned and fragrant, 5 to 10 minutes. Let cool.

IN a food processor, purée almonds, tomato, bell pepper, vinegar, garlic, salt, and cayenne until a coarse paste forms. With machine on, slowly add oil in a thin, steady stream. Process until well blended. Transfer to a bowl and refrigerate, covered, at least 2 hours or as long as 2 days. Before serving, bring to room temperature.

TO prepare the cakes: Preheat oven to 400°. Line a large baking sheet with foil or parchment paper; coat generously with butter.

IN a food processor, whirl parsley, celery, and green onions until finely chopped. In a bowl, combine crabmeat, 3 tablespoons of the bread crumbs, egg, mayonnaise, lemon juice, salt, and cayenne. Add parsley mixture and mix well.

IN a small bowl, mix almonds with remaining 5 tablespoons bread crumbs. For each cake, form about 2 tablespoons of crab mixture into a 1½- to 2-inch ball; roll in almond mixture. Arrange 1½ inches apart on the baking sheet; press down gently to form patties about ½ inch thick.

BAKE until crab cakes are firm and almonds are golden, 10 to 12 minutes. To serve, turn the crab cakes with a spatula so the browned side shows. Top each crab cake with about 2 teaspoons of romesco sauce.

MAKES 24 TO 30 CAKES

Fearless Frying

For a crisp, golden brown crust on both sides of your crab cakes, panfry them instead of baking them: Combine 2 tablespoons olive oil and 1 tablespoon butter in a large frying pan. Cook over medium heat until butter has melted and oil is hot. Working in batches, add crab cakes and cook, turning once, until lightly browned on both sides, 6 to 8 minutes total. Drain on paper towels and serve at once.

SPICY CHICKEN-WALNUT TRIANGLES

These golden pastry triangles stuffed with a sweet-savory Moroccan-style chicken filling look and taste quite professional. They take a fair amount of time to make, but you can do all the preparation in stages and keep the unbaked triangles in the refrigerator or freezer until you're ready to serve them. (For storage, freeze them on baking sheets, then transfer them to plastic freezer bags. Frozen triangles can go straight from the freezer to the oven; add a few minutes to the baking time, and test the filling to be sure it's heated through.)

PREHEAT oven to 350°. Spread walnuts on a baking sheet or in a shallow pan. Bake, stirring once or twice, until lightly browned and fragrant, 8 to 10 minutes. Let cool.

IN a medium frying pan, heat oil over medium heat. Add onion and cook until softened but not browned, about 5 minutes. Stir in chicken, cranberries, olives, chiles, garlic, salt, cumin, cinnamon, and cayenne. Cook, stirring often, until chicken is no longer pink, about 5 minutes. Taste and add salt if needed. Let cool. Stir in walnuts and cheese.

ON a flat work surface, unfold filo and cut lengthwise into 6 equal strips 2 to 3 inches wide. To prevent drying, cover filo strips with plastic wrap and top with a damp towel.

BRUSH 1 filo strip with melted butter. Place ½ heaping teaspoon of the chicken mixture in 1 corner on a narrow end of the strip.

FOLD the adjacent corner to the opposite edge, covering the filling and making a triangle. Continue folding the strip as you would fold a flag, keeping the triangular shape with each fold. Brush with butter and cover with plastic wrap to prevent drying. Repeat with remaining filo and filling. (If making in advance, refrigerate up to 8 hours. Freeze for longer storage.)

PREHEAT oven to 350°. Line a large baking sheet with foil or parchment paper; coat with vegetable oil spray. Place triangles about 1 inch apart on baking sheet. Bake until puffed and golden, 10 to 15 minutes. Let cool 5 minutes before serving.

YIELDS 36 TRIANGLES

½ CUP CHOPPED WALNUTS

1½ TABLESPOONS WALNUT OIL OR VEGETABLE OIL

½ CUP FINELY CHOPPED ONION

1 SKINLESS, BONELESS CHICKEN BREAST HALF (about 6 ounces), FINELY CHOPPED

2 TABLESPOONS SWEETENED DRIED CRANBERRIES OR RAISINS

1 TABLESPOON FINELY CHOPPED PIMIENTO-STUFFED GREEN OLIVES

2 TEASPOONS MASHED CANNED CHIPOTLE CHILES IN ADOBO SAUCE, OR ½ TEASPOON CRUSHED DRIED RED CHILES

1 SMALL CLOVE GARLIC, PRESSED OR CHOPPED

ABOUT ¼ TEASPOON SALT

½ TEASPOON GROUND CUMIN

¼ TEASPOON GROUND CINNAMON

⅛ TEASPOON CAYENNE PEPPER

½ CUP (about 2 ounces) SHREDDED MONTEREY JACK CHEESE

6 SHEETS FILO DOUGH, THAWED

½ CUP UNSALTED BUTTER, MELTED

WALNUT-PEPERONATA WONTONS

1½ CUPS CHOPPED WALNUTS

2 RED BELL PEPPERS
(about 1 pound)

2 TABLESPOONS ROASTED
GARLIC WALNUT OIL

½ CUP FINELY CHOPPED ONION

1 LARGE CLOVE GARLIC,
PRESSED OR MINCED

¼ CUP CRUMBLED RICOTTA
SALATA OR FETA CHEESE

6 KALAMATA OLIVES *(about
2 tablespoons)*, PITTED AND
FINELY CHOPPED

2 TEASPOONS MINCED FRESH
LEMON THYME OR OTHER
FRESH THYME, OR PARSLEY

⅛ TEASPOON FRESHLY
GROUND PEPPER

⅛ TEASPOON CRUSHED
DRIED RED CHILES

SALT

48 WONTON WRAPPERS

2 TO 4 CUPS PEANUT OIL OR
CORN OIL FOR DEEP-FRYING

Hold the plum sauce! There's nothing Chinese about these crisp wontons with a bold Mediterranean-style filling. Think beyond Asian, and you'll find you can use wonton wrappers to make everything from homemade noodles and ravioli to dumplings and crisp-fried appetizers like these. Ricotta salata, a specialty of southern Italy (not to be confused with the more familiar fresh ricotta), is salted, pressed, and aged until it's firm enough to slice or crumble. If it's not available, you can substitute a mild feta or Mexican queso fresco.

PREHEAT oven to 350°. Spread walnuts on a baking sheet or in a shallow pan. Bake, shaking the pan once or twice, until lightly browned and fragrant, 8 to 10 minutes. Let cool.

PREHEAT oven broiler, placing rack as close to heat source as possible. Place whole peppers on a baking sheet or broiler pan; broil, turning two or three times, until skin is charred and black all over, about 10 minutes. (Alternatively, roast peppers directly over a gas flame, turning, until charred, about 5 minutes.) Remove from heat and seal in a paper bag. Set aside until cool enough to handle, at least 10 minutes. Peel off blackened skin from peppers (some skin can remain); discard stems and seeds. Chop peppers into ¼-inch pieces (you will have about 1 cup).

IN a large frying pan, warm the walnut oil over medium heat. Add peppers, onion, and garlic; cook, stirring occasionally, until softened but not brown, about 5 minutes. Let cool. Stir in cheese, olives, thyme, pepper, and chiles. Add salt if needed. (Cheese and olives vary in saltiness.)

PLACE 1 wonton wrapper with 1 corner pointing toward you. With a chopstick or finger dipped in water, lightly moisten edges of wrapper. Place about 1 teaspoon filling in center; fold nearest corner over the filling to make a triangle. Press edges to seal. As each wonton is completed, arrange in a single layer on a large baking sheet or platter and cover with plastic wrap. Repeat with remaining wrappers and filling. Cover tightly and refrigerate for 1 hour or up to 2 days; freeze for longer storage.

IN a wok or large, heavy saucepan, heat peanut oil over medium-high heat to 350°. Cook wontons in batches without crowding, turning occasionally, until crisp and golden, about 2 minutes. Drain on paper towels. If making in advance, keep warm on a wire rack over a baking sheet for up to 30 minutes in a 250° oven. Serve hot or warm, plain or with Romesco Sauce (page 36) for dipping.

YIELDS 48 WONTONS

PAPILLOTE *of* FOIE GRAS *and* LANGOUSTINES

(HUBERT KELLER)

4 SLICES *(about 3½ ounces each)*
RAW FOIE GRAS, CUT
½ INCH THICK

SALT

FRESHLY GROUND PEPPER

¼ CUP SAUTERNES WINE

20 ALMONDS

1 TABLESPOON UNSALTED
BUTTER

8 SMALL ROUND TURNIPS
(about 8 ounces total), PEELED

1½ TEASPOONS SUGAR

¾ CUP DUCK OR CHICKEN
STOCK *(page 215)*

½ POUND SMALL CHANTERELLE
MUSHROOMS, BRUSHED CLEAN
AND HALVED

1½ TEASPOONS MINCED
SHALLOT

1 SMALL HEAD *(about 1 pound)*
SAVOY OR OTHER GREEN
CABBAGE

8 FRESH LANGOUSTINES
OR JUMBO SHRIMP, SHELLED
AND DEVEINED

12 SPRIGS CHERVIL

It would be more than fair to call this a special-occasion dish. It's time-consuming to prepare, and its luxury ingredients aren't exactly a bargain. But one look at the faces of your friends as they tear open these edible "gifts" that release their heady fragrance of sautéed foie gras, Sauternes, almonds, langoustines, glazed turnips, and cabbage, and we think you'll agree: it's worth the effort. Serve this four-star first course with the rest of the bottle of Sauternes or a fruity sparkling wine.

PLACE foie gras in a single layer in a glass or other nonreactive baking dish; season both sides lightly with salt and pepper. Sprinkle with wine. Cover tightly with plastic wrap and refrigerate 45 minutes.

CUT 4 sheets of aluminum foil each 12 inches square; set aside. Place almonds in a small heat-proof bowl. Cover with boiling water and let stand for 3 minutes. Drain off water, then squeeze off the skins by squeezing almonds between your fingers and thumb.

IN a medium saucepan over medium heat, melt ½ tablespoon of the butter. Add turnips in a single layer and sprinkle with sugar. Add ½ cup of the stock; season lightly with salt and pepper. Bring mixture to a simmer. Reduce heat to medium-low and cook, covered, shaking pan occasionally, until turnips are tender, golden, and coated with a syrupy liquid, 15 to 20 minutes. Set aside.

IN a medium frying pan, heat the remaining ½ tablespoon butter over high heat. Add chanterelles and cook, tossing occasionally, until tender, about 2 minutes. Season lightly with salt and pepper. Stir in almonds and shallot; cook, stirring occasionally, until shallot is softened, about 2 minutes. Transfer mixture to a plate and set aside.

BRING a large saucepan of salted water to a boil over high heat. Separate the cabbage leaves, reserving 8 pale inner leaves (save the rest of the cabbage for another use). Cut out and discard the coarse stem from the center of each leaf. Plunge the leaves into the boiling water and cook until limp and flexible but not soft, 6 to 8 minutes. Drain, then plunge the leaves into ice water to refresh them. Drain again and spread the leaves in a single layer on towels to dry.

PREHEAT oven to 450°. Heat a nonstick frying pan over very high heat. With a metal spatula, lift foie gras from the wine; reserve wine. Working in batches if necessary, cook foie gras without crowding until very lightly browned, about 30 seconds on each side; drain on paper towels.

FOLD each sheet of aluminum foil in half; reopen as you would a book. On one-half of each piece, lay 2 cabbage leaves, overlapping them slightly; season lightly with salt and pepper. Top cabbage with a slice of foie gras. Arrange the chanterelles and almonds around the cabbage leaves. Season langoustines lightly with salt and pepper; place 2 on each slice of foie gras. Slice each turnip in half lengthwise and place 4 pieces, along with 3 chervil sprigs, on each serving. Top each papillote with 1 tablespoon of the remaining wine and 1 tablespoon of the remaining broth. Fold over the foil, crimping the edges all around to seal securely.

ARRANGE papillotes on a baking sheet and bake until packets are puffed and sizzling hot, about 7 minutes. Immediately place 1 papillote on each of 4 warm serving plates. With the tip of a sharp knife, cut an X on the top of each papillote. Let guests use their forks to unfold the packets at the table.

SERVES 4

ROASTED BEET SALAD *with* APPLE, DANDELION LEAVES, *and* ALMONDS

(CHARLIE TROTTER)

½ CUP SLIVERED ALMONDS

1 LARGE WHITE OR
YELLOW BEET *(10 to 12 ounces)*

1 LARGE SHALLOT, PEELED

6 TABLESPOONS OLIVE OIL

1 LARGE POBLANO CHILE
(4 to 5 ounces)

2 TABLESPOONS WATER

SALT

FRESHLY GROUND PEPPER

1 TABLESPOON RICE VINEGAR

1 SMALL GALA APPLE
(5 to 6 ounces), CORED AND CUT
INTO MATCHSTICK-SIZE PIECES

20 DANDELION LEAVES

All of the elements of this fanciful first-course salad can be prepared ahead of time, making it easy to assemble at the last minute. Look for white beets at specialty produce stores; if you can't find them, you can use golden beets. Just avoid red beets, which would bleed and overpower this delicate presentation.

PREHEAT oven to 350°. Spread almonds on a baking sheet or in a shallow pan. Bake, stirring once or twice, until lightly browned and fragrant, 5 to 10 minutes. Chop coarsely and set aside. Increase oven temperature to 375°.

PLACE beet in a small baking dish and bake until tender, 2 to 2½ hours. When beet is cool enough to handle, peel off and discard the skin. Cut the beet into matchstick-size pieces.

WHILE the beet is baking, in a small ramekin or baking dish, combine the shallot with 3 table-spoons of the oil, turning to coat. Bake until shallot is tender when pierced with the tip of a sharp knife, about 30 minutes. Remove shallot from pan, reserving the oil. Remove and discard the shallot's tough outer layer; cut shallot into thin slices.

PREHEAT oven broiler, placing the rack as close to the heat source as possible. Place the chile on a baking sheet or broiler pan; broil, turning once or twice, until skin is charred and black all over, about 10 minutes.(Alternatively, roast chile directly over a gas flame, turning, until charred,

about 5 minutes.) Remove from heat and seal in a paper bag. Set aside until cool enough to handle, at least 10 minutes. Peel off blackened skin from chile (some skin can remain); discard stem and seeds. Cut chile in half. Coarsely chop one half; set aside the remaining half.

PLACE the chopped chile in a blender. Pour in the water and the oil from baking the shallot. Purée until smooth, then press through a fine sieve. Season to taste with salt and pepper. Scrape chile purée into a small bowl and refrigerate, covered.

CUT the remaining chile half into small cubes; place in a large bowl and add the vinegar. Slowly whisk in the remaining 3 tablespoons oil; season to taste with salt and pepper. Mix in the beet, shallot, and apple. If desired, add salt and pepper.

PLACE 5 dandelion leaves on each of 4 plates. Arrange the beet-and-apple mixture on top of the greens; scatter almonds around the greens. Drizzle the reserved chile purée on top of and around the salads; sprinkle salads with pepper.

SERVES 4

ASPARAGUS SALAD *with* SESAME-GLAZED WALNUTS

(MARTIN YAN)

2½ TO 3 POUNDS ASPARAGUS

1 TEASPOON WALNUT OIL
OR VEGETABLE OIL

¾ TEASPOON SALT

3 TABLESPOONS RICE VINEGAR

2 TABLESPOONS ASIAN PLUM
SAUCE

1½ TABLESPOONS SOY SAUCE

1 TABLESPOON HONEY

¾ TEASPOON DRY MUSTARD
POWDER

1 TABLESPOON ASIAN
SESAME OIL

⅔ CUP PREPARED SESAME-
GLAZED WALNUTS

If Yan can cook with walnuts, so can you! We asked the world's favorite Chinese chef for an easy salad idea, and he created this winning combination: tender-crisp asparagus in a sweet soy vinaigrette topped with a scattering of crunchy glazed walnuts.

TRIM off and discard tough ends from asparagus; cut diagonally into 1½-inch pieces. In a large frying pan or saucepan over high heat, bring about 2 inches of water to a boil. Add asparagus, walnut oil, and salt. Cook until asparagus is tender-crisp, 1 to 3 minutes. Drain immediately and plunge into ice water; drain again and pat dry with paper towels. Cover and refrigerate until ready to serve, up to 8 hours.

TO make dressing: In a small bowl, whisk together vinegar, plum sauce, soy sauce, honey, and mustard. Whisk in sesame oil until well blended.

JUST before serving, toss asparagus and dressing in a large bowl. Arrange asparagus on a serving platter and top with walnuts.

SERVES 4 TO 6

Asparagus Tips

When spring rolls around, I make more than spring rolls! I make asparagus as many ways as I can think of, from stir-fries to salads. Here are two tips I always pass along to my students. First, when serving whole spears, unless you're using the most slender and tender asparagus, use a vegetable peeler to peel the base of each spear, starting about halfway down; this makes the whole stalk more palatable, and it looks beautiful, too. Second, wait until the last minute to toss asparagus with any acid-based dressing so that it retains its bright green color. —M.Y.

SPINACH SALAD *with* BACON, ALMONDS, *and* WARM GOAT CHEESE

How could you possibly improve upon a classic salad of baby spinach leaves tossed in a honey-mustard vinaigrette with toasted almonds and bacon? How about adding a little cake of meltingly warm, almond-encrusted goat cheese, and perhaps some crusty bread and a glass of crisp chardonnay on the side?

PREHEAT oven to 350°. Spread almonds on a baking sheet or in a shallow pan. Bake, stirring once or twice, until lightly browned and fragrant, 5 to 10 minutes. Let cool. Chop ¼ cup of the almonds; reserve the rest.

IN a large frying pan, cook bacon over medium heat, stirring occasionally, until browned and crisp, 6 to 8 minutes. Drain on paper towels.

IN a large bowl, whisk together mustard, honey, and vinegar. Gradually whisk in 6 tablespoons of the oil. Season to taste with salt and pepper. Add the reserved ½ cup slivered almonds, the bacon, spinach, and onion, tossing gently to coat. Divide salad equally among 4 plates.

ON a small plate, mix the chopped almonds with the chives. Roll the edges of the goat cheese rounds in the nut mixture, pressing in gently. In a small frying pan, warm the remaining 2 tablespoons oil over medium-high heat. Add cheese rounds and cook, turning once, until they are softened but still retain their shape, about 1 minute total. Top each salad with a slice of hot cheese and serve at once.

SERVES 4

¾ CUP SLIVERED ALMONDS

5 OUNCES *(about 5 slices)* THICK-SLICED BACON, CUT CROSSWISE INTO 1-INCH PIECES

2 TEASPOONS DIJON MUSTARD

2 TEASPOONS HONEY

1 TABLESPOON SHERRY VINEGAR OR WHITE WINE VINEGAR

½ CUP EXTRA-VIRGIN OLIVE OIL OR WALNUT OIL *(or a combination)*

ABOUT ¼ TEASPOON SALT

ABOUT ⅛ TEASPOON FRESHLY GROUND PEPPER

10 OUNCES *(about 8 cups, loosely packed)* BABY SPINACH LEAVES, WELL RINSED AND DRIED

½ SMALL RED ONION, THINLY SLICED

2 TABLESPOONS CHOPPED FRESH CHIVES

1 LOG *(4 ounces)* FRESH GOAT CHEESE *(chèvre)*, PLAIN, GARLIC, OR HERB-FLAVORED, CUT CROSSWISE INTO 4 EQUAL SLICES

PAN–SEARED SEA SCALLOPS
with GRAPEFRUIT, ENDIVE, *and* WALNUTS
(MARK FRANZ)

1 CUP WALNUTS

2 CUPS LOOSELY PACKED FRESH
FLAT-LEAF PARSLEY

3 TABLESPOONS PLUS
2 TEASPOONS FRESH LEMON
JUICE

½ CUP PLUS 2 TABLESPOONS
EXTRA-VIRGIN OLIVE OIL

COARSE-GRAINED SALT

FRESHLY GROUND PEPPER

2 WHITE OR PINK GRAPEFRUITS

2 LARGE HEADS BELGIAN
ENDIVE *(6 to 8 ounces total),*
CUT INTO THIN STRIPS

2 TABLESPOONS WALNUT OIL
OR VEGETABLE OIL

8 LARGE SEA SCALLOPS
(about 1 pound total), RINSED
AND PATTED DRY

In this elegant starter, the seared scallops are topped with a dollop of walnut-parsley coulis that tastes as bright and fresh as it looks. The recipe makes more coulis than you'll need, but that's a good thing—save what's left over to serve with any simply cooked food. It's right at home on grilled or roasted chicken or fish, and even grilled steak or lamb chops.

PREHEAT oven to 350°. On a large baking sheet, spread walnuts in an even layer. Bake, stirring once or twice, until light golden brown and fragrant, 10 to 12 minutes. Chop coarsely.

TO make the walnut-parsley coulis: In a blender or food processor, combine the parsley, ½ cup of the walnuts, and 3 tablespoons of the lemon juice. Process until finely chopped, scraping the bowl once. With the motor running, add ½ cup of the oil in a thin, steady stream; process until a thick purée forms. Season to taste with salt and pepper.

IN a medium bowl, whisk the remaining 2 teaspoons lemon juice with the remaining 2 tablespoons oil; season to taste with salt and pepper. Slice the ends off the grapefruits. With a sharp knife, carefully cut away the rind and white pith. With a small, sharp knife, slice between the membranes to release the grapefruit segments; discard the seeds. To the bowl, add the grapefruit segments, endive, and the remaining ⅓ cup walnuts, tossing gently to mix with the dressing.

HEAT a large frying pan over high heat. Add the walnut oil; when it shimmers, carefully add the scallops. Cook, turning once, until golden brown on both sides and almost opaque throughout, about 4 minutes total. Remove from heat; let scallops remain in pan to complete cooking while you assemble the salad,

TO serve, place a scallop on each side of 4 dinner plates (2 scallops per plate); place a dollop of the walnut-parsley coulis over each scallop. With tongs, mound the salad in the center of each plate. Serve at once.

SERVES 4

BABY LIMA BEAN SALAD *with* SHRIMP *and* ALMONDS

½ CUP CHOPPED ALMONDS

7 TABLESPOONS EXTRA-VIRGIN OLIVE OIL

1 PACKAGE *(20 ounces)* FROZEN BABY LIMA BEANS, THAWED

1 TABLESPOON MINCED FRESH ROSEMARY

1 TEASPOON MINCED FRESH THYME

ABOUT ¾ TEASPOON SALT

2 LARGE CLOVES GARLIC, MINCED

1 CUP WATER

1 POUND MEDIUM SHRIMP, SHELLED AND DEVEINED

2 LARGE TOMATOES *(about 1 pound total)*, SEEDED AND CUT INTO ½ INCH CUBES

3 TABLESPOONS FRESH LEMON JUICE

ABOUT ½ TEASPOON FRESHLY GROUND PEPPER

LETTUCE LEAVES *(optional)*

LEMON WEDGES FOR GARNISH

ROSEMARY SPRIGS FOR GARNISH

Baby lima beans are more tender and less starchy than their more mature siblings, and their delicate flavor makes a fine match with the subtle sweetness of shrimp and walnuts. You can even peel off the outer skin to reveal the bright green beans. Serve this salad as a first course, or as part of a composed salad or an antipasto platter. Or set it out at a picnic along with a nice bottle of chilled Sauvignon Blanc.

PREHEAT oven to 350°. Spread almonds on a baking sheet or in a shallow pan. Bake, stirring once or twice, until lightly browned and fragrant, 8 to 10 minutes. Let cool.

IN a large frying pan, heat 1 tablespoon of the oil over medium heat. Add lima beans, rosemary, thyme, ½ teaspoon of the salt, and half of the garlic. Cook, stirring, until garlic is fragrant, 1 to 2 minutes. Pour in water; increase heat to medium-high and bring to a boil. Cook uncovered, stirring occasionally, until beans are just tender and liquid has evaporated, 3 to 5 minutes. Spoon bean mixture into a large bowl. Stir in 4 tablespoons more oil and let cool.

IN the same pan, warm the remaining 2 tablespoons oil over medium heat. Add the remaining garlic and cook, stirring, until fragrant, about

1 minute. Add shrimp and ¼ teaspoon salt. Increase heat to medium-high and cook, stirring, until shrimp are pink and opaque throughout, 3 to 4 minutes. Stir in tomatoes and cook, stirring, until just heated through, about 1 minute. Remove from heat and stir in the lemon juice. Let cool.

ADD shrimp and cooking juices to the lima bean mixture, tossing gently to mix. Taste for seasoning, adding salt and pepper as needed.

JUST before serving, stir in almonds. With a slotted spoon, spoon salad onto lettuce leaves or directly onto a platter. Garnish with lemon wedges. Serve at cool room temperature.

SERVES 4 TO 6

CAESAR SALAD *with* GREEN ONIONS *and* WALNUTS

Walnuts with Rosemary and Parmesan

1 EGG WHITE

2 CUPS WALNUTS

2 TABLESPOONS MINCED FRESH ROSEMARY

1 TEASPOON COARSE-GRAINED SALT

¼ TEASPOON CAYENNE PEPPER

½ CUP FRESHLY GRATED PARMESAN CHEESE

Double-Garlic Croutons

3 SLICES FRENCH OR ITALIAN BREAD, CUT ABOUT ½ INCH THICK

1½ TABLESPOONS ROASTED GARLIC WALNUT OIL

1 CLOVE GARLIC, HALVED

3 ROMAINE LETTUCE HEARTS
(about 1 pound total)

(Ingredients continue on opposite page)

What can you do to the king of salads to take it right over the top? Easy. Top it with walnuts. Lovers of pesto sauce know that nuts, herbs, and Parmesan cheese are a match made in heaven (or, better yet, northern Italy). The seasoned walnuts used here are addictive on their own, and they make a fantastic complement to the garlicky croutons. This recipe makes plenty so you can enjoy them both ways. If you prefer, however, you can use plain toasted walnuts and packaged croutons. Real Parmigiano-Reggiano or another good Italian grana cheese is worth the splurge in this simple salad.

TO make the walnuts: Preheat oven to 300°. Line a large baking sheet with foil or parchment paper; coat with vegetable oil spray. In a large bowl, whisk egg white until frothy. Add walnuts, rosemary, salt, and cayenne, tossing to coat evenly. Spread nuts in a single layer on the prepared baking sheet. Bake until very lightly browned, about 10 minutes. Sprinkle walnuts with Parmesan cheese; bake until walnuts are crisp and cheese has melted, 5 to 10 minutes. Let cool. You should have 2 cups. Serve slightly warm or at room temperature. If making in advance, store airtight at room temperature up to 1 week.

TO make the croutons: Preheat oven to 425°. Brush both sides of bread with oil and place on a baking sheet. Bake, turning once, until golden brown, 10 to 15 minutes.

WHEN bread is cool enough to handle, rub each slice with garlic, pressing the garlic against the rough surface of the toast to distribute the flavor. Cut bread into ¾-inch squares. Let cool. If making in advance, store airtight at room temperature up to 3 days.

TO make the salad: Tear each lettuce leaf crosswise into 4 or 5 pieces; discard the tough stem ends. Rinse lettuce well and wrap in a clean dish towel.

TO make the dressing: In a large salad bowl, whisk together the lemon juice, mustard, garlic, salt, pepper, hot-pepper sauce, and Worcestershire. Reserve 6 anchovy fillets; chop the remainder. Add chopped anchovies to salad bowl, mashing with the back of a spoon. Gradually whisk in the oil to make a thick dressing.

BRING a small pan of water to a boil over medium-high heat. With a slotted spoon, gently lower the egg into the water; cook exactly 2 minutes. Crack the egg into the dressing and whisk until completely blended. If any solid egg white sticks to the shell, scoop it out with a spoon; chop finely and add to the dressing.

ADD lettuce to the bowl, tossing to coat. Add croutons, green onion, walnuts, and ⅓ cup of the Parmesan cheese; toss gently. Sprinkle remaining cheese on top. Garnish salad with remaining anchovy fillets and serve at once.

SERVES 4 TO 6

Caesar Dressing

2 TABLESPOONS FRESH LEMON JUICE

1 TEASPOON DIJON MUSTARD

1 CLOVE GARLIC, PRESSED OR MINCED

⅛ TEASPOON SALT

⅛ TEASPOON FRESHLY COARSE-GROUND PEPPER

⅛ TEASPOON HOT-PEPPER SAUCE, SUCH AS TABASCO

⅛ TEASPOON WORCESTERSHIRE SAUCE

1 CAN *(2 ounces)* FLAT ANCHOVY FILLETS, DRAINED

¼ CUP EXTRA-VIRGIN OLIVE OIL OR WALNUT OIL

1 EGG

ABOUT ¾ CUP THIN DIAGONAL SLICES GREEN ONION

½ CUP FRESHLY GRATED PARMESAN CHEESE

APPLE *and* RADICCHIO SALAD

(BRADLEY OGDEN)

Spicy Glazed Walnuts

2 TABLESPOONS UNSALTED
BUTTER

3 TABLESPOONS SUGAR

3 TABLESPOONS WATER

½ TEASPOON SALT

½ TEASPOON FRESHLY
GROUND PEPPER

⅛ TEASPOON CAYENNE PEPPER

⅔ CUP WALNUTS

Basil Balsamic Vinaigrette

¼ CUP FINELY DICED RED
ONION

2 CLOVES GARLIC, MINCED

⅛ TEASPOON DRY MUSTARD
POWDER

¼ CUP CHOPPED FRESH
BASIL

¼ CUP CHOPPED FRESH FLAT-
LEAF PARSLEY

¼ CUP BALSAMIC VINEGAR

¼ CUP OLIVE OIL

3 TABLESPOONS FRESH LEMON
JUICE

1 TEASPOON FINELY GRATED
LEMON ZEST

½ TEASPOON COARSE-GRAINED
SALT

½ TEASPOON FRESHLY
GROUND PEPPER

*(Ingredients continue on
opposite page)*

To make a perfect salad for a brisk fall day, chef Bradley Ogden balances the mildly bitter taste of radicchio with sweet-spicy glazed walnuts, blue cheese, tart apples, and a sparkling balsamic vinaigrette. These nuts are highly recommended for topping any salad made with fruit or cheese. They also make a tasty party snack. The dressing can be used on all kinds of salads, especially those with more robust greens. Try it with thinly shaved fennel, apples, and walnuts, or with chilled hearts of romaine with sliced beets and orange segments.

TO make the walnuts: Line a baking sheet with parchment paper or foil. Melt butter in a large, heavy frying pan over medium heat. Stir in the sugar, water, salt, pepper, and cayenne. Bring to a boil. Add walnuts, stirring to coat well. Cook, stirring constantly, until sugar begins to caramelize and nuts are glazed, about 5 minutes. Spread walnuts in a single layer on the prepared baking sheet; separate walnuts with a fork if needed. Let cool completely.

TO make the vinaigrette: In a small bowl, toss together the onion, garlic, and mustard. Add the basil, parsley, vinegar, oil, lemon juice, lemon zest, salt, and pepper; mix until well blended. Let stand 30 minutes at room temperature to blend flavors. Taste, adjusting seasonings as needed.

TO assemble the salad: Remove any limp outer leaves from the radicchio. Cut radicchio in half through the stem end, then cut each half into thin strips.

IN a large bowl, combine the radicchio, apples, blue cheese, and walnuts. Toss gently to mix. Add ½ cup of the vinaigrette and toss again to coat. Taste, adding more dressing, salt, and pepper as needed. (Reserve leftover vinaigrette for another use.) Garnish with radicchio leaves and apple slices and serve at once.

SERVES 4 TO 6

1 HEAD RADICCHIO
(about 10 ounces)

3 APPLES *(about 18 ounces total)*,
SUCH AS FUJI OR GRAVENSTEIN,
CORED AND CUT INTO ½-INCH
CUBES

¾ CUP *(about 3 ounces)* CRUMBLED
BLUE CHEESE, SUCH AS MAYTAG
BLUE

COARSE-GRAINED SALT

FRESHLY GROUND PEPPER

RADICCHIO LEAVES FOR GARNISH

APPLE SLICES FOR GARNISH

ROASTED SWEET CORN SALAD

½ CUP CHOPPED PECANS

3 LARGE OR 4 MEDIUM EARS
OF CORN, SHUCKED

6 TABLESPOONS EXTRA-VIRGIN
OLIVE OIL

SALT

FRESHLY GROUND PEPPER

1 TABLESPOON FRESH LIME
JUICE

FINELY GRATED ZEST OF 1 LIME

1 TABLESPOON WHITE WINE
VINEGAR

1 TEASPOON SUGAR

¼ TEASPOON GROUND
CINNAMON

HOT-PEPPER SAUCE, SUCH AS
TABASCO

1 ENGLISH CUCUMBER, CUT
INTO ½-INCH CUBES

4 RIPE TOMATOES *(about 1 pound
total)*, CUT INTO ½-INCH CUBES

2 FIRM-RIPE AVOCADOS,
PITTED, PEELED, AND CUT
INTO ½-INCH CUBES

4 CUPS LOOSELY PACKED
ARUGULA OR WATERCRESS

1 CUP *(4 ounces)* CRUMBLED
FETA CHEESE

Roasting fresh corn until it's slightly browned and caramelized is a wonderful way to bring out its natural sweetness. Make all the elements of this colorful salad in advance and toss them together with a light hand just before serving. This salad also works beautifully as a relish, served with grilled fish or chicken.

PREHEAT oven to 350°. Spread pecans on a baking sheet or in a shallow pan. Bake, stirring once or twice, until lightly browned and fragrant, 5 to 10 minutes. Let cool. Increase oven temperature to 450°.

WITH a sharp knife, cut the kernels from the ears of corn. (You will have about 2 cups kernels.) Toss kernels with 2 tablespoons of the olive oil; season with ¼ teaspoon salt and ⅛ teaspoon pepper. Spread the kernels in a single layer on a baking sheet. Bake, stirring once or twice and watching carefully to avoid burning, until golden brown, 15 to 20 minutes. Let cool.

TO make the dressing: In a blender, combine ¼ cup of the roasted kernels, lime juice, lime zest, vinegar, sugar, and cinnamon. Blend until smooth. With the blender running, add the remaining 4 tablespoons olive oil in a thin, steady stream. Season to taste with salt, pepper, and hot-pepper sauce.

TO assemble the salad: In a large bowl, combine remaining 1¾ cups corn, cucumber, tomatoes, and avocados. Add dressing, tossing to coat. Arrange arugula on a large platter. With a slotted spoon, arrange salad on top. Sprinkle with cheese and pecans.

SERVES 6 TO 8

Keep Your Ears to the Ground

To cut the kernels from an ear of corn, hold the ear at an angle, with the pointed end resting on the work surface. Hold a sharp knife (such as a chef's knife) with the blade parallel to the cob and carefully slice downward, cutting away from yourself. To help keep the kernels from flying all over the kitchen, work over a rimmed baking sheet.

DIAMOND WALDORF SALAD

The classic Waldorf is defined by four essential ingredients: apples, celery, walnuts, and mayonnaise. On the principle that you can't have too much of a good thing, we've upped the walnut ante by adding a homemade walnut-oil mayonnaise. To save time, you can, of course, use prepared mayonnaise; to perk it up, try adding a splash of lemon juice and a few drops of honey. ❦ Besides being the secret ingredient in our Diamond Waldorf Salad, this mayonnaise makes a mean chicken salad. Just toss cubes of roasted or poached chicken with diced celery, toasted walnuts, and, if you like, a pinch of curry powder or a dollop of orange marmalade. To make a walnut aioli for dipping raw veggies, simply replace the walnut oil with roasted garlic walnut oil.

TO make the mayonnaise: In a food processor, combine the egg, lemon juice, mustard, salt, and cayenne. Process until blended, 2 to 3 seconds. In a measuring cup, combine olive oil and walnut oil. With motor running, add oil a few drops at a time. When about ½ cup of the oil has been added, the mayonnaise will begin to thicken; add the remaining oil in a slow, steady stream. Taste, processing in more lemon juice or salt if needed. Use at once, or refrigerate, covered, up to 5 days.

TO assemble the salad: Preheat oven to 350°. On a large baking sheet, spread walnuts in an even layer. Bake, stirring once or twice, until light golden brown and fragrant, 10 to 12 minutes. Let cool. Chop coarsely.

IN a large bowl, combine apples, celery, grapes, ¾ cup of the mayonnaise, and parsley. Toss gently to mix. (Reserve leftover mayonnaise for another use.) If making in advance, cover and refrigerate up to 2 days.

JUST before serving, stir in the walnuts.

SERVES 6

Walnut Mayonnaise

1 EGG

ABOUT 3 TABLESPOONS FRESH LEMON JUICE

1 TEASPOON DIJON MUSTARD

ABOUT ½ TEASPOON SALT

⅛ TEASPOON CAYENNE PEPPER

⅔ CUP OLIVE OIL OR VEGETABLE OIL

⅓ CUP WALNUT OIL

1½ CUPS WALNUTS

2 FUJI OR OTHER CRISP, FLAVORFUL APPLES (*about 12 ounces total*), CORED AND CUT INTO ¾-INCH CUBES

3 STALKS CELERY, CUT INTO ½-INCH CUBES (*about 1½ cups*)

1 CUP HALVED SEEDLESS RED OR GREEN GRAPES (*about 24 grapes*)

¼ CUP CHOPPED FRESH FLAT-LEAF PARSLEY

ENTRÉES

Farmers have more time to think than city people do. And that's why I've always thought and said that farmers are the smartest people in the world.

HARRY S. TRUMAN

NUT-CRUSTED SALMON *with* GARLICKY GREENS *and* WALNUTS

4 SKINLESS SALMON FILLETS
(4 to 6 ounces each), ABOUT
½ INCH THICK

SALT

FRESHLY GROUND PEPPER

3 TABLESPOONS MAYONNAISE

3 TABLESPOONS FRESHLY
GRATED PARMESAN CHEESE

1 TEASPOON FRESH
LEMON JUICE

⅛ TEASPOON CAYENNE PEPPER

1 CUP SLICED WALNUTS

1½ POUNDS SWISS CHARD,
TOUGH ENDS REMOVED

4 CLOVES GARLIC, MINCED

3 TABLESPOONS UNSALTED
BUTTER

1½ TEASPOONS ROASTED
GARLIC WALNUT OIL, WALNUT
OIL, OR OLIVE OIL

LEMON WEDGES FOR GARNISH

Don't you love it when a recipe is really easy but yields dramatic results? That's what we have here: a quick topping for salmon (it goes well on snapper and halibut, too) that you can whip up from ingredients you probably have in your kitchen right now. It becomes golden and lightly puffed when baked and tastes much more complex than the handful of ingredients that goes into it. The chard rounds out the flavors; if you can't find chard, the same method works perfectly for spinach.

LINE a baking sheet with foil or parchment paper; coat with vegetable oil spray. Lightly season both sides of salmon with salt and pepper; arrange fillets 2 inches apart on the baking sheet.

IN a small bowl, blend mayonnaise, Parmesan, lemon juice, and cayenne. Spread mixture evenly over the fillets, then sprinkle 2 tablespoons walnuts over each. (If making in advance, cover with plastic wrap and refrigerate up to 4 hours.)

COARSELY chop chard stems and leaves separately and rinse in cold water; drain in a colander, but do not pat dry. In a large frying pan or saucepan, combine chard stems and garlic. Cover and cook over medium heat, stirring once or twice, 2 to 3 minutes. Add chard leaves and cook until wilted, 3 to 5 minutes. Transfer to a colander. Preheat oven to 400°.

IN the same pan, melt butter in the oil over medium heat. Add the remaining ½ cup walnuts and cook, stirring, until lightly browned and fragrant, 3 to 5 minutes. Add chard and garlic; cook, stirring, until heated through. Season to taste with salt and pepper.

BAKE fish until walnuts are lightly browned and fish is just opaque throughout, 5 to 8 minutes. To serve, divide chard equally among 4 warm dinner plates. Top each with a salmon fillet and garnish with lemon wedges.

SERVES 4

BAKED HALIBUT *with* TARATOR SAUCE

(HEIDI KRAHLING)

Tarator Sauce

¾ CUP PINE NUTS

1 CUP WALNUTS

2 CUPS LOOSELY PACKED FRESH
CILANTRO LEAVES

2 OR 3 CLOVES GARLIC

½ TEASPOON PAPRIKA

½ TEASPOON CAYENNE PEPPER

5 TABLESPOONS TAHINI
(Middle Eastern sesame seed paste)

⅓ CUP FRESH LEMON JUICE

½ CUP WATER

ABOUT ½ TEASPOON SALT

ABOUT ¼ TEASPOON FRESHLY
GROUND PEPPER

6 HALIBUT FILLETS *(5 to 6 ounces
each)*, ABOUT 1 INCH THICK

SALT

FRESHLY GROUND PEPPER

CILANTRO SPRIGS FOR GARNISH

LEMON WEDGES FOR GARNISH

Tarator is a rich, creamy sauce that turns up all over the Middle East. Its ingredients usually include finely ground nuts, garlic, and lemon. Chef Heidi Krahling bakes fish under a light coating of the sauce, which produces wonderfully moist and flavorful fillets. She likes to serve the halibut with sautéed greens; a pilaf of rice, bulgur, or couscous; and a salad of baby greens. This dish can also be served at room temperature, making it ideal for a buffet or a party. ❀ This recipe makes more sauce than you'll need to prepare the halibut, so you'll have plenty of extra sauce to serve alongside the fish or to use as a dip for fresh vegetables or warm pita triangles. If you're not sure how you feel about tahini (the creamy sesame seed paste sold in cans in the ethnic foods sections of many supermarkets), start with ¼ cup and add more to taste.

TO make the sauce: Preheat oven to 325°. Place pine nuts in a small pan and bake, shaking once or twice, until just golden, 5 to 7 minutes. Let cool. Increase oven temperature to 350°.

SPREAD walnuts on a baking sheet or in a shallow pan. Bake, stirring once or twice, until lightly browned and fragrant, 10 to 12 minutes. Let cool.

IN a food processor, combine pine nuts, walnuts, cilantro, garlic, paprika, and cayenne. Turn machine on and off until nuts are finely chopped; with a spatula, scrape down the sides of the bowl. Add tahini and lemon juice; whirl until well mixed. With the machine running, add water in a thin, steady stream until a thick purée forms. Season to taste with salt and pepper. If making in advance, cover and refrigerate up to 3 days.

TO bake the fish: Preheat oven to 425°. Line a large baking sheet with foil or parchment paper; coat with vegetable oil spray. Season both sides of fish with salt and pepper, then arrange fillets 2 inches apart on the baking sheet. Spread 1 to 2 tablespoons sauce over each fillet.

BAKE until fish is opaque throughout, 8 to 10 minutes. Garnish with cilantro sprigs and lemon wedges. Serve with remaining sauce, if desired, or reserve sauce for another use.

SERVES 6

MEXICAN-STYLE SEA BASS
with ALMOND-SERRANO SAUCE

Nuts and seeds, along with chiles, garlic, onions, and lime, are mainstays of Mexican sauces. This succulent sauce for baked fish has them all. Serve it warm with tortillas and rice to sop up every bit of the sauce.

PREHEAT oven to 325°. Spread almonds on a baking sheet or in a shallow pan. Bake, stirring once or twice, until lightly browned and fragrant, 5 to 10 minutes. Let cool slightly, then chop coarsely. Increase temperature to 400°.

COAT the bottom of a 2-quart baking dish with ½ tablespoon of the butter. Season both sides of sea bass with salt and pepper. Put fish in the baking dish.

IN a medium frying pan, melt 2 tablespoons of butter over medium heat. Add cumin, green onions, chiles, and garlic. Cook, stirring occasionally, until fragrant, about 1 minute. Stir in lime juice and cook 1 minute longer. Let cool slightly, then stir in almonds and cilantro. Spoon mixture over fish fillets and dot with remaining 1½ tablespoons butter.

COVER dish tightly with foil and bake until fish is opaque throughout, 15 to 20 minutes. To serve, spoon some of the cooking juices over each fillet. Garnish with cilantro sprigs and lime wedges.

SERVES 4

¾ CUP SLIVERED ALMONDS

¼ CUP UNSALTED BUTTER

4 SEA BASS FILLETS *(5 to 6 ounces each)*, CUT ABOUT 1 INCH THICK

SALT

FRESHLY GROUND PEPPER

2 TEASPOONS GROUND CUMIN

¾ CUP SLICED GREEN ONION

1 OR 2 SERRANO OR JALAPEÑO CHILES, SEEDED *(if desired)* AND FINELY CHOPPED

2 TO 3 CLOVES GARLIC, MINCED

¼ CUP FRESH LIME JUICE

⅓ CUP LOOSELY PACKED CHOPPED FRESH CILANTRO, PLUS 4 SPRIGS FOR GARNISH

LIME WEDGES FOR GARNISH

PEPPER-PECAN-ENCRUSTED TUNA *with* FRESH MANGO SALSA

Mango Salsa

2 RIPE MANGOES *(about ¾ pound each)*, PEELED AND CUT INTO ½-INCH SLICES

2 TABLESPOONS FINELY CHOPPED RED ONION

2 TABLESPOONS FRESH LIME JUICE

¼ CUP LOOSELY PACKED CHOPPED FRESH CILANTRO OR MINT

⅛ TEASPOON SALT

⅛ TEASPOON SUGAR

½ CUP PECAN CHIPS

4 TUNA STEAKS *(6 to 8 ounces each)*, ABOUT 1 INCH THICK

4 TEASPOONS BOURBON *(optional)*

1½ TEASPOONS COARSE-GRAINED SALT

2 TABLESPOONS FRESHLY CRACKED PEPPER

CILANTRO SPRIGS FOR GARNISH

We love the way everything works together in this simple dish. The tangy salsa cools the fire of the cracked peppercorns, the bourbon subtly enhances the flavor of the pecans, and the texture of the crisp nut crust makes a delightful contrast with the tender seared tuna. The brief marinating period helps take the chill off the fish so that, when it's cooked, its rare center isn't cold. You can use less pepper if you like, but do crack it yourself instead of using cracked pepper from a jar—the flavor will be much more lively and fresh. If you don't have a pepper mill that gives a very coarse grind, put the peppercorns in a skillet (to keep them from rolling around) and crush them under a heavy pot.

TO make the salsa: In a medium bowl, combine mangoes, onion, lime juice, cilantro, salt, and sugar. Toss gently to mix. Cover and refrigerate up to 1 hour to blend flavors.

MEANWHILE, prepare the fish: Preheat oven to 350°. Spread pecans on a baking sheet or in a shallow pan. Bake, stirring once or twice, until lightly browned and fragrant, 5 to 10 minutes. Let cool.

RUB each side of each tuna steak with ½ tea-spoon bourbon; season steaks lightly with ½ teaspoon of the salt. In a small bowl, combine pecans with the pepper. Divide mixture evenly among tuna steaks, pressing gently into both sides. Let stand 30 minutes at room temperature.

SPRINKLE a 10- to 12-inch frying pan with remaining 1 teaspoon salt and place over medium-high heat. When pan is hot, add fish without crowding. Pressing fish onto pan with a spatula, cook 2 minutes to sear. Turn fish over and cook until seared on the outside but still pink in the center, about 2 minutes longer. Transfer fish to a clean work surface. Let sit 1 minute, then cut fish on an angle into ½-inch slices. Spoon salsa off-center on each of 4 dinner plates. Arrange the tuna slices on the plates, over-lapping them slightly.

SERVES 4

TROUT SAUTÉ *with* LEMON
BUTTER *and* ALMONDS

4 WHOLE TROUT *(10 to 12 ounces each)*, CLEANED AND BONED, HEADS AND TAILS LEFT ON, RINSED AND PATTED DRY

SALT

FRESHLY GROUND PEPPER

½ CUP MILK

½ CUP ALL-PURPOSE FLOUR OR ⅓ CUP INSTANT FLOUR, SUCH AS WONDRA

¼ CUP UNSALTED BUTTER

1 TABLESPOON WALNUT OIL OR OLIVE OIL

½ CUP SLICED ALMONDS

⅓ CUP CHOPPED FRESH FLAT-LEAF PARSLEY

¼ CUP FRESH LEMON JUICE

LEMON WEDGES FOR GARNISH

After a blissful day of biking through the French countryside, stop beside a stream, catch a few trout, and prepare them in this simple, time-honored method. More realistically, omit the French countryside, stop by the supermarket on the way home from work, pick up the fish, and rent a copy of *Forget Paris* to watch after dinner. Coho fillets can be substituted for the trout.

SEASON trout inside and out with salt and pepper. Place milk and flour in separate shallow pans or plates. Dip fish in milk, then in flour to coat. Shake excess flour from fish.

IN a large frying pan, melt 2 tablespoons of the butter in the oil over medium-high heat. Working in batches if necessary, cook trout without crowding, turning once, until crisp and golden brown on the outside and opaque throughout, 7 to 9 minutes total. Remove fish to a warm platter. Discard any fat left in the pan.

IN the same pan, melt the remaining 2 tablespoons butter over medium heat. Add almonds and cook, stirring, until light golden brown and fragrant, about 3 minutes. Stir in parsley and lemon juice, scraping any brown bits from the bottom of the pan. Spoon mixture over fish and serve at once. Garnish with lemon wedges.

SERVES 4

Toasting Walnuts in the Shell

The great chef Jacques Pépin loves the whole experience of cracking open walnuts and eating them right from the shell. But he also loves the flavor of toasted nuts, so he came up with this simple technique that combines the best of both: Preheat the oven to 375°. For 4 servings, spread 4 cups in-shell walnuts on a baking sheet and roast them. After 20 minutes, carefully remove one nut, holding it with a dish towel or pot holder, and crack it open. The meat should be lightly toasted and aromatic. If it still looks pale inside, roast a few minutes longer. Let the nuts cool, and serve them in a bowl with nutcrackers and some fruit and cheese on the side. Bonus: this little trick also makes the shells easier to crack.

MUSHROOM–WALNUT LOAF
with PIPÉRADE SAUCE

2 CUPS SLICED WALNUTS

2 TABLESPOONS WALNUT OIL

¾ CUP FINELY CHOPPED ONION

2 CLOVES GARLIC

2 CUPS CHOPPED MUSHROOMS

2 CUPS COOKED WHITE RICE

5 EGGS, LIGHTLY BEATEN

2 CUPS *(about 8 ounces)* SHREDDED
MONTEREY JACK CHEESE

1 CUP *(8 ounces)* LARGE-CURD
COTTAGE CHEESE

½ CUP FRESHLY GRATED
PARMESAN CHEESE

2 TABLESPOONS CHOPPED
FRESH FLAT-LEAF PARSLEY

1 TABLESPOON CHOPPED
FRESH MARJORAM

1½ TEASPOONS SALT

¼ TEASPOON FRESHLY
GROUND PEPPER

(sauce recipes on page 74)

After much searching and experimentation, we've come up with a vegetarian "meat loaf" that we think is just as satisfying as the carnivore version. Whip up a batch of mashed potatoes and some Green Beans with Green Onions and Hazelnuts (page 106), and you've got a fresh new take on the all-American blue-plate special. If you prefer a milder, creamier sauce, try the walnut-pepper variation (page 74). Both sauces are also terrific for dressing up plain cooked vegetables such as broccoli, cauliflower, green beans, or asparagus.

TO make the mushroom-walnut loaf: Preheat oven to 350°. Spread walnuts on a baking sheet or in a shallow pan. Bake, stirring once or twice, until lightly browned and fragrant, 5 to 10 minutes. Let cool. Increase oven temperature to 375°. Coat a 5-by 9-inch loaf pan with vegetable oil spray and set aside.

IN a large frying pan, heat walnut oil over medium heat. Add onion and cook, stirring occasionally, until softened but not browned, 3 to 5 minutes. Add garlic and mushrooms; cook, stirring occasionally, until mushroom liquid evaporates, 5 to 6 minutes. Let cool slightly.

IN a large bowl, combine walnuts, rice, and eggs. Stir in jack cheese, cottage cheese, Parmesan, parsley, and marjoram until well blended. Stir in mushroom mixture, salt, and pepper. Mix well.

PACK mixture into loaf pan; bake until golden brown on top and firm to the touch, about 45 minutes. Let sit 10 minutes, then unmold onto a serving platter. Serve warm or at room temperature, cut into thick slices, with pipérade sauce on the side.

SERVES 4 TO 6

(continues)

Pipérade Sauce

3 TABLESPOONS OLIVE OIL

1 TEASPOON CHOPPED
FRESH THYME

1 ONION, HALVED AND
THINLY SLICED

1 RED BELL PEPPER, STEMMED,
SEEDED, AND CUT LENGTHWISE

½ CUP DRY WHITE WINE

¼ CUP WALNUT OIL

1 TABLESPOON WHITE WINE
OR CHAMPAGNE VINEGAR

1 TEASPOON CHOPPED FRESH
FLAT-LEAF PARSLEY

SALT

FRESHLY GROUND PEPPER

Walnut-Pepper Sauce

½ CUP WALNUTS

3 CUPS WATER

1 RED BELL PEPPER, STEMMED,
SEEDED, AND CHOPPED

1 ONION, HALVED AND
THINLY SLICED

2 CLOVES GARLIC

SALT

FRESHLY GROUND PEPPER

(Mushroom-Walnut Loaf with Pipérade Sauce continued from page 72)

TO make the pipérade sauce: In a medium frying pan, heat oil and thyme over medium heat. Add onion and cook, stirring occasionally, until softened but not browned, 3 to 5 minutes. Add bell pepper and cook, stirring, until softened, 5 to 7 minutes.

POUR in wine; increase heat to high. Cook, stirring to scrape up any brown bits from the bottom of the pan, until wine has reduced slightly, about 2 minutes. Remove from heat.

STIR in walnut oil, vinegar, and parsley. Season to taste with salt and pepper. Refrigerate, covered, for up to 3 days. Serve slightly chilled or at room temperature.

Variation

WALNUT-PEPPER SAUCE

PREHEAT oven to 350°. Spread walnuts on a baking sheet or in a shallow pan. Bake, stirring once or twice, until lightly browned and fragrant, 10 to 12 minutes. Let cool.

IN a medium saucepan, combine water, bell pepper, onion, and garlic over medium-high heat. When water comes to a boil, reduce heat to low and cook, stirring occasionally, until vegetables are tender, about 20 minutes. Strain through a fine sieve, reserving the cooking liquid.

IN a food processor or blender, whirl pepper-onion mixture and walnuts until smooth. With machine on, gradually pour in about ¼ cup of the cooking liquid. Mixture should be just thick enough to coat the back of a spoon; add more cooking liquid if needed. Season to taste with salt and pepper. Refrigerate, covered, for up to 3 days. Serve slightly chilled or at room temperature.

YIELDS 1½ CUPS

Sprinkle, Sprinkle Little Nut

World's easiest nut recipe (no kidding): Make something; sprinkle it with some nuts. A salad, a sandwich, a piece of fish or chicken, a bowl of soup—even a frozen pizza—there's almost no kind of food that doesn't benefit from a handful of toasted nuts. Whisk some ground nuts into salad dressing; they'll practically disappear, but you'll have a thicker, richer dressing. Drizzle a little walnut oil and a few chopped toasted walnuts on any steamed vegetable. Add any nut to any grain dish. Have fun, and remember, you really can't go wrong. One quick toss, and you've got flavor, texture, and something even better: a little finishing flourish that says you care about the food you cook. Is that so nutty?

CIRCASSIAN CHICKEN

(JOYCE GOLDSTEIN)

3 CUPS WALNUTS

3 POUNDS CHICKEN BREAST
HALVES ON THE BONE (about 6),
SKIN ON

4 CUPS WATER

2 CUPS CHOPPED ONION

1 CARROT, PEELED AND CUT
INTO 1-INCH PIECES

1 SPRIG THYME OR FLAT-LEAF
PARSLEY

1 SMALL BAY LEAF

2 WHOLE CLOVES

SALT

¼ CUP UNSALTED BUTTER

4 TEASPOONS MINCED GARLIC

3 TABLESPOONS SWEET PAPRIKA

1 TEASPOON CAYENNE PEPPER

2 SLICES FIRM WHITE
SANDWICH BREAD, CRUSTS
REMOVED

2 TABLESPOONS FRESH
LEMON JUICE

FRESHLY GROUND PEPPER

2 TABLESPOONS WALNUT OIL

2 TABLESPOONS CHOPPED
FRESH FLAT-LEAF PARSLEY

This is one of Turkey's national dishes: a creamy, spicy chicken salad that's also served throughout the Middle East, usually as part of a spread of *mezze* or "small plates." This version, created by chef and cookbook author Joyce Goldstein and served with romaine lettuce leaves and pita triangles for scooping, is perfect for a lunch, picnic, or light dinner. The bread and nuts tend to absorb liquid as the dressing sits. The final drizzle of paprika-infused walnut oil intensifies the dressing's walnut flavor and adds a beautiful splash of color.

PREHEAT oven to 350°. Spread walnuts on a large baking sheet or in a shallow pan. Bake, stirring once or twice, until lightly browned and fragrant, 10 to 12 minutes. Let cool slightly. Pick out 6 to 12 walnut halves and reserve for garnish.

IN a Dutch oven or large saucepan, combine chicken, water, half the onion, the carrot, thyme, bay leaf, and cloves. Bring to a boil over medium-high heat. Reduce heat to low and cook, uncovered, until chicken is white throughout but still juicy, 20 to 25 minutes. With tongs or a slotted spoon, remove chicken from broth and set aside. Pour broth through a fine sieve placed over a medium saucepan. Discard vegetables, bay leaf, cloves, and other solids.

WHEN chicken is cool enough to handle, remove skin and bones; return skin and bones to the strained broth. Cook broth over medium heat until reduced to 2 cups. Strain and discard the chicken skin and bones. With your fingers, shred chicken into strips about 1½ inches long. Transfer chicken to a large bowl and season lightly with salt; cover and set aside.

IN a medium frying pan, melt butter over medium heat. Add remaining onion and cook, stirring occasionally, until very soft but not browned, about 8 minutes. Stir in garlic, 2 tablespoons of the paprika, and the cayenne; cook until fragrant, 2 to 3 minutes.

MOISTEN bread with water until softened; squeeze dry. In a food processor, whirl the softened bread and walnuts until walnuts are finely chopped. Add the onion mixture and process until well mixed. With the machine on, pour in the broth and process until smooth. Add lemon juice. Season to taste with salt and pepper. Add half of this sauce to the chicken, tossing gently to coat. Scrape mixture onto a serving platter and cover with the remaining sauce.

IN a small frying pan, combine walnut oil with the remaining 1 tablespoon paprika. Cook over low heat, stirring, just until heated through, about 1 minute; drizzle over chicken. Sprinkle with parsley and garnish with reserved toasted walnut halves. Serve at cool room temperature.

SERVES 6

CHICKEN ENCHILADAS *in*
ALMOND CREAM

If you think enchiladas have to be bland and soggy and red all over, these will come as a big surprise. They're made from soft corn tortillas rolled around a filling of roasted green chiles, chicken, and cheese, then baked in a delicate, creamy almond sauce. That's a whole different enchilada.

1½ CUPS SLIVERED ALMONDS

2 CUPS WHIPPING CREAM

½ CUP CHICKEN STOCK *(page 215)*

SALT

2 POBLANO CHILES

2 ANAHEIM CHILES

1 JALAPEÑO CHILE

4 TO 5 TABLESPOONS VEGETABLE OIL

1 ONION, HALVED AND THINLY SLICED

1 POUND SKINLESS, BONELESS CHICKEN BREAST HALVES *(about 3)*, THINLY SLICED

1 TABLESPOON CHOPPED FRESH CILANTRO

1 TABLESPOON CHOPPED FRESH OREGANO, OR 1 TEASPOON DRIED

1 TABLESPOON CHOPPED FRESH FLAT-LEAF PARSLEY

2 CLOVES GARLIC, MINCED

FRESHLY GROUND PEPPER

8 CORN TORTILLAS

2 CUPS *(8 ounces)* SHREDDED MONTEREY JACK CHEESE

PREHEAT oven to 350°. Spread almonds on a baking sheet or in a shallow pan. Bake, stirring once or twice, until lightly browned and fragrant, 5 to 10 minutes. Let cool.

IN a medium saucepan, combine cream, stock, and 1¼ cups of the almonds. Cook over medium-high heat until bubbles appear around edges of pan; do not let mixture boil. Remove from heat and let stand 30 minutes to develop flavors. Pour into a blender and pulse machine on and off until almonds are very finely chopped. Season to taste with ½ to ¾ teaspoon salt.

PREHEAT oven broiler, placing the rack as close to the heat source as possible. Place the chiles on a baking sheet or broiler pan; broil, turning once or twice, until skin is charred and black all over, about 10 minutes. Remove from heat and seal in a paper bag. Set aside until cool enough to handle, at least 10 minutes. Peel blackened skin from chiles (some skin can remain); discard stems and seeds. Cut chiles into thin strips about 1½ inches long (you should have about ¾ cup).

IN a large frying pan, heat 2 tablespoons oil over medium heat. Add onion and cook, stirring, until softened but not browned, 5 to 7 minutes.

If pan seems dry, heat 1 more tablespoon oil before adding the chicken. Cook chicken, stirring, until lightly browned but still juicy, 5 to 7 minutes. Stir in chiles, cilantro, oregano, parsley, and garlic. Cook, stirring, until garlic is fragrant, about 1 minute. Season to taste with salt and pepper.

PREHEAT oven to 350°. In a small frying pan, heat 2 tablespoons oil over medium heat. Soften tortillas, one at a time, by quickly turning them in the oil to coat both sides, 2 to 3 seconds total. Drain between paper towels.

PLACE 1 tortilla on a clean surface. Place a heaping ⅓ cup chicken filling and 2 tablespoons cheese on the lower third of a tortilla and roll up. Place seam side down in a shallow 2- to 2½-quart baking dish. Repeat with remaining tortillas. Pour almond cream over enchiladas, coating with sauce. Sprinkle with remaining 1 cup cheese and ¼ cup toasted almonds.

BAKE, uncovered, until sauce is bubbly and enchiladas are heated through, 20 to 30 minutes.

SERVES 4

FARMHOUSE CHICKEN STEW *with* BUTTERMILK-WALNUT DUMPLINGS

¼ CUP FLOUR

1½ TEASPOONS SALT

½ TEASPOON GROUND PEPPER

½ TEASPOON SWEET PAPRIKA

1 CHICKEN *(3½ to 4 pounds)*, CUT INTO 8 PIECES

2 TABLESPOONS OLIVE OIL

1 ONION, HALVED AND SLICED

4 CUPS CHICKEN STOCK *(page 215)*

¾ POUND SMALL RED POTATOES, HALVED

12 BABY CARROTS, PEELED

½ CUP THINLY SLICED CELERY

Buttermilk-Walnut Dumplings

½ CUP SLICED WALNUTS

2 CUPS FLOUR

1½ TEASPOONS BAKING POWDER

1 TEASPOON BAKING SODA

¾ TEASPOON SALT

¼ TEASPOON GROUND PEPPER

2 TABLESPOONS SOLID VEGETABLE SHORTENING

¼ CUP CHOPPED GREEN ONION

1 CUP BUTTERMILK

1 PACKAGE *(10 ounces)* FROZEN PEAS

3 TABLESPOONS CHOPPED FRESH FLAT-LEAF PARSLEY

1 TABLESPOON CHOPPED FRESH THYME

Chicken and dumplings: the very name soothes the spirit and sets the world to rights. This recipe makes a big, old-fashioned one-pot supper—tender chicken, appealingly familiar vegetables, and, best of all, a topping of fluffy homemade dumplings. You can make the stew in advance, but the dumplings do need to be cooked as soon as you mix the dough.

TO make the stew: In a paper bag, mix flour, 1 teaspoon of the salt, pepper, and paprika. Add chicken to bag, 1 or 2 pieces at a time, and shake until well coated. Shake off excess flour.

IN a Dutch oven, heat oil over medium-high heat. Add chicken, in batches if needed to prevent crowding. Cook, turning once or twice, until browned on all sides, about 10 minutes. Remove chicken and set aside.

REDUCE heat to medium. Add onion to pot and cook, stirring occasionally, until softened, 5 to 7 minutes. Discard any fat left in pot.

ADD the remaining ½ teaspoon salt, stock, potatoes, carrots, and celery. Bring to a boil over high heat, scraping up any brown bits from the bottom. Return chicken to pot and bring to a boil. Immediately reduce heat to low, cover, and cook until chicken is just white throughout, about 20 minutes.

MEANWHILE, make the dumplings: Preheat oven to 350°. Spread walnuts on a baking sheet or in a shallow pan. Bake, stirring once or twice, until lightly browned and fragrant, 5 to 10 minutes. Let cool.

IN a medium bowl, gently whisk together flour, baking powder, baking soda, salt, and pepper. With a pastry blender or 2 knives, cut in shortening until it is the size of small peas. Stir in walnuts and green onions. Make a well in the center, pour in the buttermilk, and stir just until dough comes together.

TO cook the dumplings: Skim off any fat from top of the stew. Stir in peas, parsley, and thyme. Increase heat to medium and bring to a simmer.

FOR each dumpling, dip a large spoon into the simmering liquid, use it to scoop out about ¼ cup of dough, and then gently drop the dough onto the top of the stew, preferably on a piece of chicken. Repeat with remaining dough. You should have about 12 dumplings.

COVER pan tightly and reduce heat to low. Cook, without lifting the cover, until dumplings are puffed, firm to the touch, and cooked through, about 20 minutes. Serve immediately.

SERVES 4 TO 6

LEMON CHICKEN BREASTS *with* SLICED
WALNUTS *and* HERBS

4 SKINLESS, BONELESS
CHICKEN BREAST HALVES
(about 1½ pounds total)

¼ CUP FRESH LEMON JUICE

2 TABLESPOONS WALNUT OIL
OR OLIVE OIL

1 CLOVE GARLIC, MINCED

⅓ CUP SLICED WALNUTS

½ TEASPOON SALT

¼ TEASPOON FRESHLY
GROUND PEPPER

2 TABLESPOONS UNSALTED
BUTTER

⅓ CUP CHICKEN STOCK
(page 215)

1 TEASPOON MINCED
LEMON ZEST

2 TABLESPOONS DIJON
MUSTARD

2 TO 3 TABLESPOONS FINELY
CHOPPED FRESH HERBS
*(any combination of rosemary, thyme,
basil, oregano, and flat-leaf parsley)*

You could become known for a dish like this. The chicken is moist and flavorful, and the herbed walnut sauce provides an irresistible crunchy counterpoint. Serve it with steamed green beans and buttermilk mashed potatoes or Couscous Pilaf with Lentils and Pine Nuts (page 118).

WITH a smooth meat mallet or other heavy object, pound chicken breasts until about ½ inch thick. In a heavy-duty 1-gallon plastic food storage bag or a large bowl, combine 2 tablespoons of the lemon juice, 1 tablespoon of the walnut oil, and garlic. Add chicken to the bag, turning to coat. Seal bag securely. Marinate chicken up to 2 hours at room temperature, or up to 24 hours in the refrigerator.

IN a large frying pan, toast walnuts, stirring, over medium heat until lightly browned and fragrant, 3 to 5 minutes. Remove from pan and let cool.

REMOVE chicken from bag, discarding marinade. Pat chicken dry; season with salt and pepper. In the same frying pan over medium heat, melt 1 tablespoon of the butter in the remaining 1 tablespoon walnut oil. Add chicken and cook, turning, until golden brown on the outside and white throughout but still juicy, 6 to 8 minutes. Transfer chicken to a plate and keep warm.

ADD the remaining 2 tablespoons lemon juice, stock, and lemon zest to pan. Increase heat to high and bring to a boil. Cook, scraping any brown bits from the bottom of the pan, until liquid has reduced slightly, 1 to 2 minutes. Reduce heat to low. Add the remaining 1 tablespoon butter and the mustard, whisking until well blended. Stir in herbs and toasted walnuts. Return chicken and any accumulated juices to the frying pan, turning to coat with walnut mixture. Cook until heated through, 1 to 2 minutes longer. Remove chicken breasts to warm dinner plates; top with any walnuts remaining in the pan.

SERVES 4

CHICKEN, PECAN, *and*
WILD RICE CASSEROLE

This creamy, satisfying one-dish chicken dinner can be assembled ahead of time and baked at the last minute, making it just the thing for a weeknight at home or one very lucky potluck. This is an extremely "forgiving" recipe that can easily be adjusted to your taste. Since the brown and wild rice are cooked, you can substitute the same quantity of white rice, a prepared blended rice, or even cooked bulgur.

PREHEAT oven to 350°. Spread pecans on a baking sheet or in a shallow pan. Bake, stirring once or twice, until lightly browned and fragrant, 7 to 10 minutes. Let cool slightly, then chop coarsely.

IN a large frying pan, heat 2 tablespoons of the oil over medium-high heat. Add chicken and cook, stirring, until lightly browned on the outside and white throughout but still juicy, 5 to 7 minutes. Season to taste with salt and pepper. With a slotted spoon, transfer chicken to a large bowl.

ADD the remaining 2 tablespoons oil to pan. Add onion and cook, stirring occasionally, until lightly browned on the edges, about 5 minutes. Leave onion in pan.

TO the pan, add mushrooms, celery, and bell pepper. Cook, stirring, until softened but not browned, 5 to 7 minutes. Season lightly with salt and pepper. Add to chicken mixture; then add ½ cup of the pecans, wild rice, brown rice, crème fraîche, stock, corn, green onions, tarragon, parsley, and cayenne. Toss gently to mix well. Taste, adding more salt and pepper if needed.

BUTTER a 2-quart baking dish. Add chicken mixture and sprinkle with the remaining ½ cup pecans. Bake, uncovered, until heated through, 20 to 30 minutes. Serve immediately.

SERVES 4 TO 6

1 CUP PECANS

¼ CUP VEGETABLE OIL

1 POUND SKINLESS, BONELESS CHICKEN BREAST HALVES *(about 3)*, THINLY SLICED

SALT

FRESHLY GROUND PEPPER

1 RED ONION, HALVED AND THINLY SLICED

½ POUND MUSHROOMS, SLICED

½ CUP CHOPPED CELERY

1 RED BELL PEPPER, STEMMED, SEEDED, AND CUT INTO ½ -INCH SQUARES

1 CUP COOKED WILD RICE

1 CUP COOKED BROWN RICE

1 CUP CRÈME FRAÎCHE OR SOUR CREAM

2 CUPS CHICKEN STOCK *(page 215)*

⅔ CUP FRESH OR THAWED FROZEN CORN KERNELS

¼ CUP SLICED GREEN ONION

2 TABLESPOONS MINCED FRESH TARRAGON, OR ½ TEASPOON DRIED

¼ CUP CHOPPED FRESH FLAT-LEAF PARSLEY

½ TEASPOON CAYENNE PEPPER *(optional)*

CRISPY PECAN CHICKEN BREASTS

(KIMBALL JONES)

½ CUP CHOPPED PECANS OR
PECAN HALVES

4 SKINLESS, BONELESS
CHICKEN BREAST HALVES
(about 1½ pounds total)

½ TEASPOON SALT

¼ TEASPOON FRESHLY
GROUND PEPPER

6 TABLESPOONS FLOUR

1 EGG

1 TABLESPOON WHIPPING
CREAM

¼ CUP YELLOW CORNMEAL

½ TEASPOON CAYENNE PEPPER

⅛ TEASPOON GROUND CUMIN

⅛ TEASPOON GROUND
CINNAMON

VEGETABLE OIL FOR FRYING

FLAT-LEAF PARSLEY SPRIGS FOR
GARNISH

LEMON WEDGES FOR GARNISH
(optional)

Kimball Jones, executive chef at Northern California's Wente Vineyards, created this uptown homage to down-home fried chicken: sautéed chicken breast fillets with a golden cumin-scented pecan-cornmeal crust. Serve with Brussels Sprouts with Sweet Bell Peppers and Walnuts (page 107) and a bowl of Romesco Sauce (page 36) on the side. If any chicken is left over, slice it and arrange it over a simple salad. We recommend spinach, toasted pecans, and thinly sliced red onions in an oil-and-lemon dressing.

IN a food processor, whirl pecans, pulsing on and off, until finely ground.

WITH a smooth meat mallet or other heavy object, pound chicken breasts until about ½ inch thick. Season with salt and pepper. Dredge chicken in 4 tablespoons of the flour; shake off any excess.

IN a shallow bowl, whisk egg and cream until well blended. In another shallow bowl or pan, combine pecans, cornmeal, the remaining 2 tablespoons flour, and cayenne, cumin, and cinnamon. One at a time, dip chicken breasts in egg mixture, then in the pecan-flour mixture, pressing in gently to coat all sides completely. Transfer to a wire rack.

IN a large frying pan, heat ¼ inch oil over medium-high heat until hot. Working in batches if necessary, cook chicken without crowding, turning once, until golden brown on the outside and white throughout but still juicy on the inside, 5 to 7 minutes. Drain on paper towels and serve at once; garnish with parsley sprigs and lemon wedges.

SERVES 4

ROASTED STUFFED ROCK
CORNISH GAME HENS

(JACQUES PÉPIN)

1½ CUPS WATER

⅓ CUP BULGUR WHEAT*

½ CUP CHOPPED WALNUTS

2 CORNISH GAME HENS
(1¼ to 1¾ pounds each)

1 TABLESPOON PLUS 1 TEASPOON
CANOLA OIL

1¼ CUPS CHOPPED LEEK
(white and tender green parts only)

¾ CUP CHOPPED ONION

1½ TEASPOONS MINCED GARLIC

ABOUT 1 TEASPOON FINELY
CHOPPED JALAPEÑO CHILE

1 GRANNY SMITH APPLE
(about 7 ounces), CORED AND
CUT INTO ⅜-INCH PIECES

2 TEASPOONS FINELY CHOPPED
FRESH THYME, OR
½ TEASPOON DRIED

¾ TEASPOON SALT

¼ TEASPOON FRESHLY
GROUND PEPPER

SAUTÉED APPLE SLICES FOR
GARNISH

*Bulgur is cracked wheat that has been
steamed and dried; it needs only to be
reconstituted in water.

This recipe, from renowned television chef and cookbook author Jacques Pépin, calls for partially boning the game hens. Don't worry. Once you get the hang of it, the technique of removing the breastbone and rib cage is actually fairly simple, and the result is an attractively plump hen that's easier to eat and holds more of the nutty bulgur-apple stuffing. If you're timid about boning, ask your butcher to do it for you. Pépin suggests buying bulgur wheat from a bulk bin at a health food store: "It's usually less expensive than the kind sold in boxes. Be sure to buy true bulgur, not just cracked wheat, which is uncooked."

IN a small saucepan, bring 1 cup of the water to a boil over high heat. Stir in bulgur and remove pan from heat. Let sit 1 hour, then drain in a fine sieve; you should have about 1 cup.

MEANWHILE, preheat oven to 350°. Spread walnuts on a baking sheet or in a shallow pan. Bake, stirring once or twice, until lightly browned and fragrant, 8 to 10 minutes. Let cool.

TO bone the game hens: Start from the neck opening. Without tearing the skin, cut around the wishbone and remove it. Cut at the shoulder joints and push with your fingers to separate the breast meat from the bone. Remove the rib cage and breastbone but leave the legs and wings intact. (Reserve the bones to make stock or soup.)

IN a large frying pan, heat 1 tablespoon of the oil over medium heat. Add leek and onion; cook, stirring occasionally, until softened but not browned, about 3 minutes. Add garlic, jalapeño to taste, apple, thyme, ½ teaspoon of the salt, the pepper, and bulgur. Cook, stirring, until any additional moisture from the bulgur is absorbed. Let cool completely. Stir in walnuts.

PREHEAT oven to 425°. Stuff game hens with the bulgur-walnut mixture. Use a skewer or string to enclose the stuffing.

SPREAD the remaining 1 teaspoon oil in the bottom of a small roasting pan. Place hens in pan and sprinkle with the remaining ¼ teaspoon salt. Roast until golden brown on the outside and cooked throughout, about 40 minutes, basting every 15 minutes with the juices and fat in the bottom of the pan.

REMOVE hens to a plate. Pour out and discard any fat that has accumulated in the roasting pan. Add the remaining ½ cup water to the pan and bring to a boil, stirring to release any browned bits in the pan.

REMOVE skewers and cut hens in half. Arrange any extra stuffing on 4 warmed plates. Set hens on top and spoon over cooking juices. Garnish with sautéed apple slices.

SERVES 4

OLD-FASHIONED ROAST TURKEY *with* NEW-FASHIONED DRESSING

1 WHOLE TURKEY
(12 to 14 pounds)

SALT

FRESHLY GROUND PEPPER

ABOUT 9 CUPS LOOSELY PACKED
TURKEY DRESSING, COOLED
(recipes follow; optional)

2 TABLESPOONS WALNUT OIL,
ROASTED GARLIC WALNUT OIL,
OLIVE OIL, OR MELTED BUTTER

1 CUP TURKEY OR CHICKEN
STOCK *(page 215)*

2 CUPS DRY WHITE WINE OR
DRY VERMOUTH *(or 2 more cups
stock)*

Basic Pan Gravy

DRIPPINGS FROM ROAST
TURKEY

6 TABLESPOONS FLOUR

4 CUPS TURKEY OR CHICKEN
STOCK *(page 215)*

SALT

FRESHLY GROUND PEPPER

Every cook, every book, every magazine will tell you it has come up with the perfect way to roast a turkey—rotating it every 15 minutes, basting constantly, never basting at all, sealing it in a bag. Which source are you going to believe? We say, stop the madness! There is no right answer, and no matter what you do, your turkey will turn out just fine, especially if you keep it simple and focus your energy on the really flavorful stuff, like an imaginative dressing and a nice tasty gravy—which is exactly what you'll find on these pages.

POSITION rack on the lowest shelf in the oven. Preheat oven to 325°.

WHEN ready to cook, remove the wrapping from the turkey. Remove the neck and giblets from the breast and neck cavities; if desired, use them to make turkey gravy or stock. Rinse turkey inside and out with cold water and pat dry. Lightly season the breast and neck cavities with salt and pepper. If you will be stuffing the turkey, turn it on its breast and loosely fill the neck cavity with cool dressing. Pull skin over the neck cavity to close, and fold wings behind the back to secure the neck skin in place. (Alternatively, secure neck skin with a metal skewer.) If you will be stuffing the turkey, loosely fill the breast cavity with cool stuffing. Place any remaining stuffing in a buttered baking dish; cover and refrigerate to bake as a side dish.

PLACE turkey, breast side up, on a flat rack in a shallow roasting pan. If using a standard meat thermometer, insert it deeply into the thickest part of the thigh next to the body but not touching the bone. Rub turkey skin with oil; season with salt and pepper. Pour stock and vermouth into the roasting pan. Roast the turkey, basting every 30 to 45 minutes with juices from the pan, until a meat thermometer registers 180°, and juices run clear, not pink, when the thigh is pierced with a fork, about 3 hours. The stuffing inside should register at least 160° in its center.

TO ensure easier carving and more tender meat, transfer roasted turkey to a large, warm serving platter or carving board and let sit at least 20 minutes (or as long as 1 hour) before slicing. If you have stuffed the turkey, remove all the dressing before serving.

TO prepare oven for baking dressing in separate baking dish, carefully move the rack to the center of the oven and increase oven temperature to 350°. Follow the baking instructions for each recipe.

TO make the gravy: Drain all but 6 tablespoons of fat from the pan. Place over medium heat. Add flour, whisking until smooth. Cook until the flour turns golden, about 2 minutes. Gradually stir in stock and bring to a boil, scraping up any brown bits from the bottom of the pan with a wire whisk. Reduce heat to low and cook, stirring occasionally, until slightly thickened, 2 to 3 minutes. Season with salt and pepper. Pour into a warmed sauceboat.

SERVES 12 TO 14

TIPS

Stuffing unstuffed: Dressing baked in a pan can be every bit as delicious and moist as dressing stuffed into the bird, and it's much easier to prepare. The trick is to baste it with a bit of the turkey drippings. If you do stuff the neck and body cavities, do it just before roasting, and remove the dressing as soon as the bird is done to avoid bacterial growth and potential health hazards.

Aroma therapy: If you choose not to stuff the bird, place a few aromatics (pieces of onion, a stalk or two of celery, a wedge of apple or orange, or some fresh herbs) inside the body cavity to add flavor to the meat and basting juices. (Discard these ingredients once the turkey is cooked.)

Go natural: When removing the neck and giblets, we recommend getting rid of any other extra manufacturer-supplied contraptions as well, such as pop-up thermometers (notoriously unreliable) and metal leg clamps (not nice to look at, and they get very hot).

Brining a turkey before roasting adds flavor and helps keep the meat moist and tender. To make a simple brine, combine 1 cup kosher salt per gallon of water. Make enough brine to cover the turkey completely, and place the container (a rectangular plastic storage tub works well) in the refrigerator or a cool spot (around 40°) for at least 6 hours or overnight. Drain and rinse the turkey, and pat it dry before proceeding.

ESTIMATED TURKEY ROASTING TIMES*

Weight	Unstuffed	Stuffed
8 to 12 pounds	2¾ to 3 hours	3 to 3½ hours
12 to 14 pounds	3 to 3¾ hours	3½ to 4 hours
14 to 18 pounds	3¾ to 4¼ hours	4 to 4¼ hours
18 to 20 pounds	4¼ to 4½ hours	4¼ to 4¾ hours
20 to 24 pounds	4½ to 5 hours	4¾ to 5¼ hours
24 to 29 pounds	5 to 5½ hours	5¼ to 5¾ hours

* To prevent overcooking, always take a temperature reading about 30 minutes before you expect the turkey to be ready.

ITALIAN DRESSING *with* PEARS, PINE NUTS, *and* PROSCIUTTO

¼ CUP OLIVE OIL

1 CUP PINE NUTS

3 OUNCES THINLY SLICED PROSCIUTTO, COARSELY CHOPPED *(about ¾ cup)*

6 OUNCES BABY SPINACH LEAVES *(about 8 cups, loosely packed)*

¾ CUP DRY MARSALA

3 CLOVES GARLIC, MINCED

2 CUPS CHOPPED ONION

1 FENNEL BULB *(1 pound)*, TRIMMED AND CHOPPED

6 CUPS ¾-INCH DRY BREAD CUBES *(about 11 ounces)*

2 BOSC PEARS *(about 1 pound total)*, STEMMED, CORED, AND COARSELY CHOPPED

¾ CUP DRIED FRUIT, SUCH AS GOLDEN RAISINS, OR CHOPPED DRIED PEARS

3 TABLESPOONS CHOPPED FRESH FLAT-LEAF PARSLEY

1½ TABLESPOONS MINCED FRESH ROSEMARY, OR 2 TEASPOONS DRIED

ABOUT 1½ CUPS TURKEY OR CHICKEN STOCK *(page 215)*

ABOUT 1 TEASPOON SALT

ABOUT ½ TEASPOON FRESHLY GROUND PEPPER

ABOUT ¼ CUP DRIPPINGS FROM ROASTED TURKEY *(optional)*

If you've ever enjoyed pears with prosciutto, this dressing's for you. The combination of Marsala, figs, pears, fennel, prosciutto, and pine nuts gives it a luxuriously sweet-savory flavor that goes well with poultry, pork, or veal. It's made with dry Marsala as opposed to the sweet dessert variety often used in zabaglione and other Italian *dolci*. If you're serving this dressing with turkey, use dry Marsala in place of the white wine in the master recipe as well.

PREHEAT oven to 350°. Coat a shallow 2½-quart baking dish with vegetable oil spray and set aside. In a large frying pan or Dutch oven, heat 2 tablespoons of the oil over medium heat. Add pine nuts and prosciutto. Cook, stirring, until pine nuts are light golden brown, about 5 minutes. Add spinach and ¼ cup of the Marsala. Cook, covered, just until spinach has wilted, 2 to 3 minutes. Stir in garlic and cook, uncovered, until fragrant, 30 seconds to 1 minute. Scrape mixture into a large bowl and set aside.

IN the same frying pan, heat the remaining 2 tablespoons oil over medium-high heat. Add onion and fennel; cook, stirring, until softened, 5 to 7 minutes. Add to the pine nut mixture along with the bread cubes, pears, dried fruit, parsley, and rosemary. Pour in 1 cup of the stock and the remaining ½ cup Marsala; toss gently to mix. Bread should be moist but not soggy; add stock as needed, depending on dryness of bread. Season with salt and pepper; toss again. (If dressing will be used to stuff a turkey, cover and let cool. Don't stuff turkey until just before roasting.)

SPOON dressing into baking dish and cover with foil. Bake, covered, until heated through, about 30 minutes. If a crusty topping is desired, remove foil and drizzle with turkey drippings. Continue baking, uncovered, until lightly browned on top, about 15 minutes longer.

YIELDS ABOUT 12 CUPS

WILD MUSHROOM DRESSING *with* WALNUTS *and* BRAZIL NUTS

Nuts and mushrooms were made for each other, and in this dressing they're very happy together. The dried porcini and assorted fresh mushrooms ensure a match made in heaven. Instead of those little half-ounce packets sold in the produce section of supermarkets, look for dried mushrooms in bulk; they're a much better buy and are often fresher and more flavorful.

PREHEAT oven to 350°. Coat a shallow 2½-quart baking dish with vegetable oil spray and set aside. Spread walnuts and Brazil nuts on large baking sheet or in a shallow pan. Bake, stirring once or twice, until lightly browned and fragrant, 10 to 12 minutes. Let cool slightly, then chop coarsely.

PLACE dried mushrooms in a small bowl; add warm water to cover. Let stand until softened, about 30 minutes. Remove mushrooms, squeezing out excess liquid. Chop mushrooms coarsely. Place a fine sieve over a 2-cup measuring cup. Strain the liquid into the cup.

MELT half the butter in a large frying pan over medium heat. Add onion and celery; cook, stirring occasionally, until softened but not browned, 5 to 7 minutes. Stir in parsley, thyme, and sage; cook 1 minute longer. Scrape mixture into a large bowl.

IN the same frying pan, melt the remaining ¼ cup butter over medium heat. Add rehydrated and fresh mushrooms. Cook, stirring, until mushrooms are tender and lightly browned on the edges, 5 to 7 minutes. Stir in garlic, ½ teaspoon salt, and pepper; cook 1 minute longer. Add mixture to the onion and celery, then add walnuts, Brazil nuts, and bread pieces.

ADD enough turkey stock to the mushroom liquid to equal 2 cups. Pour over the bread mixture, tossing gently to mix. Bread should be moist but not soggy; add stock as needed, depending on the dryness of the bread. Taste, adding more salt if needed. (If dressing will be used to stuff a turkey, cover and let cool. Don't stuff turkey until just before roasting.)

SPOON dressing into baking dish and cover with foil. Bake, covered, until heated through, about 30 minutes. If a crusty topping is desired, remove foil and drizzle with turkey drippings. Continue baking, uncovered, until lightly browned on top, about 15 minutes longer.

YIELDS ABOUT 12 CUPS

⅔ CUP WALNUTS

⅔ CUP BRAZIL NUTS

½ OUNCE DRIED PORCINI OR OTHER DRIED WILD MUSHROOMS

ABOUT 1 CUP WARM WATER

½ CUP UNSALTED BUTTER

1½ CUPS CHOPPED ONION

1½ CUPS CHOPPED CELERY

2 TABLESPOONS CHOPPED FRESH FLAT-LEAF PARSLEY

1½ TABLESPOONS CHOPPED FRESH THYME, OR 1½ TEASPOONS DRIED

1½ TABLESPOONS CHOPPED FRESH SAGE, OR 1½ TEASPOONS DRIED

1 POUND ASSORTED FRESH MUSHROOMS *(such as shiitake, cremini, and portabella)*, SLICED OR CHOPPED

2 CLOVES GARLIC, MINCED

½ TO 1 TEASPOON SALT

¼ TEASPOON FRESHLY GROUND PEPPER

6 CUPS COARSELY TORN DRY BREAD CUBES *(about 11 ounces)*

ABOUT 1 CUP TURKEY OR CHICKEN STOCK *(page 215)*

ABOUT ¼ CUP DRIPPINGS FROM ROASTED TURKEY *(optional)*

KENTUCKY CORN BREAD—
PECAN DRESSING

1½ CUPS PECANS OR
SPICY PECANS *(page 94)*,
COARSELY CHOPPED

½ CUP UNSALTED BUTTER

2 CUPS CHOPPED ONIONS

1½ CUPS CHOPPED CELERY

¼ CUP CHOPPED FRESH
FLAT-LEAF PARSLEY

2 TABLESPOONS CHOPPED
FRESH SAGE, OR
2 TEASPOONS DRIED

1½ TABLESPOONS CHOPPED
FRESH THYME, OR
1½ TEASPOONS DRIED

1½ CUPS STEMMED, SEEDED, AND
CHOPPED RED BELL PEPPERS

3 CLOVES GARLIC, MINCED

6 CUPS CRUMBLED DRY
CORN BREAD *(11 to 12 ounces)*

ABOUT 2½ CUPS TURKEY OR
CHICKEN STOCK *(page 215)*

2 TABLESPOONS BOURBON
(optional)

1 TEASPOON SALT

FRESHLY GROUND PEPPER

ABOUT ¼ CUP DRIPPINGS FROM
ROASTED TURKEY *(optional)*

This recipe calls for crumbled corn bread. We recommend following the recipe you'll find on any cornmeal box and letting it sit out for a day. Avoid packaged corn bread mixes, which will give you an overly sweet dressing. For extra flavor, add crumbled cooked bacon or sausage or chopped ham.

PREHEAT oven to 350°. (If using Spicy Pecans, skip the next step.) Spread pecans on a baking sheet or in a shallow pan. Bake, stirring once or twice, until lightly browned and fragrant, 7 to 10 minutes. Let cool. Chop coarsely.

MELT ¼ cup of the butter in a large frying pan over medium heat. Add onions and celery; cook, stirring occasionally, until softened but not browned, 5 to 7 minutes. Stir in parsley, sage, and thyme; cook 1 minute longer. Scrape mixture into a large bowl.

IN the same frying pan, melt the remaining ¼ cup butter over medium heat. Add bell peppers. Cook, stirring, until softened but not browned, 3 to 5 minutes. Stir in garlic; cook 1 minute longer. Scrape mixture into bowl with onions and celery; add pecans and crumbled corn bread.

POUR in 2 cups of the stock and the bourbon. Toss gently to mix. Corn bread should be moist but not soggy; add the remaining ½ cup stock, or more depending on the dryness of the corn bread. Season with salt and pepper; toss again. (If dressing will be used to stuff a turkey, cover and let cool. Don't stuff turkey until just before roasting.)

SPOON dressing into baking dish and cover with foil. Bake, covered, until heated through, about 30 minutes. If a crusty topping is desired, remove foil and drizzle with turkey drippings. Continue baking, uncovered, until lightly browned on top, about 15 minutes longer.

YIELDS ABOUT 12 CUPS

ROAST PORK LOIN *with* A GOLDEN ALMOND CRUST

(GARY DANKO)

If throwing a roast in the oven is easy, adding a nutty coating is not a whole lot harder—and it makes for a decidedly more dramatic and delectable presentation. Take this elegant pork roast with a crunchy mustard-almond crust, for example. It's a fine choice for a fancy dinner party or just a relaxed supper at home. Try the deceptively complex three-ingredient sauce on grilled chicken, veal, or pork chops, too.

PREHEAT oven to 350°. Season pork with salt and pepper, and rub with mustard.

IN a food processor, whirl bread crumbs, almonds, parsley, herbs, and garlic, pulsing the machine on and off until finely chopped.

PAT almond mixture over roast, pressing to coat well. Place on a rack in a shallow roasting pan; cook until crust is lightly browned and a meat thermometer inserted into the center of the roast registers 155° to 160°, 1½ to 2 hours. Transfer roast to a cutting board and let stand 10 minutes before slicing. Spoon mustard sauce over sliced pork.

WHILE the pork roasts, make the sauce: In a medium saucepan, simmer chicken stock over medium heat until reduced to 1 cup. (If making in advance, refrigerate, covered, up to 3 days. To finish sauce, reheat the reduced stock over low heat while the cooked roast rests.) Reduce heat to low and whisk in 2 tablespoons of the mustard. Taste, adding more mustard as desired. Whisk in butter, a few pieces at a time, until butter is incorporated and sauce is smooth.

SERVES 6 TO 8

1 BONELESS PORK LOIN ROAST *(about 4 pounds)*

SALT

FRESHLY GROUND PEPPER

2 TO 3 TABLESPOONS DIJON MUSTARD

1 CUP FRESH BREAD CRUMBS

½ CUP SLIVERED ALMONDS

¼ CUP COARSELY CHOPPED FRESH FLAT-LEAF PARSLEY

1 TEASPOON HERBES DE PROVENCE

2 CLOVES GARLIC, SMASHED WITH THE FLAT SIDE OF A KNIFE AND PEELED

Dijon Mustard Sauce

4 CUPS CHICKEN STOCK *(page 215)*

2 TO 3 TABLESPOONS DIJON MUSTARD

¼ CUP UNSALTED BUTTER, CUT INTO SMALL PIECES

PAN-SEARED PORK MEDALLIONS *with* GINGER-PEAR-PECAN SAUCE

½ CUP PECANS

1 PORK TENDERLOIN
(about 1½ pounds)

SALT

FRESHLY GROUND PEPPER

2 TABLESPOONS OLIVE OIL

1 TABLESPOON UNSALTED
BUTTER

1 MEDIUM ONION, CHOPPED

1 TEASPOON GRATED
FRESH GINGER

1 FIRM-RIPE PEAR *(about
½ pound)*, PREFERABLY BOSC,
PEELED, CORED, AND CUT
INTO ½-INCH CUBES

1 TABLESPOON GINGER
PRESERVE *(chop any large pieces)*

⅓ CUP CHICKEN STOCK *(page 215)*

1 TEASPOON FRESH
LEMON JUICE

If you're a fan of the sweet-savory combination of pork and applesauce (and who isn't?), try this quick sauté. Its magic ingredients are ginger preserve (which you can find with the jams and jellies in most supermarkets), pecans, and chunks of fresh pear. When cooked with the pan juices from the pork, they blend together to make a beautiful fruity glaze.

PREHEAT the oven to 350°. Spread pecans on a baking sheet or in a shallow pan. Bake, stirring once or twice, until lightly browned and fragrant, 7 to 10 minutes. Let cool slightly, then chop coarsely.

CUT tenderloin crosswise into medallions about 1 inch thick. Season with salt and pepper. In a large frying pan, heat oil over medium-high heat. Add pork and cook, turning once, until browned on the outside with no trace of pink in the center, 6 to 8 minutes total. Transfer pork to a plate and keep warm.

IN the same pan, melt butter over medium heat. Add onion and ginger; cook, stirring occasionally, until softened but not brown, about 5 minutes. Add pear, pecans, and ginger preserve. Cook, stirring, until pecans are crisp and glazed, 3 to 4 minutes. Add chicken stock and lemon juice; increase heat to high. Cook, scraping any brown bits from the bottom of the pan, until liquid has reduced slightly, 1 to 2 minutes. Return pork and any accumulated juices to the frying pan, turning to coat with sauce. Remove pork to a warm serving platter and top with pear-pecan sauce.

SERVES 3 OR 4

LAMB MEDALLIONS *with* A SPICY PECAN CRUST

(PATRICK O'CONNELL)

Spicy Pecans

¼ CUP UNSALTED BUTTER

3 TABLESPOONS SUGAR

2 TEASPOONS GROUND CUMIN

½ TEASPOON CAJUN SEASONING

½ TEASPOON CAYENNE PEPPER

4 CUPS PECANS

Barbecue Sauce

1 CUP KETCHUP

1 MEDIUM ONION, QUARTERED

½ CUP WHITE WINE VINEGAR

½ CUP PACKED BROWN SUGAR

¼ CUP WORCESTERSHIRE SAUCE

2 TEASPOONS DRY MUSTARD
POWDER

1 TEASPOON HOT-PEPPER SAUCE
(such as Tabasco)

3 RACKS OF LAMB, *(about 1½
pounds each)*

SALT

FRESHLY GROUND PEPPER

For more than two decades, this has been one of the most popular versions of rack of lamb on the menu at one of America's favorite dining rooms, the Inn at Little Washington, in Washington, Virginia. The racks are basted with a tangy barbecue sauce and grilled. Then they're removed from the bone, given a second coating of sauce, rolled in spicy pecans, and sliced into medallions to be served with crispy shoestring sweet potatoes and marinated cabbage slaw. The quick, no-cook barbecue sauce goes with everything from ribs to burgers. The recipe makes extra, so slather away. ❧ "We serve these pecans slightly warm with cocktails," says Chef Patrick O'Connell. "Our guests find them addictive, and so will your friends."

TO make the pecans: Fit a wire rack over a baking sheet and set aside. In a large frying pan, melt butter over medium-high heat until it begins to foam. Add sugar, cumin, Cajun seasoning, and cayenne, stirring to blend. Stir in the pecans. Cook, stirring and tossing, until pecans are well coated and lightly browned, 3 to 4 minutes. Scrape nuts onto the wire rack; let cool. (If making in advance, cool completely and store airtight at room temperature up to 5 days.)

TO make the barbecue sauce: In a food processor, process ketchup, onion, vinegar, brown sugar, Worcestershire sauce, dry mustard, and hot-pepper sauce until smooth. (If making in advance, cover and refrigerate up to 3 days.)

TO grill the lamb: Preheat a stovetop or indoor grill, or preheat an oven broiler, placing the rack 5 to 6 inches from the heat source. Season lamb with salt and pepper, and brush each lamb rack with about 6 tablespoons of the barbecue sauce. Grill or broil the lamb, turning once, just

enough to crisp and lightly char the exterior, 2 to 3 minutes per side. (The lamb will finish cooking in the oven.) Remove lamb to a roasting pan or large baking sheet. Preheat oven to 400°.

ROAST lamb until medium-rare (140° to 145° on a meat thermometer), 15 to 20 minutes. Remove lamb to a cutting board and let stand 5 to 10 minutes.

TO assemble the medallions: Chop 1½ cups of the pecans. (Reserve remaining pecans for another use.) Place about ¾ cup of the barbecue sauce and the chopped pecans in separate shallow pans or bowls. (Reserve remaining sauce for another use.) With a thin, sharp knife, cut along the bones of each rack to release the tenderloin in one piece; trim off and discard any fat. Roll the boneless loins in the barbecue sauce, then in the pecans, pressing to coat. Slice each tenderloin crosswise into 6 medallions.

SERVES 6

HAZELNUT, BEEF, *and*
GREEN BEAN STIR-FRY

1 POUND BEEF FLANK STEAK

2 TABLESPOONS SOY SAUCE

1 TABLESPOON PLUS
1 TEASPOON CORNSTARCH

1 TEASPOON ASIAN SESAME OIL

⅓ CUP DRY VERMOUTH, DRY
SHERRY, OR STOCK

1 TABLESPOON CHINESE BLACK
BEAN GARLIC SAUCE

1 TEASPOON SUGAR

⅛ TO ¼ TEASPOON CRUSHED
DRIED RED CHILES

½ CUP CHOPPED HAZELNUTS

2 TABLESPOONS PEANUT OIL
OR VEGETABLE OIL

4 GREEN ONIONS,
CUT DIAGONALLY INTO
1-INCH PIECES

2 TEASPOONS MINCED FRESH
GINGER

1 CLOVE GARLIC, MINCED

½ POUND GREEN BEANS,
ENDS TRIMMED, CUT INTO
2-INCH PIECES

Follow this recipe, and you'll have a fantastic steak stir-fry that tastes every bit as good as anything you'd get at a Chinese restaurant. The hazelnuts add a pleasant crunch and a surprising amount of flavor. If you're not a fan of flank steak, any tender cut of beef (such as strip steak, top round, or sirloin) can be used; just be sure to slice the meat thinly across the grain. When asparagus is in season, try substituting it for the green beans. Serve with steamed rice. And don't forget the fortune cookies.

CUT steak in half lengthwise, then cut crosswise on an angle into thin slices. In a medium bowl, combine beef, 1 tablespoon of the soy sauce, 1 tablespoon of the cornstarch, and the sesame oil.

IN a small bowl, stir together the vermouth, the remaining 1 tablespoon soy sauce and 1 teaspoon cornstarch, black bean garlic sauce, sugar, and crushed chiles; set aside.

HEAT a wok or large frying pan over medium-high heat. Toast hazelnuts, stirring, until lightly browned and fragrant, 3 to 4 minutes. Remove hazelnuts from wok and set aside to cool. Raise heat to high.

POUR 1 tablespoon of the oil into the hot wok, swirling to coat. Add beef and cook, stirring and tossing, until it is barely pink, 1 to 2 minutes. With a slotted spoon, remove to a plate. Reduce heat to medium-high.

POUR remaining 1 tablespoon of oil into wok, swirling to coat. Add green onions, ginger, and garlic. Cook, stirring, until fragrant, about 30 seconds. Add green beans and cook, stirring and tossing, until bright green, 30 seconds to 1 minute.

STIR sauce to blend, then add to wok along with beef. Cook, stirring and tossing, until beans are tender-crisp and sauce thickens, 1 to 2 minutes. Serve topped with hazelnuts.

SERVES 3 TO 4

BRAISED BEEF BRACIOLE
with WALNUT–RICE FILLING

½ CUP WALNUTS

5½ TABLESPOONS WALNUT OIL,
ROASTED GARLIC WALNUT OIL,
OR OLIVE OIL *(or a combination)*

1 CUP COARSELY CHOPPED
MUSHROOMS

⅓ CUP LONG-GRAIN
WHITE RICE

1 CLOVE GARLIC, MINCED

½ TEASPOON SALT

¼ TEASPOON FRESHLY
GROUND PEPPER

⅔ CUP WATER

3 TABLESPOONS CHOPPED FRESH
FLAT-LEAF PARSLEY

6 BEEF TOP ROUND STEAKS,
CUT ABOUT ¼ INCH THICK
(about 1½ pounds total)

6 THIN SLICES *(about 6 ounces total)*
PROVOLONE CHEESE

3 TABLESPOONS FLOUR

1 ONION, SLICED

1 CARROT, PEELED AND
COARSELY CHOPPED

2 TABLESPOONS TOMATO PASTE

1 CAN *(10½ ounces, about 1¼ cups)*
BEEF STOCK

¾ CUP CHIANTI OR OTHER
DRY RED WINE

¼ CUP CHOPPED FRESH BASIL
OR FLAT-LEAF PARSLEY

The term *braciole* is often used to describe thin-cut steaks wrapped around a savory filling and then rolled, browned, and slowly braised in a flavorful sauce. Sensational is the English word for how it tastes, especially this version with its stuffing of provolone and mushroom-walnut pilaf. Top round steaks are sometimes sold as sandwich steaks; if you can't find them, thin-cut sirloin steaks will also work. You can make this dish a day or two ahead of time, and, like most braised dishes, its flavor will actually improve on reheating. Just don't slice the beef rolls until you're ready to serve.

PREHEAT oven to 350°. Spread walnuts on a baking sheet or in a shallow pan. Bake, stirring once or twice, until lightly browned and fragrant, 10 to 12 minutes. Let cool slightly; then chop coarsely.

IN a small saucepan, heat 2 tablespoons of the oil over medium heat. Add mushrooms, rice, garlic, ¼ teaspoon salt, and ⅛ teaspoon pepper. Cook, stirring, until mushrooms are just tender, about 4 minutes. Add water and bring to a boil. Reduce heat to low and cook, covered, until rice is just tender, about 15 minutes. Let cool, then stir in the walnuts and 2 tablespoons of the parsley.

TRIM any excess fat from the steaks. With a smooth meat mallet or other heavy object, pound steaks until about ⅛ inch thick. Lay 1 slice provolone on each beef slice.

DIVIDE rice mixture equally among steaks, placing about ⅓ cup on the lower third of each. Roll steaks up, tucking in sides to enclose filling. Tie with string or fasten with toothpicks.

IN a shallow bowl, mix flour with the remaining ¼ teaspoon salt and ⅛ teaspoon pepper. Dredge meat rolls in flour mixture to coat; shake off excess.

IN a Dutch oven or flameproof casserole, heat 2 tablespoons of the oil over medium-high heat. Add beef rolls and cook, turning occasionally, until browned all over, about 10 minutes. Remove meat and set aside.

IN the same pan, heat the remaining 1½ tablespoons oil over medium-high heat. Add onion, carrot, and tomato paste. Cook, stirring, until vegetables are softened, about 5 minutes. Increase heat to high and pour in beef stock and wine; bring to a boil. Cook, stirring to scrape all the brown bits from bottom of pan.

REDUCE heat to low. Add beef rolls and cook, covered, until meat and vegetables are tender, 50 to 60 minutes. Use tongs or a slotted spoon to transfer beef rolls to a clean work surface.

COOK stock-onion mixture over high heat until thickened slightly, 3 to 5 minutes. Remove from heat and stir in 3 tablespoons of the basil. Remove string from rolls; cut diagonally into thick slices. Arrange slices in a single layer in warm, shallow bowls or plates. Spoon sauce over top and sprinkle with remaining 1 tablespoon basil.

SERVES 6

SPEZZATINO
with ORZO *and* WALNUTS

This Italian-style beef and mushroom stew will surprise you: it cooks in just about an hour (the secret is cutting the beef into thin slices). You can start it in the morning or on the weekend and then pop it in the oven to bake when you get home from work. We like how the late-in-the-game addition of orzo (small rice-shaped pasta) and walnuts brings the whole dish together and turns it into a hearty one-pot meal.

PREHEAT oven to 350°. Spread walnuts on a baking sheet or in a shallow pan. Bake, stirring once or twice, until lightly browned and fragrant, 8 to 10 minutes. Let cool.

INCREASE oven temperature to 375°.

TRIM excess fat from beef. Cut into thin slices; season with about 1 teaspoon salt and ½ teaspoon pepper. In a Dutch oven or large, flameproof casserole, heat 2 tablespoons of the oil over medium-high heat. Add beef and cook, stirring occasionally, until browned, about 3 minutes. With slotted spoon, remove beef from pan and set aside. In same pan, heat remaining 2 tablespoons oil. Add onion and cook, stirring occasionally, until softened but not brown, about 5 minutes. Stir in mushrooms and garlic; cook until mushrooms are lightly browned, 4 to 5 minutes. Return beef to pan. Stir in tomatoes and their liquid and the water; bring to a boil. Cover and bake until beef is just tender when pierced with a fork, about 45 minutes.

STIR in orzo and walnuts. Bake, covered, until orzo is tender but still firm, about 15 minutes or as package directs. Stir in basil and parsley. Taste, adding more salt and pepper if needed. Spoon into warm, shallow bowls. Sprinkle each serving with Parmesan cheese.

SERVES 4 TO 6

½ CUP CHOPPED OR SLICED WALNUTS

1½ POUNDS BONELESS BEEF TRI-TIP

SALT

FRESHLY GROUND PEPPER

¼ CUP OLIVE OIL

1 MEDIUM ONION, HALVED AND THINLY SLICED

½ POUND CREMINI OR OTHER MUSHROOMS, QUARTERED

2 CLOVES GARLIC, MINCED

1 CAN *(28 ounces)* DICED TOMATOES

2½ CUPS WATER OR BEEF STOCK *(page 215)*

1 CUP ORZO OR RISO *(rice-shaped pasta)*

⅓ CUP CHOPPED FRESH BASIL

¼ CUP CHOPPED FRESH FLAT-LEAF PARSLEY

⅓ CUP FRESHLY GRATED PARMESAN CHEESE

VEGETABLES, GRAINS & PASTA

I went down into
the garden of nuts
to see the fruits
of the valley,
and to see whether
the vine flourished
and the pomegranates
budded.

SOLOMON'S SONG 6:11

GRILLED SUMMER VEGETABLES
with HERBED YOGURT–WALNUT SAUCE

Herbed Yogurt–Walnut Sauce

½ CUP WALNUTS

1 CUP PLAIN YOGURT

1 CUP PEELED, SEEDED, AND
CHOPPED ENGLISH CUCUMBER

1 TABLESPOON FRESH
LEMON JUICE

2 TABLESPOONS CHOPPED
FRESH MINT

2 TABLESPOONS CHOPPED
FRESH CILANTRO

2 TABLESPOONS CHOPPED FRESH
FLAT-LEAF PARSLEY

1 CLOVE GARLIC, MINCED

2 TEASPOONS SUGAR

SALT AND FRESHLY GROUND
PEPPER

2 RED BELL PEPPERS

1 EGGPLANT *(about 1 pound)*,
CUT LENGTHWISE INTO
½-INCH SLICES

1 POUND ZUCCHINI, CUT
LENGTHWISE INTO ½-INCH
SLICES

3 PORTABELLA MUSHROOM
CAPS *(about 1 pound total)*

1 LARGE ONION, CUT CROSS-
WISE INTO ½-INCH SLICES

1 POUND FIRM-RIPE TOMATOES
(about 4 medium), CUT CROSSWISE
INTO ½-INCH SLICES

EXTRA-VIRGIN OLIVE OIL

SALT

FRESHLY GROUND PEPPER

(Ingredients continue on opposite page)

Grilled vegetables were made for entertaining—whether it's summertime or just plain supper-time. You can serve them either warm or at room temperature as part of a fancy meal or a casual barbecue, and cooking them outdoors means the kitchen stays cool. Add a quick homemade walnut sauce and call it a mélange. ❀ The creamy Greek-inspired Herbed Yogurt-Walnut Sauce goes with just about any vegetable you can think of. It's wonderful with red meat, too, especially grilled or roasted lamb. You can also spread it on a sandwich or a burger, or serve it as a dip with pita bread triangles, crisp vegetables, or golden fried falafel. Or try the variation—a quick herb-and-walnut oil infusion. It can be drizzled on any kind of cooked vegetable and will add a bit of splash to mild-flavored fish as well.

TO make the sauce: Preheat oven to 350°. Spread walnuts on a baking sheet or in a shallow pan. Bake, stirring once or twice, until lightly browned and fragrant, 10 to 12 minutes. Let cool slightly, then chop finely.

IN a medium bowl, stir together walnuts, yogurt, cucumber, lemon juice, mint, cilantro, parsley, garlic, and sugar. Season to taste with salt and pepper. Refrigerate, covered, for 30 minutes to blend flavors. Serve slightly chilled.

TO grill the vegetables: Light a hot fire in an outdoor grill, or preheat a stovetop or indoor grill. Brush peppers, eggplant, zucchini, mush-rooms, onion, and tomatoes with oil; season with salt and pepper.

GRILL peppers, turning, until skin is charred and black all over, 12 to 15 minutes. Remove from heat and seal in a paper bag. Set aside until cool enough to handle, at least 10 minutes. Peel blackened skin from peppers (some skin can remain); discard stems and seeds. Cut peppers lengthwise into ½-inch strips.

GRILL remaining vegetables, turning, until browned and tender but still firm: eggplant and zucchini, 5 to 7 minutes; mushrooms, 5 to 7 minutes; onion, 5 to 6 minutes; and tomatoes, 1 to 3 minutes.

CUT mushrooms into ½-inch slices, and separate onion slices into rings. Arrange peppers, eggplant, zucchini, mushrooms, onion, and tomatoes on a serving platter. Serve warm or at room tempera-ture. Just before serving, drizzle with sauce, or serve sauce on the side.

SERVES 6 TO 8

Variation

HERB-AND-WALNUT OIL

PREHEAT oven to 350°. Spread walnuts on a baking sheet or in a shallow pan. Bake, stirring once or twice, until lightly browned and fragrant, 8 to 10 minutes. Let cool.

IN a medium bowl, stir together walnuts, walnut oil, olive oil, parsley, lemon juice, basil, chives, rosemary, and garlic. Season to taste with salt and pepper. Let stand 30 minutes at room temperature to blend flavors. (If making in advance, refrigerate, covered, up to 3 days. Return sauce to room temperature before serving.)

Herb-and-Walnut Oil

½ CUP CHOPPED WALNUTS

½ CUP WALNUT OIL

¼ CUP EXTRA-VIRGIN OLIVE OIL

2 TABLESPOONS CHOPPED FRESH FLAT-LEAF PARSLEY

1 TABLESPOON FRESH LEMON JUICE

1 TABLESPOON CHOPPED FRESH BASIL

1 TABLESPOON FINELY CHOPPED FRESH CHIVES

1 TEASPOON FINELY CHOPPED FRESH ROSEMARY

1 CLOVE GARLIC, PRESSED OR MINCED

SALT

FRESHLY GROUND PEPPER

GREEN BEANS *with* GREEN ONIONS *and* HAZELNUTS

1 POUND GREEN BEANS,
ENDS TRIMMED

2 TABLESPOONS UNSALTED
BUTTER

1 CUP CHOPPED HAZELNUTS

1 CUP CHOPPED GREEN ONION

SALT

FRESHLY GROUND PEPPER

Remember green beans amandine? This simple, sophisticated take on that classic side dish is made with crisp-tender green beans and hazelnuts. It's a combination that also works well as a room-temperature salad. Simply substitute olive oil for the butter when sautéing. Let everything cool to room temperature, then, at the last minute, toss in a little lemon juice or rice vinegar, salt, and pepper.

BRING a large pot of salted water to a boil over high heat. Add green beans and cook until tender-crisp, 2 to 4 minutes. Drain immediately in a colander, then plunge into a bowl of ice water to stop the cooking and retain color. Drain again.

IN a large frying pan, melt butter over medium heat. Add hazelnuts and cook, stirring occasionally, until lightly browned and fragrant, 3 to 5 minutes. Add green onions and green beans; cook, stirring, until the onions are softened but not browned and beans are heated through, 1 to 2 minutes. Season to taste with salt and pepper.

SERVES 4

BRUSSELS SPROUTS *with*
SWEET BELL PEPPER *and* WALNUTS

Do yourself and the people of Belgium a favor. Give brussels sprouts a second chance. We all remember them from childhood as bitter, cabbagey little pieces of punishment on a plate. But they can actually be sublimely tender and tasty. The trick is to buy young, very fresh ones (a farmers' market is your best bet for this) and to avoid overcooking them.

TRIM off and discard any dark areas at the base of each brussels sprout. Cut each sprout in half. Stem and seed bell peppers and cut into ½-inch squares.

BRING a large pot of salted water to a boil over high heat. Add brussels sprouts and cook until tender but still firm, 7 to 10 minutes. Drain.

IN a large frying pan, toast walnuts over medium heat, stirring, until lightly browned and fragrant, about 3 minutes. Remove from pan and set aside.

IN the same frying pan, melt butter in walnut oil over medium heat. Add bell pepper, shallot, and garlic; cook, stirring occasionally, until softened but not browned, about 5 minutes. Stir in brussels sprouts, walnuts, thyme, and sugar. Cook, stirring, until sprouts are lightly glazed and heated through, about 2 minutes longer. Season to taste with salt and pepper

SERVES 4 TO 6

1 POUND BRUSSELS SPROUTS

1 SMALL YELLOW OR RED BELL PEPPER

½ CUP SLICED WALNUTS

1 TABLESPOON UNSALTED BUTTER

1 TABLESPOON ROASTED GARLIC WALNUT OIL OR WALNUT OIL

¼ CUP THINLY SLICED SHALLOT

1 LARGE CLOVE GARLIC, THINLY SLICED

1 TEASPOON CHOPPED FRESH THYME

½ TEASPOON SUGAR

SALT

FRESHLY GROUND PEPPER

ZUCCHINI RIBBONS *with* ALMONDS
and SHAVED PECORINO

1½ POUNDS ZUCCHINI
(about 6 medium)

2 TABLESPOONS OLIVE OIL

½ CUP SLICED ALMONDS

¼ CUP THINLY SLICED SHALLOT

1 SMALL CLOVE GARLIC,
THINLY SLICED

SALT

FRESHLY GROUND PEPPER

1 SMALL CHUNK *(1 to 2 ounces)*
PECORINO ROMANO CHEESE

Something delightful happens to zucchini when you slice it into noodle-thin ribbons and quickly sauté it. It takes on a delicately crunchy texture and, because more of its surface area is exposed, it develops a lot more flavor than the usual slices or chunks. If you don't want to invest in a costly French mandoline (a planelike slicing contraption), a plastic vegetable slicer with metal blades will work just as well. When good sweet cherry tomatoes (such as Sweet 100) are in season, throw in a handful along with the zucchini for an extra burst of flavor and color.

WITH a mandoline, vegetable slicer, or knife, cut zucchini lengthwise into long, thin strands.

IN a large frying pan, heat oil over medium-high heat. Add almonds, shallot, and garlic; cook, stirring, until lightly browned, 2 to 3 minutes. Add zucchini and cook, stirring, until tender, 2 to 3 minutes. Season to taste with salt and pepper. Transfer to a warm shallow bowl or serving platter. With a swivel-bladed vegetable peeler, shave cheese over the top.

SERVES 4

WALNUT-STUFFED ARTICHOKES

(MOLLIE KATZEN)

6 LARGE ARTICHOKES, TRIMMED,
COOKED UNTIL TENDER,
DRAINED, AND COOLED

1 CUP GROUND WALNUTS

1 TO 2 TABLESPOONS OLIVE OIL

1½ CUPS CHOPPED ONION

½ TEASPOON SALT

¼ CUP DRY WHITE WINE
OR DRY VERMOUTH (optional)

1 LARGE CLOVE GARLIC,
MINCED

½ CUP FINE DRY BREAD
CRUMBS

½ TEASPOON DRIED THYME

½ TEASPOON PAPRIKA

2 TEASPOONS DRY MUSTARD
POWDER

¼ CUP FINELY CHOPPED FRESH
FLAT-LEAF PARSLEY

2 TABLESPOONS FRESH
LEMON JUICE

FRESHLY GROUND PEPPER

How do you improve upon something as perfect as an artichoke? "Stuff it," suggests cookbook author and cooking show host Mollie Katzen. And so saying, she created this bread crumb, onion, and herb stuffing that tastes like everyone's favorite part of Thanksgiving dinner. She suggests cooking and prepping the artichokes ahead of time and then stuffing and baking them just before serving. Make some Walnut Mayonnaise (page 57), Romesco Sauce (page 36), or Herbed Yogurt-Walnut Sauce (page 104) to serve in individual ramekins for dipping.

TRIM the stems from the artichokes so they stand upright. Grasp the central leaf cluster at the tip and pull it out, forming a cavity in the middle of each artichoke. With a small spoon, scrape out and discard the fuzzy choke.

PREHEAT oven to 350°. Spread walnuts on a baking sheet or in a shallow pan. Bake, stirring once or twice, until lightly browned and fragrant, 5 to 10 minutes. Let cool. Reduce oven temperature to 325°.

IN a medium frying pan, heat oil over medium heat. Add onion and salt. Cook, stirring occasionally, until onion is softened but not browned, about 5 minutes. Add wine and cook until reduced slightly, about 5 minutes. Add garlic, bread crumbs, thyme, paprika, and dry mustard.

Cook, stirring frequently, until garlic is fragrant and crumbs are lightly browned, about 5 minutes. Remove frying pan from heat and stir in walnuts, parsley, and lemon juice. Season to taste with pepper.

DIVIDE walnut mixture evenly among the artichokes, firmly packing the filling into the middle of each. (If there is any extra filling, force it between some of the larger leaves.) Place stuffed artichokes upright in a shallow baking pan. Cover loosely with foil and bake until filling is heated through, about 30 minutes. Serve hot, warm, or at room temperature.

SERVES 6

CREAMY POLENTA
with WALNUTS

½ CUP SLICED WALNUTS

2½ CUPS CHICKEN OR
VEGETABLE STOCK *(page 215–216)*,
OR WATER

1 CUP MILK

1 TEASPOON SALT

¾ CUP INSTANT POLENTA
OR YELLOW CORNMEAL

2 OUNCES *(about ½ cup)*
FRESHLY GRATED PARMESAN
CHEESE, PREFERABLY ITALIAN

3 TABLESPOONS UNSALTED
BUTTER, AT ROOM
TEMPERATURE

FRESHLY GROUND PEPPER

4 TEASPOONS WALNUT OIL OR
ROASTED GARLIC WALNUT OIL

Instant comfort, Italian style. In shopping for this dish, look for Parmigiano-Reggiano cheese imported from Italy; its flavor is richer and nuttier than that of domestic versions. You'll be surprised what a difference good cheese and a sprinkling of lightly toasted walnuts can make in a humble bowl of polenta. Some other easy ideas: add a drizzle of Walnut Pesto (page 126), sliced mushrooms sautéed in butter, or crumbled goat cheese and chopped tomatoes.

PREHEAT oven to 350°. Spread walnuts on a baking sheet or in a shallow pan. Bake, stirring once or twice, until lightly browned and fragrant, 5 to 10 minutes. Let cool.

IN a large saucepan, bring stock, milk, and salt to a boil over medium-high heat. Stir in polenta in a slow, steady stream. Reduce heat to medium-low and cook, stirring often, until mixture has thickened and polenta tastes creamy, 5 to 10 minutes.

REMOVE from heat and stir in cheese, butter, and pepper. Spoon into 4 warm shallow bowls or plates. Drizzle each serving with 1 teaspoon oil and sprinkle with 2 tablespoons toasted walnuts.

SERVES 4

COUNTRY WALNUT MASHED POTATOES

(TODD ENGLISH)

It's not easy to improve on the perfection of mashed potatoes. But Todd English has figured out a way. He folds in a purée of sautéed walnuts and sour cream, then adds a final accent of freshly grated Parmesan. The result: potatoes that are slightly tangy, extra-rich, and wonderfully toasty, with flecks of ground walnuts giving them the look and texture of a rustic country bread. Serve these at a special dinner alongside a juicy roasted rack of beef or lamb, or with pan-seared scallops. Or set out a big bowlful, family style, to warm up a weeknight dinner.

1 TABLESPOON UNSALTED BUTTER

½ CUP CHOPPED WALNUTS

¼ TO ½ CUP SOUR CREAM

4 LARGE RED-SKINNED POTATOES (1½ to 2 pounds total), PEELED AND CUT INTO LARGE CUBES

1 TEASPOON COARSE-GRAINED SALT

½ TEASPOON FRESHLY GROUND PEPPER

1 TABLESPOON FRESHLY GRATED PARMESAN CHEESE

IN a small frying pan, melt butter over medium-high heat. Add walnuts and cook, stirring, until golden brown, about 3 minutes. In a food processor, whirl walnuts and butter with ¼ cup sour cream until smooth.

PLACE potatoes in a large saucepan with enough cold water to cover them by 1 inch. Bring to a boil over high heat. Cook over medium heat until potatoes are tender when pierced with the tip of a sharp knife, 10 to 12 minutes. Drain potatoes in a colander, then transfer to a medium bowl. Mash with a fork or potato masher, gradually adding the walnut–sour cream mixture. For a creamier texture, add up to ¼ cup more sour cream if desired; mix in salt, pepper, and Parmesan.

SERVES 4

MOROCCAN-SPICED WALNUT RICE

½ CUP CHOPPED OR SLICED
WALNUTS

2 TABLESPOONS OLIVE OIL

1 ONION, HALVED AND
THINLY SLICED

1 TEASPOON GROUND CUMIN

1 TEASPOON GROUND
CORIANDER

1 TEASPOON GROUND
CINNAMON

½ TEASPOON GROUND
TURMERIC

1 CUP LONG-GRAIN
CONVERTED WHITE RICE

1 CAN *(14½ ounces)* DICED
TOMATOES

1 CUP WATER

¼ CUP PITTED, SLICED
KALAMATA OLIVES

1 TABLESPOON CHOPPED
FRESH OREGANO, OR
1 TEASPOON DRIED

2 TABLESPOONS CHOPPED FRESH
FLAT-LEAF PARSLEY

2 TEASPOONS FINELY
GRATED ORANGE ZEST

SALT

FRESHLY GROUND PEPPER

Nuts and spice and everything rice. That's what this tomatoey Middle Eastern pilaf is made of. Its complex flavors make an excellent match for simply roasted or grilled chicken, fish, lamb, pork, or steak. It can be made ahead and served at room temperature. If you do this, however, you may need to add some more liquid as the rice absorbs moisture as it sits.

PREHEAT oven to 350°. Spread walnuts on a baking sheet or in a shallow pan. Bake, stirring once or twice, until lightly browned and fragrant, 8 to 10 minutes. Let cool.

IN a medium saucepan, heat oil over medium-high heat. Add onion and cook, stirring, until lightly browned, about 5 minutes. Add cumin, coriander, cinnamon, and turmeric. Cook, stirring, until fragrant, 1 to 2 minutes. Stir in rice and cook until well coated, about 2 minutes.

STIR in tomatoes and their liquid, water, olives, oregano, parsley, and orange zest. Bring to a boil. Cover and reduce heat to low. Cook, covered, until rice is tender and liquid is absorbed, about 15 minutes. Stir in walnuts. Season to taste with salt and pepper.

SERVES 4

COCONUT-MACADAMIA RICE PILAF

Kids can't get enough of this sweet, tropical rice pilaf made with pineapple, toasted coconut, and buttery macadamia nuts. And we have yet to find a grownup who doesn't feel pretty much the same way. Serve it with teriyaki chicken or salmon, or pair it with pork or just about any entrée that goes well with fruit.

PREHEAT oven to 350°. Spread macadamias on a baking sheet or in a shallow pan. Bake, stirring once or twice, until lightly browned and fragrant, 5 to 7 minutes. Let cool. Increase oven temperature to 325°.

SPREAD coconut on a baking sheet or in a shallow pan. Bake, stirring occasionally, until lightly browned, 8 to 10 minutes. Let cool.

IN a medium saucepan, heat oil over medium heat. Add onion and cook, stirring, until softened but not browned, 3 to 5 minutes. Add ginger and cook 1 minute. Add rice and 1 teaspoon salt; stir until rice is coated with oil and ginger

is fragrant, about 1 minute. Add water and reserved pineapple juice; bring to a boil. Cover and reduce heat to low. Cook, covered, until rice is tender and liquid is absorbed, about 20 minutes. Stir in pineapple, green onion, cilantro, and parsley. Season to taste with salt and pepper.

IN a small bowl, toss together the toasted macadamias and coconut; stir three-fourths of this mixture into the pilaf and sprinkle the remainder on top.

SERVES 4 TO 6

½ CUP CHOPPED MACADAMIAS

½ CUP SWEETENED SHREDDED COCONUT

2 TABLESPOONS VEGETABLE OIL

¾ CUP CHOPPED YELLOW ONION

1 TABLESPOON MINCED FRESH GINGER

1 CUP LONG-GRAIN CONVERTED WHITE RICE

ABOUT 1 TEASPOON SALT

1½ CUPS WATER

1 CAN (8 ounces) UNSWEETENED CRUSHED PINEAPPLE, DRAINED, JUICE RESERVED

½ CUP SLICED GREEN ONION

2 TABLESPOONS CHOPPED FRESH CILANTRO

2 TABLESPOONS CHOPPED FRESH FLAT-LEAF PARSLEY

FRESHLY GROUND PEPPER

WILD MUSHROOM RISOTTO
with PINE NUTS

1 OUNCE DRIED PORCINI
MUSHROOMS OR OTHER DRIED
WILD MUSHROOMS

ABOUT 1 CUP WARM WATER

½ CUP PINE NUTS

5 TABLESPOONS OLIVE OIL

½ POUND FRESH MUSHROOMS
(wild, cultivated, or a combination),
SLICED OR COARSELY CHOPPED

3 TABLESPOONS DRY WHITE
WINE OR DRY MADEIRA

ABOUT 3½ CUPS CHICKEN OR
VEGETABLE STOCK *(page 215–216)*

1 TABLESPOON CHOPPED FRESH
THYME, OR 1 TEASPOON DRIED

½ CUP FINELY CHOPPED ONION

1½ CUPS ARBORIO RICE

¼ CUP DRY WHITE WINE
OR DRY VERMOUTH

ABOUT 1 CUP FRESHLY
GRATED PARMESAN CHEESE

2 TABLESPOONS UNSALTED
BUTTER, CUT INTO PIECES

SALT

FRESHLY GROUND PEPPER

Risotto? Isn't that tricky to make and loaded with cream? No, and no. Try this delicious version, made in the classic way, and see for yourself. True risotto is a luscious, satisfying entrée or first course that gets most of its creaminess when the starch is slowly released from the short-grain rice. Sure, it involves a few minutes of standing and stirring. But pour yourself a glass of whatever wine you're using in the risotto, and think of it as a little meditation break at the end of a busy day.

PLACE dried mushrooms in a small bowl; add warm water to cover. Let sit until softened, about 30 minutes. Remove mushrooms, squeezing out excess liquid. Chop mushrooms coarsely. Place a fine sieve over a 4-cup measuring cup. Strain the liquid into the cup.

PREHEAT oven to 325°. Place pine nuts in a small pan and bake, shaking once or twice, until just golden, 5 to 7 minutes. Let cool.

IN a large frying pan, heat 3 tablespoons of the oil over medium-high heat. Add fresh mushrooms and cook, stirring occasionally, until lightly browned, 5 to 7 minutes. Stir in the rehydrated mushrooms. Add the 3 tablespoons white wine and cook 1 minute, scraping up any brown bits from the bottom of the pan. Set aside.

ADD enough stock to the dried mushroom liquid to make 4 cups. Pour into a medium saucepan and keep warm over low heat.

IN a large saucepan, heat the remaining 2 tablespoons oil over medium heat. Stir in the thyme and onion. Cook, stirring occasionally, until onion is softened but not browned, 3 to 5 minutes. Add rice and cook, stirring often, until coated with oil and translucent, 2 to 3 minutes.

POUR in the ¼ cup white wine and bring to a boil over high heat, scraping up any brown bits from the bottom of the pan. Cook, stirring often, until wine is absorbed, 1 to 2 minutes. Reduce heat to medium. Pour in 1 cup of the warm mushroom liquid and cook, stirring often, until absorbed. Continue adding liquid, 1 cup at a time, stirring often, until it is absorbed and rice is creamy and tender but still firm in the center, 15 to 20 minutes total.

STIR in mushrooms, ¼ cup of the pine nuts, ⅓ cup Parmesan, and the butter. Cook, stirring, until mushrooms are heated through and butter has melted, 1 to 2 minutes. Season to taste with salt and pepper. Divide risotto equally among 4 warm, shallow bowls or plates and top with the remaining ¼ cup pine nuts. Pass remaining Parmesan cheese at the table.

SERVES 4

COUSCOUS PILAF *with*
LENTILS *and* PINE NUTS

5 CUPS WATER

1 CUP DRIED FRENCH
GREEN LENTILS

1 CUP PINE NUTS

2 TABLESPOONS EXTRA-VIRGIN
OLIVE OIL

SALT

1⅔ CUPS *(10 ounces)* QUICK-
COOKING COUSCOUS

½ CUP SWEETENED DRIED
CRANBERRIES

½ CUP THINLY SLICED
GREEN ONION

½ CUP CHOPPED FRESH MINT

ABOUT 2 TABLESPOONS FRESH
LEMON JUICE

¼ CUP CHOPPED FRESH
FLAT-LEAF PARSLEY

1 TABLESPOON FINELY
GRATED ORANGE ZEST

1 TABLESPOON FINELY
GRATED LEMON ZEST

If you're a fan of tabbouleh (a Middle Eastern minted bulgur salad), give this bright-flavored couscous salad a try. It's made with French green lentils *(lentilles de Puy),* which have more flavor and hold their shape better than the brown kind, and quick-cooking couscous, tossed with mint, citrus zest, olive oil, toasted pine nuts, and tangy dried cranberries. Serve it at a barbecue or picnic or as part of a Mediterranean buffet with other salads and vegetables, such as Grilled Summer Vegetables with Herbed Yogurt-Walnut Sauce (page 104), Green Beans with Green Onions and Hazelnuts (page 106), or Walnut-Stuffed Artichokes (page 110). You can make this dish ahead, but you may need to add more lemon juice and olive oil if you do, because the lentils and couscous absorb a great deal of liquid as they sit.

IN a medium saucepan, bring 3 cups of the water to a boil over high heat. Add lentils and reduce heat to medium-low. Cook until lentils are tender but still firm, 30 minutes or as package directs. Drain in a colander, rinse under cold water, and drain again.

PREHEAT oven to 325°. Place pine nuts in a small pan and bake, shaking once or twice, until golden, 5 to 7 minutes. Let cool.

IN a medium saucepan, combine the remaining 2 cups water, 1 tablespoon of the olive oil, and ½ teaspoon salt. Bring to a boil over high heat. Stir in couscous, cover, and remove from heat. Let sit 5 minutes.

SCRAPE couscous into a large bowl and separate grains with a fork. Let cool slightly. Add lentils, pine nuts, the remaining 1 tablespoon olive oil, cranberries, green onions, mint, lemon juice, parsley, orange zest, and lemon zest. Toss gently to mix well. Taste, adding more salt or lemon juice if desired. Serve at cool room temperature.

SERVES 4 TO 6

LINGUINE PRIMAVERA
with ALMONDS

In Italian, *primavera* means "spring." And spring, of course, means asparagus. Seize the season with this bountiful pasta that comes with a clever technique built in: blanching the vegetables right in the pasta water. Using a pasta pot with a built-in strainer basket (so you don't have to fish the vegetables out a few at a time) makes the task a whole lot easier. While the pasta is cooking, the blanched veggies are sautéed with pancetta, almonds, mushrooms, and cherry tomatoes. And finally, the pasta is tossed in a Parmesan cream sauce and topped with the vegetables. Happy primavera.

2 CUPS BROCCOLI FLORETS

½ POUND GREEN BEANS, ENDS TRIMMED

1 POUND THIN ASPARAGUS, CUT INTO 2-INCH PIECES

1 POUND DRIED LINGUINE OR OTHER RIBBON-SHAPED PASTA

3 TABLESPOONS OLIVE OIL

½ POUND PANCETTA, CHOPPED OR CUT INTO ¼-INCH CUBES

1½ CUPS SLIVERED ALMONDS, COARSELY CHOPPED

1 ONION, THINLY SLICED

2 CUPS SLICED MUSHROOMS

4 CLOVES GARLIC, MINCED

1 CUP (*½ pound*) SMALL CHERRY TOMATOES, STEMMED

1 CUP WHIPPING CREAM

1½ CUPS FRESHLY GRATED PARMESAN CHEESE

SALT

FRESHLY GROUND PEPPER

6 TABLESPOONS THINLY SLICED FRESH BASIL

IN a large pot of boiling salted water over high heat, cook broccoli 1 minute; add green beans and cook 1 minute; add asparagus and cook 30 seconds longer. With a slotted spoon, remove all the vegetables; plunge immediately into a large bowl of ice water to stop the cooking and retain the color. Drain well.

IN the same pot of boiling water, cook linguine until tender but still firm, 10 to 12 minutes or as package directs. Drain, reserving 1 cup of cooking water.

IN a large frying pan, heat 1 tablespoon of the oil over medium-high heat. Add pancetta and cook, stirring occasionally, until browned and crisp, 5 to 7 minutes. Add almonds and cook, stirring, until lightly browned and fragrant, 2 to 3 minutes. Remove from pan.

IN the same frying pan, heat the remaining 2 tablespoons oil over medium-high heat. Add onion; cook, stirring occasionally, until lightly browned, about 5 minutes. Add mushrooms and garlic; cook, stirring occasionally, until mushroom juices have been reabsorbed, about 10 minutes. Stir in the blanched broccoli, green beans, and asparagus, and the almond-pancetta mixture. Cook, stirring and tossing, until vegetables are just heated through, 1 to 2 minutes. Stir in cherry tomatoes and remove from heat.

IN a medium saucepan, heat cream over medium-high heat. Remove pan from heat and stir in Parmesan. Keep warm.

IN a large, warm mixing bowl, toss linguine with Parmesan cream and the reserved cooking water. Taste, adding salt and pepper if needed. Divide linguine equally among warm, shallow bowls or plates, and top with the vegetable-almond mixture. Sprinkle with basil.

SERVES 4 TO 6

PENNE *with* CHARD, GOAT CHEESE, *and* PECANS

1½ CUPS PECANS

3 TABLESPOONS OLIVE OIL

1 LARGE RED ONION, HALVED
AND THINLY SLICED

⅛ TEASPOON CRUSHED DRIED
RED CHILES

1½ POUNDS GREEN SWISS
CHARD, TOUGH RIBS REMOVED,
CUT CROSSWISE INTO THIN
STRIPS

2 CUPS *(1 pound)* SMALL CHERRY
TOMATOES, STEMMED

SALT

FRESHLY GROUND PEPPER

1 POUND DRIED PENNE OR
OTHER TUBE-SHAPED PASTA

1 LOG *(5 to 8 ounces)* FRESH
GOAT CHEESE, CRUMBLED

Want to get rich quick? Try this pasta with an "instant" creamy sauce that's as simple as tossing hot penne with a little of the pasta water (which contains both salt and a bit of starch from the pasta) and some fresh goat cheese. To make your own variation, all it takes is some sautéed chard, pecans, red onion, and small cherry tomatoes (such as Sweet 100), and suddenly you've turned a package of pasta into penne from heaven.

PREHEAT oven to 350°. Spread pecans on a baking sheet or in a shallow pan. Bake, stirring once or twice, until lightly browned and fragrant, 7 to 10 minutes. Let cool slightly; then chop coarsely.

IN a large frying pan or Dutch oven, heat oil over medium heat. Add onion and chiles; cook, stirring, until onion is softened but not browned, 3 to 5 minutes. Stir in chard. Cover and cook just until chard has wilted, about 3 minutes. Add tomatoes and cook, uncovered, stirring occasionally, until chard is tender and tomatoes pop, about 2 minutes longer. Season to taste with salt and pepper. Remove from heat.

IN a large pot of boiling salted water, cook penne until tender but still firm, about 10 minutes or as package directs. Drain penne, reserving 1 cup of the cooking water. Turn penne into a large, warm mixing bowl. Add the reserved water, chard mixture, 1 cup of the toasted pecans, and ½ cup of the goat cheese. Toss gently to mix. Taste, adding more salt and pepper if needed.

DIVIDE pasta equally among warm, shallow bowls or plates. Top each with some of the remaining goat cheese and toasted pecans.

SERVES 4 TO 6

SPAGHETTI ALLE NOCI
(SPAGHETTI *with* WALNUTS)

1½ CUPS WALNUTS

1 SLICE FIRM WHITE SANDWICH
BREAD, TORN INTO SEVERAL
PIECES

1 POUND DRIED SPAGHETTI

¼ CUP EXTRA-VIRGIN
OLIVE OIL

2 TABLESPOONS WALNUT OIL

3 CLOVES GARLIC, MINCED

⅛ TEASPOON CRUSHED DRIED
RED CHILES

½ CUP CHOPPED FRESH
FLAT-LEAF PARSLEY

ABOUT 1 CUP FRESHLY GRATED
ASIAGO OR PARMESAN CHEESE

SALT

FRESHLY GROUND PEPPER

Every cook's repertoire should include a few emergency dishes—the kind that can be pulled out of a hat on short notice from ingredients that are always in the kitchen. This simple pasta with toasted walnuts, bread crumbs, olive oil, and garlic is just such a dish. But do yourself a favor: don't wait for an emergency to make it.

PREHEAT oven to 350°. Spread walnuts on a baking sheet or in a shallow pan. Bake, stirring once or twice, until lightly browned and fragrant, 10 to 12 minutes. Let cool slightly, then chop coarsely.

IN a food processor, whirl bread pieces until coarse crumbs form.

IN a large pot of boiling salted water, cook spaghetti until tender but still firm, about 10 minutes or as package directs. Drain, reserving ½ cup of the cooking water.

MEANWHILE in a large frying pan, heat olive oil and walnut oil over medium heat. Add garlic and cook, stirring, until fragrant, 30 seconds to 1 minute. Stir in chiles, walnuts, and bread crumbs. Cook, stirring occasionally, until bread crumbs are lightly browned and crisp, 5 to 7 minutes. Stir in pasta water and parsley; cook until hot, 1 to 2 minutes longer. Remove from heat.

ADD spaghetti to the frying pan, stirring and tossing to coat. Add ½ cup of the grated cheese and toss again. Taste, adding salt and pepper if needed. Divide spaghetti equally among 4 warm shallow bowls or plates. Pass the extra cheese at the table.

SERVES 4

Worth Its Salt

Don't omit the step of adding salt to pasta water. As pasta (which is made without salt) cooks and absorbs some of the cooking water, the salt adds a great deal of flavor. Use about 1 tablespoon of salt per 3 quarts of water. Once the pasta is done, save a little of the water, which now contains some starch released during cooking. Add a splash to a pasta sauce as a convenient finishing touch that both thickens and adds flavor.

SWEET POTATO RAVIOLI *in*
WALNUT–SAGE BROWN BUTTER

Sweet Potato Ravioli

1 TABLESPOON UNSALTED
BUTTER

1 TABLESPOON MINCED
SHALLOT

1 SMALL SWEET POTATO OR
YAM *(8 ounces)*, COOKED, PEELED,
AND MASHED

1 CUP *(about 4 ounces)*
CRUMBLED FETA CHEESE

1 TEASPOON FINELY CHOPPED
FRESH FLAT-LEAF PARSLEY

SALT

FRESHLY GROUND PEPPER

1 EGG, SEPARATED

1 TABLESPOON WATER

40 WONTON WRAPPERS

Walnut–Sage Brown Butter

½ CUP UNSALTED BUTTER,
CUT INTO PIECES

½ CUP SLICED WALNUTS

⅓ CUP FINELY CHOPPED
FRESH SAGE

SALT

FRESHLY GROUND PEPPER

FRESH SAGE LEAVES FOR
GARNISH

Yes, homemade ravioli. But don't panic. With purchased wonton wrappers, it's easy to create these traditional northern Italian stuffed pastas with a delicate sweet potato filling. And take our word for it—no one will ever know you didn't roll out your own, especially if you use a fluted cookie cutter or a juice glass to trim the finished ravioli into rounds. Cooking the sweet potato in the microwave is another time-saving step. Be sure to cook the ravioli at a gentle boil to keep them from falling apart. ❧ The easy brown butter sauce can be used with any kind of homemade or purchased ravioli or tortellini. It's also really good drizzled over grilled or pan-broiled chicken breast, turkey breast scallops, pork, or veal.

TO make the ravioli: In small frying pan, melt butter over medium heat. Add shallot and cook, stirring occasionally, until softened but not browned, 1 to 2 minutes. Scrape into a large bowl.

STIR in sweet potato, feta, and parsley. Season to taste with salt and pepper. Mix in egg yolk until well blended.

IN a small bowl, whisk egg white with water until well blended.

LAY half the wonton wrappers on a clean work surface. Place 1 tablespoon sweet potato mixture in the center of each. With a brush or your fingertip, moisten wrapper edges with egg white mixture. Top each with another wonton wrapper; with a fork or your fingers, press to seal. (If making in advance, place ravioli in a single layer on a baking sheet and cover tightly with plastic wrap. Refrigerate up to 24 hours.)

TO make the brown butter: In a large frying pan, melt butter over medium heat. Add walnuts and cook, stirring, until nuts are golden and butter is lightly browned but not burned, about 3 minutes. Stir in sage and remove from heat. Season to taste with salt and pepper. Keep warm.

TO cook the ravioli: Bring a large pot of salted water to a low boil over high heat. Working in batches, cook ravioli until wrappers are tender but firm, 2 to 3 minutes. (Cooked ravioli will rise to the surface.) Carefully remove with a slotted spoon, then drain in a colander.

ADD ravioli to frying pan with brown butter, tossing gently to coat. Divide ravioli equally among 4 warm, shallow bowls or plates; top with remaining brown butter and sage leaves.

SERVES 4 AS A FIRST COURSE OR
LIGHT SUPPER

FETTUCCINE *with* WALNUT PESTO
and TOASTED WALNUTS

Walnut Pesto

½ CUP WALNUTS

1½ CUPS PACKED FRESH BASIL

½ CUP FRESHLY GRATED
PARMESAN CHEESE

2 CLOVES GARLIC

¾ CUP EXTRA VIRGIN
OLIVE OIL

¼ CUP WALNUT OIL OR
ROASTED GARLIC WALNUT OIL

2 TO 3 TEASPOONS FRESH
LEMON JUICE

½ TO 1 TEASPOON SALT

½ CUP SLICED WALNUTS

1 POUND DRIED FETTUCCINE
OR OTHER RIBBON-SHAPED
PASTA

FRESHLY GRATED PARMESAN
CHEESE

Keep a batch or two of walnut pesto in the fridge or the freezer and a package of fettuccine in the cupboard, and you'll always have at least one speedy, splendid dinner up your sleeve. Tossing in some toasted sliced walnuts adds a bit of flavor and crunch. Try it, and you'll never serve "just plain" pesto again. Make a little extra pesto, and you'll find all kinds of things to do with it. Use it to dress a pasta salad; drizzle it over sliced tomatoes, steamed new potatoes, green beans, chicken, fish, or steak; stir it into vegetable soup; or spread it on crostini, topped with goat cheese and toasted walnuts.

TO make the pesto: Preheat oven to 350°. Spread walnuts on a baking sheet or in a shallow pan. Bake, stirring once or twice, until lightly browned and fragrant, 10 to 12 minutes. Let cool.

IN a food processor or blender, combine walnuts, basil, Parmesan, and garlic. Process until a coarse paste forms. With machine on, add olive oil and walnut oil in a thin, steady stream. Add 2 teaspoons lemon juice and ½ teaspoon salt. Taste, adding more lemon juice and salt if needed. Use at once, or refrigerate in a covered glass container up to 3 days; freeze for longer storage. (If making in advance, return to room temperature before using.)

TO make the fettuccine: Preheat oven to 350°. Spread walnuts on a baking sheet or in a shallow pan. Bake, stirring once or twice, until lightly browned and fragrant, 5 to 10 minutes. Let cool.

IN a large pot of boiling salted water, cook fettuccine until tender but still firm, about 10 minutes or as package directs. Drain, then turn into a large, warm mixing bowl. Add walnuts and about ¾ cup of the pesto, tossing to mix well. Taste, adding more pesto if desired. Divide fettuccine equally among 4 warm, shallow bowls or plates. Top each with Parmesan. Pass extra pesto and grated Parmesan at the table.

SERVES 4

Pesto Presto

An easy way to store pesto is in resealable plastic bags. Fill each bag with 1 cup pesto. Seal the top most of the way, lay the bag flat, and gently press out all of the air. Seal each bag and freeze flat. Frozen in this way, pesto thaws quickly. If you need less than a whole bagful, you can easily break off a chunk and reseal the bag.

PIZZA *with* CARAMELIZED ONIONS, WALNUTS, *and* GORGONZOLA

Here's a very contemporary pizza that really delivers: a chewy crust, sweet caramelized onions, walnuts, and Gorgonzola, topped at the last minute with a delicate little watercress salad. The crust is a snap to make in a food processor. You can make the dough up to 24 hours ahead and keep it, covered with plastic wrap, in the refrigerator. When you're ready to use it, just punch it down and proceed. You can also freeze the dough after the kneading stage, then thaw it overnight in the refrigerator and punch it down just before you top it. No pizza pan? No problem. Make a rectangular pizza on a baking sheet and cut it into squares.

Food Processor Pizza Dough

1 CUP WARM WATER
(110° to 115°)

2¼ TEASPOONS *(¼ ounce)* ACTIVE DRY YEAST

¼ TEASPOON SUGAR

ABOUT 3 CUPS FLOUR

1 TEASPOON SALT

1 TABLESPOON OLIVE OIL

6 TABLESPOONS OLIVE OIL

4 LARGE ONIONS, HALVED AND THINLY SLICED

1 CUP CHOPPED WALNUTS

SALT

FRESHLY GROUND PEPPER

8 TO 12 OUNCES GORGONZOLA OR OTHER BLUE CHEESE

2 TABLESPOONS EXTRA VIRGIN OLIVE OIL

2 TEASPOONS FRESH LEMON JUICE OR WHITE WINE VINEGAR

4 CUPS LOOSELY PACKED WATERCRESS

TO make the dough: In a small bowl, combine ¼ cup of the warm water with the yeast and sugar. Let stand in a warm place until yeast becomes bubbly, 5 to 10 minutes.

IN a food processor, combine 2½ cups flour and salt. With motor running, add yeast mixture in a slow, steady stream. Pour in the remaining ¾ cup water and 1 tablespoon olive oil. Process until dough forms a ball on the blade, then process 30 seconds longer.

TRANSFER dough to a lightly floured work surface. Knead by hand until smooth, 1 to 2 minutes, adding remaining ½ cup flour if necessary to make a soft, pliable dough. Lightly coat a large bowl with olive oil. Add dough, turning to coat with oil. Cover and let rise in a warm, draft-free place until puffed but not quite doubled in bulk, 1 to 2 hours.

TO prepare the topping: Preheat oven to 450°. In a large frying pan, heat oil over medium heat. Add onions and cook, stirring often, until golden brown, about 20 minutes. Stir in walnuts and season lightly with salt and pepper.

TO assemble and bake the pizzas: Coat 2 pizza pans or baking sheets with vegetable oil spray. Punch down risen dough. Divide into 2 equal portions. With a rolling pin or your hands, spread half the dough over each pan, making a circle 9 to 10 inches in diameter. Spread half the onion–walnut mixture evenly over each circle; crumble cheese on top. Bake until crust is browned and crisp and topping is bubbly and hot, 12 to 15 minutes. Slide pizzas onto a clean work surface and cut into wedges.

IN a medium bowl, whisk together extra virgin olive oil and lemon juice; season lightly with salt and pepper. Add watercress, tossing to coat. Mound half of salad on top of each pizza.

SERVES 4

VEGETABLE-WALNUT TART *with* FETA CHEESE

1 CUP WALNUTS

¾ CUP *(about 3 ounces)*
CRUMBLED FETA CHEESE

2 TABLESPOONS UNSALTED
BUTTER, AT ROOM
TEMPERATURE

2 TABLESPOONS CHOPPED FRESH
FLAT-LEAF PARSLEY

1 TABLESPOON CHOPPED
FRESH OREGANO, OR
1 TEASPOON DRIED

SALT

FRESHLY GROUND PEPPER

1 FROZEN PUFF PASTRY SHEET
(half of a 17.3-ounce package),
THAWED AS PACKAGE DIRECTS

1 EGG, BEATEN

1 SMALL ZUCCHINI
(3 to 4 ounces), THINLY SLICED

2 MEDIUM TOMATOES *(about 12
ounces total),* SLICED

Do you suffer from "crust-o-phobia"? Don't despair. Pick up some frozen puff pastry dough, and, before you know it, you'll be fearlessly turning out beautiful tarts like this one. It makes an impressive first course or an elegant brunch entrée with a salad of baby greens or frisée and bacon on the side.

PREHEAT oven to 350°. Spread walnuts on a baking sheet or in a shallow pan. Bake, stirring once or twice, until lightly browned and fragrant, 10 to 12 minutes. Let cool. Increase oven temperature to 375°.

IN a food processor or blender, whirl walnuts, cheese, butter, parsley, and oregano, pulsing the machine on and off, until walnuts are finely chopped and mixture is well blended. Season to taste with salt and pepper.

ON a lightly floured surface, roll pastry into a 10-inch square. (For dough folding instructions, see page 217.) Place on a lightly buttered or parchment-lined baking pan.

SPREAD nut mixture evenly over the base. Alternate zucchini and tomato slices on top, overlapping slightly. Season with pepper. Bake until pastry is puffed and golden and topping is heated through, 20 to 25 minutes. Cut into squares.

SERVES 4

Variation

GOAT CHEESE AND WALNUT TART

USE ingredients for Vegetable-Walnut Tart with Feta Cheese, but make these changes: Omit feta cheese and replace with 3 tablespoons freshly grated Parmesan cheese; increase parsley to 3 tablespoons; omit oregano; add 1 small log (about 5 ounces) fresh goat cheese.

IN a food processor or blender, whirl toasted walnuts with Parmesan cheese, parsley, and butter. Pulse machine on and off until walnuts are finely chopped and mixture is well blended. Season to taste with salt and pepper.

ROLL and fold pastry, then brush with egg as directed in master recipe. (For dough folding instructions, see page 217.)

SPREAD nut mixture evenly over the base. Arrange tomato and zucchini on top. Crumble goat cheese on top. Bake until pastry is puffed and golden and topping is heated through, 20 to 25 minutes. Cut into squares.

SERVES 4

DESSERTS

*I have often thought that
if heaven had given me choice
of my position and calling,
it should have been on
a rich spot of earth,
well watered, and near
a good market for the
productions of the garden.*

THOMAS JEFFERSON

WALNUT-CHEESE CUSTARD

(GERALD HIRIGOYEN)

1½ CUPS SLICED WALNUTS

1½ TABLESPOONS UNSALTED
BUTTER, AT ROOM
TEMPERATURE

4 EGGS

¾ CUP SUGAR

2 CUPS WHIPPING CREAM

1 CUP (6 ounces) GRATED
SHEEP'S MILK CHEESE,
SUCH AS MANCHEGO

There's only one thing to say about this remarkable Basque-style dessert: Make it! It's unlike any custard you've ever tasted—like a cross between cheesecake and panna cotta, with the texture of bread pudding—but much nuttier and much easier to prepare than any of these. You can also bake it in a shallow 3-quart gratin dish. Serve with a few fresh berries and a glass of tawny port.

PREHEAT oven to 350°. Spread walnuts on a baking sheet or in a shallow pan. Bake, stirring once or twice, until lightly browned and fragrant, 5 to 10 minutes. Let cool. Increase oven temperature to 375°.

GENEROUSLY coat 8 (6-ounce) ramekins or custard cups with the butter. In a large bowl, whisk eggs and sugar until well blended. Stir in cream, then walnuts and cheese. Divide custard equally among ramekins. Arrange filled ramekins on a baking sheet. Bake until custard no longer jiggles when a ramekin is gently shaken, 25 to 35 minutes. Let cool to room temperature before serving.

SERVES 8

BLUEBERRY-ALMOND BREAD PUDDING

This moist, creamy bread pudding is definitely more pudding than bread—a far cry from those dry, heavy versions that get sawed into squares and served with a gooey sauce. This one is dependably creamy and flavorful, thanks to a rich custard base, buttery cubes of egg bread, crunchy toasted almonds, and tart blueberries. It's a perfect way to use up stale bread, and an equally perfect reason to let bread go stale. For an elegant presentation, bake in individual ramekins; set each ramekin on a small plate and garnish with a dusting of powdered sugar, a few fresh blueberries, and a sprig of mint.

PREHEAT oven to 350°. Spread almonds on a baking sheet or in a shallow pan. Bake, stirring once or twice, until lightly browned and fragrant, 5 to 10 minutes. Let cool. Reduce oven temperature to 325°.

WITH 1 tablespoon of the butter, generously coat a 9- by 13-inch (or other shallow 2½-quart) baking dish; set aside. In a large frying pan, melt remaining 7 tablespoons butter over medium heat. Add bread cubes, stirring and tossing to coat well. Cook, stirring occasionally, just until golden, about 5 minutes. Let cool.

IN a large bowl, combine half-and-half, sugar, egg yolks, eggs, vanilla, almond extract, salt, and cinnamon.

SPREAD bread cubes in baking dish. Sprinkle with ½ cup almonds and the blueberries. Slowly pour in egg mixture. With a spatula, gently press down bread cubes to coat well with custard. Let stand 5 minutes. Scatter the remaining ½ cup almonds on top.

SET the baking dish inside a large roasting pan. Pour in enough boiling water to reach halfway up the sides of the baking dish. Bake until custard no longer jiggles when dish is gently shaken, 40 to 45 minutes. Carefully lift pudding from the water bath and cool at least 20 minutes on a wire rack. Serve slightly warm, at room temperature, or chilled.

SERVES 8 TO 10

Frozen Berry Blues

When fresh blueberries are in season, stock up and freeze them to use throughout the year. Don't wash them; just remove any stems or leaves. Spread them on a baking sheet and flash-freeze until firm; then package them airtight in 2-cup or quart-size containers or freezer bags. Use them frozen in your favorite recipes; there's no need to defrost.

1 CUP SLICED ALMONDS

½ CUP UNSALTED BUTTER, AT ROOM TEMPERATURE

8 OUNCES 1- OR 2-DAY-OLD CHALLAH, BRIOCHE, OR OTHER RICH EGG BREAD, CUT INTO ¾-INCH CUBES *(about 6 cups)*

4 CUPS HALF-AND-HALF

1 CUP SUGAR

6 EGG YOLKS

2 EGGS

1 TABLESPOON VANILLA EXTRACT

⅛ TEASPOON ALMOND EXTRACT

¼ TEASPOON SALT

⅛ TEASPOON GROUND CINNAMON

2 CUPS FRESH OR UNSWEETENED FROZEN BLUEBERRIES

NECTARINE CRISP *with* WALNUT TOPPING

Walnut Topping

2 CUPS WALNUTS

1 CUP FLOUR

½ CUP PACKED DARK BROWN
SUGAR

½ CUP GRANULATED SUGAR

½ TEASPOON GROUND
CINNAMON

1 CUP CHILLED UNSALTED
BUTTER, CUT INTO ½-INCH
PIECES

1 CUP ROLLED OATS
(regular or quick-cooking; not instant)

1 TEASPOON VANILLA EXTRACT

⅓ CUP SUGAR

¼ CUP FLOUR

2 POUNDS *(about 8 medium)*
FIRM-RIPE NECTARINES OR
PEACHES, PITTED AND SLICED

1 TABLESPOON VANILLA
EXTRACT

1 TABLESPOON GRATED
LEMON ZEST

2 TABLESPOONS FRESH
LEMON JUICE

A good fruit crisp is sensational. You get all the satisfaction of a freshly baked fruit pie with about half the work. This recipe can be made with all kinds of fruit. Nectarines are a top choice because they're juicy and flavorful and don't require peeling. Peaches are also good, though they do need to be peeled. Once summer's over, you can use apples, pears, or just about anything frozen. And any time of year, you can always toss in a handful of fresh or frozen berries or sweetened dried cranberries. The topping freezes beautifully; just shape it into cylinders and wrap it in plastic wrap. When you're ready to use it, simply crumble the still-frozen topping directly on the fruit. If you go in for gilding the lily, top each serving of warm crisp with whipped cream, ice cream, frozen yogurt, crème fraîche, or a drizzle of heavy cream.

TO prepare the topping: Preheat oven to 350°. Spread walnuts on a baking sheet or in a shallow pan. Bake, stirring once or twice, until lightly browned and fragrant, 10 to 12 minutes. Let cool.

IN a food processor, combine flour, brown sugar, granulated sugar, and cinnamon. Whirl briefly to blend. Add walnuts. Process, pulsing machine on and off, until very coarsely chopped. Add butter, oats, and vanilla. Process, pulsing on and off, until just mixed; bits of butter will still be visible. Scrape mixture into a bowl, cover, and chill until firm, at least 30 minutes or as long as 3 days. Freeze for longer storage.

TO assemble and bake the crisp: Preheat oven to 350°. Butter a 9- by 13-inch (or other shallow 2½-quart) baking dish.

IN a large bowl, combine sugar and flour; whisk gently to blend. Add nectarines; toss gently to mix. Add vanilla, lemon zest, and lemon juice; toss again. Spread mixture in baking dish.

COARSELY crumble chilled topping and sprinkle evenly over fruit. Place dish on a baking sheet and bake until topping is golden brown and nectarine mixture is hot and bubbly, about 1 hour. Let cool at least 20 minutes before spooning into shallow bowls or onto plates. Serve hot, warm, or at room temperature.

SERVES 8 TO 10

Variation

RHUBARB-STRAWBERRY CRISP WITH WALNUT TOPPING

REPLACE 2 pounds nectarines with 1½ pounds rhubarb, cut into 1-inch pieces, and ½ pound ripe strawberries washed, hulled, and halved. Increase the sugar to ⅔ cup and omit the lemon zest and juice.

KEY LIME CHEESECAKE *with* TOASTED WALNUT CRUST

(NORMAN VAN AKEN)

Toasted Walnut Crust

¾ CUP GROUND WALNUTS

14 GRAHAM CRACKERS
(each 2½ inches square),
BROKEN INTO PIECES

⅓ CUP SUGAR

1 TEASPOON GROUND
CINNAMON

1 TEASPOON FRESHLY
GRATED NUTMEG

⅓ CUP UNSALTED BUTTER,
MELTED

4 EGGS, SEPARATED

¾ CUP PLUS 2 TABLESPOONS
SUGAR

1 POUND CREAM CHEESE, AT
ROOM TEMPERATURE

1 CUP SOUR CREAM

½ TEASPOON VANILLA EXTRACT

¼ CUP KEY LIME JUICE

The key to the refreshingly tart flavor of this cheesecake is—you guessed it—Key limes. Look for these small yellow-green limes in specialty produce stores. If you can't find them, try bottled Key lime juice, now available in many supermarkets. "What few people realize," says Norman Van Aken, "is that the Key lime is the true lime, while the more familiar green Persian, or Tahitian, lime is really a hybrid lemon. Talk about making lemons from lemonade. Some marketing genius figured out how to turn lemons into limes!" Chef Van Aken recommends serving this cheesecake with a berry coulis (fresh or frozen berries pressed through a sieve to form a sauce) and a round of espressos. "You definitely won't need the lemon twist," he adds.

TO prepare the crust: Preheat oven to 350°. Spread walnuts on a baking sheet or in a shallow pan. Bake, stirring once or twice, until lightly browned and fragrant, 5 to 8 minutes. Let cool.

IN a food processor, whirl graham crackers until finely ground. Add walnuts, sugar, cinnamon, nutmeg, and melted butter; process, pulsing machine on and off, until mixture is well blended. Press mixture evenly onto the bottom and up the sides of a 10-inch-diameter springform pan with a removable bottom. Refrigerate while preparing the cheesecake.

TO assemble and bake the cheesecake: Preheat the oven to 350°. In a medium bowl, beat egg whites and 2 tablespoons sugar with an electric mixer until soft peaks form.

IN a large bowl, beat cream cheese with an electric mixer until light and fluffy, about 2 minutes. Beat in the following, one ingredient at a time and beating well after each addition: ¾ cup sugar, egg yolks, sour cream, vanilla, and lime juice. Fold egg whites into cream cheese mixture until no streaks of egg white are visible. Scrape mixture into chilled crust, smoothing the top with a spatula.

BAKE until cheesecake barely jiggles in the center when pan is gently shaken, about 1 hour. Remove from oven and place on a wire rack. Carefully run a thin knife around inside of pan to loosen crust, then release and remove pan rim. Cool, then refrigerate, covered, until well chilled, 6 hours or overnight. Serve chilled.

SERVES 12 TO 14

PECAN TART *in*
A PECAN CRUST

If you like pecan desserts, try this sophisticated tart with pecans in both the filling and the easy press-in crust. Unlike traditional pecan pies, which sometimes border on gelatinous and oversweet, this tart is long on nuts and short on filling—there's just enough to bind everything together. To save time, toast the pecans for both crust and filling together. For a triple-pecan extravaganza, serve warm with Toasted Pecan Ice Cream (page 156).

TO prepare the tart shell: Preheat oven to 350°. Spread pecan chips on a baking sheet or in a shallow pan. Bake, stirring once or twice, until lightly browned and fragrant, 5 to 10 minutes. Let cool.

IN a food processor, combine pecan chips, flour, sugar, and salt; process, pulsing the machine on and off, until pecans are very finely chopped. Add butter; process, pulsing on and off, until mixture resembles coarse meal. Add egg and vanilla; process again just until mixture comes together and begins to form a ball.

WITH vegetable oil spray, lightly coat a 7½- by 11-inch or 9-inch-diameter tart pan with a removable bottom. With your fingertips, press dough evenly onto the bottom and up the sides of the pan. Refrigerate or freeze unbaked tart shell until firm, at least 30 minutes.

TO assemble and bake the tart: Preheat oven to 350°. Spread pecan halves and chips separately on 2 baking sheets or in 2 shallow pans. Bake, stirring once or twice, until lightly browned and fragrant, 5 to 10 minutes for the chips, 7 to 10 minutes for the halves. Let cool. Reduce oven temperature to 325°.

IN a large bowl, beat eggs until blended. Add brown sugar, salt, and corn syrup; beat until sugar dissolves and mixture is well blended. Beat in butter and vanilla, then stir in pecan chips.

POUR mixture into the tart shell. Arrange neat rows of pecan halves on top. Bake until pastry is lightly browned and filling is set, 45 to 50 minutes. Let tart cool completely on a wire rack before slicing.

SERVES 6 TO 8

Press-In Pecan Tart Dough

¾ CUP PECAN CHIPS

1¼ CUPS FLOUR

¼ CUP GRANULATED SUGAR

¼ TEASPOON SALT

½ CUP CHILLED UNSALTED BUTTER, CUT INTO ½-INCH PIECES

1 EGG

½ TEASPOON VANILLA EXTRACT

ABOUT 2 CUPS PECAN HALVES

1½ CUPS PECAN CHIPS

4 EGGS

1 CUP PACKED DARK BROWN SUGAR

¼ TEASPOON SALT

½ CUP LIGHT CORN SYRUP

3 TABLESPOONS UNSALTED BUTTER, MELTED AND COOLED

1 TEASPOON VANILLA EXTRACT

APRICOT FRANGIPANE TART

Rich Tart Dough

1½ CUPS FLOUR

⅛ TEASPOON SALT

½ CUP CHILLED UNSALTED BUTTER, CUT INTO ½-INCH PIECES

1 EGG YOLK

2 TO 3 TABLESPOONS ICE WATER

1 CUP *(6 ounces)* DRIED APRICOTS

1 CUP FRESH ORANGE JUICE

1 CUP ALMONDS

⅔ CUP SUGAR

½ CUP UNSALTED BUTTER, CUT INTO ½-INCH PIECES

2 EGGS

1 TABLESPOON BRANDY

1 TEASPOON VANILLA EXTRACT

½ TEASPOON ALMOND EXTRACT

¼ CUP FLOUR

½ CUP APRICOT JAM OR PRESERVES

If you like the taste when you sink your teeth into an almond croissant and find a layer of rich, sweet almond paste, then you're sure to like frangipane, the mixture of ground nuts, butter, sugar, eggs, and flour that's used to fill and top pastries and tarts like this one. When it bakes, frangipane becomes beautifully puffed and golden and takes on a nutty, caramelized flavor. That flavor pairs perfectly with stone fruits such as peaches and apricots (of which, after all, the almond is an ancient ancestor). Here, we combine frangipane with dried apricots that have been plumped in orange juice so they stay moist and sweet during baking. You can also use fresh apricots, peaches, or nectarines, or poached pears.

TO prepare the tart shell: In a food processor, whirl flour and salt briefly to blend. Add butter; process, pulsing machine on and off, until mixture resembles coarse meal. Add egg yolk and process until blended. With machine on, add 1 tablespoon ice water. Continue adding water, a few drops at a time, just until dough comes together and begins to form a ball. Flatten dough into a 6-inch disk, wrap in plastic wrap, and refrigerate until firm, about 30 minutes.

ON a lightly floured surface, roll dough into a 12-inch-diameter circle about ⅛ inch thick. Gently ease dough into a 10-inch tart pan with a removable bottom. Pat some of the overhang back in around the edge to make the sides of the tart shell a bit thicker than the bottom. Trim off any remaining overhang. Refrigerate or freeze unbaked tart shell until firm, about 30 minutes.

TO make the filling: In a small saucepan, combine apricots with just enough orange juice to cover. Let stand 30 minutes at room temperature, then bring to a boil over medium heat. Reduce heat to low and cook until apricots are soft but still hold their shape, about 10 minutes. Remove from heat and let cool.

PREHEAT oven to 350°. Spread almonds on a baking sheet or in a shallow pan. Bake, stirring once or twice, until lightly browned and fragrant, 8 to 12 minutes. Let cool. Increase oven temperature to 375°; move oven rack to lowest position.

IN a food processor, combine almonds and sugar. Process, pulsing machine on and off, until almonds are very finely chopped. Add butter; whirl until mixture is smooth and creamy. Add eggs, brandy, vanilla, and almond extract; whirl until well blended. Add flour and process, pulsing machine on and off, just until blended.

TO assemble and bake the tart: Scrape almond
mixture into prepared tart shell; smooth top
with a spatula. Drain apricots well and arrange
on the top. Bake 15 minutes. Reduce oven
temperature to 350°; bake until filling is set
and crust is golden brown, 15 to 20 minutes.
Transfer to a wire rack.

IN a small saucepan, warm apricot jam over
low heat until liquefied. Press through a sieve
to remove any pieces of fruit. Carefully brush
warm glaze over warm tart. Let tart cool
completely before cutting.

SERVES 8 TO 10

MACAROON NUT TART

(EMILY LUCHETTI)

Sweet Tart Dough

1 TABLESPOONS GRANULATED
SUGAR

1½ CUPS FLOUR

¼ TEASPOON SALT

¾ CUP CHILLED UNSALTED
BUTTER, CUT INTO ½-INCH
PIECES

ABOUT 2 TABLESPOONS
ICE WATER

¾ CUP CHOPPED MACADAMIAS

1 CUP SWEETENED SHREDDED
COCONUT

¼ CUP PECANS

5 TABLESPOONS UNSALTED
BUTTER

½ CUP PACKED LIGHT
BROWN SUGAR

4 EGG YOLKS

⅓ CUP CANNED UNSWEETENED
COCONUT MILK

1 TEASPOON ALMOND EXTRACT

⅛ TEASPOON SALT

Emily Luchetti has a charming way of reinventing classic desserts. Here's what she does with the flavors of the much-loved macaroon: she blends macadamia nuts, pecans, and coconut in a moist, chewy caramel filling baked in a flaky tart shell. Make sure to buy unsweetened coconut milk—sold in cans in the Asian foods section of many supermarkets—rather than the sweetened kind used to make piña coladas.

TO prepare the tart shell: In a food processor, combine granulated sugar, flour, and salt; process briefly to mix. Add butter; process 5 seconds. With machine on, add ice water, processing just until dough begins to come together. Press a bit of dough between your fingers. If dough seems dry, gradually add more ice water, a few drops at a time.

ON a lightly floured surface, roll dough into a 6-by-16-inch rectangle about ¼ inch thick. Ease dough into a 4- by 14-inch tart pan. (Or, roll dough into an 11-inch-diameter circle and use a 9-inch-diameter tart pan with removable bottom.) Pat some of the overhang back in around the edge to make the sides of the tart shell a bit thicker than the bottom. Trim off any remaining overhang. Refrigerate or freeze unbaked tart shell until firm, about 30 minutes.

TO bake the tart shell partially, preheat oven to 350°. With a fork, prick bottom and sides of dough all over. Fit a 12- to 14-inch square of parchment paper (or a double thickness of

aluminum foil with a few holes poked in it) snugly against pastry in pan. Bake until edges are golden brown, about 15 minutes. Carefully lift out parchment. Bake until bottom of tart shell appears dry but not browned, about 5 minutes. Let cool on a wire rack.

TO assemble and bake the tart: Preheat oven to 350°. Spread macadamias on a baking sheet or in a shallow pan. Bake, stirring once or twice, until lightly browned and fragrant, 5 to 7 minutes. Let cool. Increase oven temperature to 325°.

SPREAD coconut on a baking sheet or in a shallow pan. Bake, stirring occasionally, until lightly browned, about 10 minutes. Let cool. Increase oven temperature to 350°.

SPREAD pecans on a baking sheet or in a shallow pan. Bake, stirring once or twice, until lightly browned and fragrant, 7 to 10 minutes. Let cool. Leave oven set at 350°.

(continues)

How to Mend a Broken Tart

If your tart shell cracks on the bottom, make a thick paste of flour and water and use it to seal the crack. Place the shell back in the oven for a few minutes to dry the "glue." – E.L.

(Macaroon Nut Tart continued from page 142)

IN a small saucepan, melt butter over medium heat. Stir in brown sugar until completely moistened. Remove from heat and set aside.

IN a large bowl, whisk together egg yolks, coconut milk, almond extract, and salt. Whisk in the brown sugar mixture. Stir in macadamias, coconut, and pecans. Scrape mixture into the tart shell and smooth the top with a spatula. Bake until tart is golden brown and just set in the center, about 20 minutes. Let cool slightly. Serve warm or at room temperature.

SERVES 6 TO 8

WARM CHOCOLATE–WALNUT TART

(JOANNE WEIR)

Short Crust Tart Dough

1½ CUPS FLOUR

2 TABLESPOONS SUGAR

¼ TEASPOON SALT

1½ TEASPOONS GRATED
LEMON ZEST

¾ CUP CHILLED UNSALTED
BUTTER, CUT INTO ½-INCH
PIECES

1 TO 1½ TABLESPOONS ICE
WATER

2 CUPS WALNUTS

5 OUNCES BITTERSWEET
CHOCOLATE, CHOPPED

¼ CUP UNSALTED BUTTER,
CUT INTO 8 EQUAL PIECES

1 CUP DARK CORN SYRUP

¼ CUP GRANULATED SUGAR

3 EGGS

2 TABLESPOONS BRANDY
OR COGNAC

1 CUP WHIPPING CREAM

3 TABLESPOONS
POWDERED SUGAR

¼ TEASPOON VANILLA EXTRACT

TOASTED WALNUT HALVES
FOR GARNISH

Here is the dark, fudgy, warm chocolate tart you have been dreaming of all your life, whether you knew it or not. Take just one bite, close your eyes, breathe deeply, smile, and you'll know you've found perfection. And by the way, if there's any left over, it's unbelievably good cold, too.

TO prepare the tart shell: In a food processor, combine flour, sugar, and salt; whirl briefly to blend. Add lemon zest and butter; pulse machine on and off until mixture resembles coarse meal. With machine on, add water, a few drops at a time, just until dough begins to form a ball. Flatten dough into a 6-inch disk, wrap in plastic wrap, and refrigerate until firm, about 30 minutes.

LIGHTLY coat a 10-inch-diameter tart pan with a removable bottom with vegetable oil spray. With your fingertips, press dough evenly onto the bottom and up the sides of the pan. Freeze until firm, about 30 minutes. Preheat oven to 400°.

WITH a fork, prick bottom and sides of tart shell all over. Fit a 12-inch square of parchment paper (or a double thickness of aluminum foil with a few holes poked in it) snugly against pastry in pan. Bake until edges of pastry are light golden brown, 10 to 15 minutes. Carefully remove parchment; reduce oven temperature to 375°. Bake until tart shell is golden brown all over, 15 to 20 minutes. Let cool on a wire rack.

TO assemble and bake the tart: Preheat oven to 350°. Spread walnuts on a baking sheet or in a shallow pan. Bake, stirring once or twice, until lightly browned and fragrant, 10 to 12 minutes. Let cool. Leave oven set at 350°.

IN a large, heatproof bowl fitted snugly over a saucepan containing 2 inches of hot water, melt chocolate and butter, stirring until smooth. Remove from heat.

IN a medium saucepan, combine corn syrup and granulated sugar. Cook over medium-high heat, stirring, until mixture boils. Stir into chocolate mixture.

IN a medium bowl, whisk eggs with brandy until foamy; stir into chocolate mixture. Add walnuts. Scrape mixture into prepared tart shell. Bake until filling is set and a toothpick inserted into the center comes out clean, 35 to 40 minutes. Let cool on a wire rack until just warm, 15 to 20 minutes.

MEANWHILE, in a large bowl, combine cream, 2 tablespoons of the powdered sugar, and vanilla. Whip until soft peaks form.

DUST tart with the remaining 1 tablespoon powdered sugar and garnish with walnut halves. Serve with the sweetened whipped cream.

SERVES 8 TO 10

WALNUT-MAPLE PIE

Picture-Perfect Pie Dough

2¼ CUPS FLOUR

¾ TEASPOON SALT

½ CUP CHILLED BUTTER,
CUT INTO ½-INCH PIECES

⅓ CUP CHILLED SOLID
VEGETABLE SHORTENING,
CUT INTO ½-INCH PIECES

6 TO 8 TABLESPOONS ICE WATER

2¼ CUPS CHOPPED WALNUTS

4 EGGS

1 CUP PURE MAPLE SYRUP

⅓ CUP PACKED DARK BROWN
SUGAR

¼ CUP UNSALTED BUTTER,
MELTED

1 TABLESPOON BRANDY, OR
1 TEASPOON VANILLA EXTRACT

¼ TEASPOON SALT

Imagine the flavors of a rich maple-nut praline baked in a pretty leaf-rimmed pie. Be sure to use a high-quality real maple syrup; the imitation variety won't work here. Serve this pie on its own, or with a big scoop of vanilla or caramel ice cream.

TO prepare the pie shell: In a food processor, process flour and salt briefly to mix. Add butter and shortening; process 5 seconds. With machine on, add 6 tablespoons ice water, processing just until dough begins to come together. Remove cover and press a bit of dough between your fingers. If dough seems dry, gradually add up to 2 tablespoons more ice water, a few drops at a time. Gather dough into a ball.

DIVIDE dough into 2 pieces: a larger piece using about two-thirds of the dough and a smaller one using the remainder. Flatten both pieces into disks about ½ inch thick. Wrap disks separately in plastic wrap and refrigerate at least 30 minutes.

ON a lightly floured surface, roll out the larger of the pastry disks into a 12-inch-diameter circle. Ease the dough into a lightly buttered 9-inch-diameter rimmed pie pan. Trim overhang to ½ inch beyond the pan rim. Roll cut edge under, pressing down gently against pan rim. Refrigerate at least 30 minutes.

ON a lightly floured surface, roll out smaller pastry disk ⅛ inch thick. With a 1½-inch cookie cutter or a small sharp knife, cut out about 25 maple or other leaf shapes, enough to fit around the rim of the pan. If desired, with the blunt edge of a knife make indentations resembling leaf veins. Use a spatula to carefully lift leaves onto a baking sheet lined with waxed paper. Refrigerate or freeze until very firm.

TO assemble and bake the pie: Preheat oven to 350°. Spread walnuts on a baking sheet or in a shallow pan. Bake, stirring once or twice, until lightly browned and fragrant, 8 to 10 minutes. Let cool. Place rack in lower third of oven; increase oven temperature to 425°.

WITH a fork, prick bottom and sides of pastry shell all over. Fit a 12-inch square of parchment paper (or a double thickness of aluminum foil with a few holes poked in it) snugly against pastry in pan. Bake 10 minutes. Carefully lift out parchment.

SEPARATE 1 egg, reserving the yolk. In a small bowl, beat egg white until foamy. Brush pastry all over with beaten egg white. Brush bottom of each leaf with egg white and apply along the pastry rim, and overlapping slightly; press down gently to seal. Brush tops of leaves with remaining beaten egg white. Bake 5 minutes longer, until pastry looks shiny and dry but not brown. Transfer to a wire rack.

IN a large bowl, whisk together the reserved egg yolk with the whole eggs, maple syrup, brown sugar, butter, brandy, and salt.

PLACE pie pan on a baking sheet; put toasted walnuts in pie shell. Pour maple mixture over walnuts, gently pressing nuts down to coat with filling. Bake pie on baking sheet until filling is puffed and firm and crust is golden brown, 30 to 35 minutes. Carefully transfer to a wire rack to cool completely. Slice into wedges with a sharp knife.

SERVES 8 TO 10

The Snack Factor

Toasted nuts are more than just a handy, healthful snack to have around. Unlike some snack foods, a handful of nuts goes a long way toward satisfying the urge to nibble. Mix them with other ingredients, such as raisins, dried cranberries, dried fruit bits, or granola to make your own trail mix. Store in an airtight container in your desk drawer or on the kitchen counter, and reach for it any time you need a quick energy boost.

ENGADINER NUSSTORTE

(NICK MALGIERI)

Pastry

3 CUPS FLOUR

½ CUP SUGAR

1 TEASPOON BAKING POWDER

1 CUP CHILLED UNSALTED BUTTER, CUT INTO ½-INCH PIECES

2 EGGS

1 EGG YOLK

2 CUPS WALNUTS

1¼ CUPS SUGAR

1 TEASPOON WATER

⅔ CUP WHIPPING CREAM

1 TABLESPOON HONEY

"The valley in southeastern Switzerland known as the Engadin has an unusual claim to fame," says renowned pastry chef Nick Malgieri. "It has produced more pastry cooks per capita than any place on earth. During the 19th century, Engadiners emigrated all over the world, and wherever they went, they'd open pastry shops and serve their famous regional specialty, a torte with a buttery double crust and a filling of walnuts in a rich caramel." If the pastry dough breaks while you're working with it, simply patch it with your fingertips. This torte is best when baked a day ahead.

TO prepare the pastry: In a food processor, whirl flour, sugar, and baking powder briefly to mix. Add butter; process, pulsing on and off, until mixture is crumbly and powdery, not sticky. Add eggs and yolk, pulsing on and off until mixture forms a ball.

DIVIDE dough into 2 pieces: a larger piece using about two-thirds of the dough and a smaller one using the remainder. Flatten both pieces into disks about ½ inch thick. Wrap disks separately in plastic wrap and refrigerate at least 30 minutes.

TO assemble and bake the torte: Preheat oven to 350°; set oven rack in lower third of oven. Spread walnuts on a baking sheet or in a shallow pan. Bake, stirring once or twice, until lightly browned and fragrant, 10 to 12 minutes. Let cool slightly, then chop coarsely. Leave oven set at 350°.

COMBINE sugar and water in a large, heavy saucepan. Cook over medium heat, stirring occasionally, until mixture is smooth and turns a deep amber color. Remove from heat and carefully stir in the cream and honey; mixture will bubble up. Return to medium heat and bring to a boil; let boil 1 minute. Remove from heat and stir in walnuts. Butter the inside of a heatproof medium bowl. Scrape in the walnut mixture and set aside to cool slightly.

BUTTER a 9-inch-diameter cake pan. Roll the larger piece of dough into a circle 13 to 14 inches in diameter. Ease dough into pan, letting edges hang over sides. Scrape in walnut mixture, smoothing the top. Roll remaining dough into a 9-inch circle; place on filling. Fold overhanging dough over top crust to form a border. Bake until pastry is firm and deep golden brown, 45 to 55 minutes. Place on a wire rack to cool completely. Wrap tightly with plastic wrap and store at room temperature about 24 hours. To serve, cut into wedges. Store any leftover torte airtight at room temperature.

SERVES 12 OR MORE

BUTTER PECAN ICE CREAM

(PATRICK O'CONNELL)

¾ CUP LIGHTLY SALTED BUTTER

1 CUP PECANS

2½ CUPS WHIPPING CREAM

1 CUP MILK

1 CUP SUGAR

9 EGG YOLKS

"As a kid, I never believed that store-bought butter pecan ice cream really contained any butter," says chef Patrick O'Connell, "and the little chunks in it never seemed to taste like pecans. As an adult, I thought about how it might have tasted in a perfect world. So this recipe is a child's fantasy of what real butter pecan ice cream should be." The secret behind the fantasy is simple and sensational: the pecans are toasted in brown butter, which freezes in little pieces that melt in your mouth.

IN a large frying pan, melt butter over medium heat. Add pecans. Cook, stirring, until pecans are lightly browned and fragrant and butter begins to turn golden brown, about 5 minutes. Immediately remove pan from heat. Place a sieve over a large heatproof bowl and strain butter from pecans. Cover pecans and set aside. Let butter cool to room temperature. (Set the sieve aside for reuse.)

IN a heavy 2-quart saucepan, combine cream, milk, and ½ cup of the sugar. Cook over medium heat, stirring occasionally, until bubbles appear around edges of pan; do not let mixture boil. Remove pan from heat.

IN the top of a double boiler or in a large heatproof bowl, whisk together egg yolks and remaining ½ cup sugar. Fit double boiler top or heatproof bowl snugly over a saucepan containing 2 inches of simmering water; whisk, stirring constantly, until egg yolk mixture becomes hot to the touch, about 110°. Slowly pour in cream mixture, whisking constantly. Strain egg yolk mixture into browned butter; whisk to blend well. Refrigerate, covered, until very cold, at least 4 hours or overnight.

STIR mixture to blend; small bits of cold butter will remain. Pour into the canister of an ice cream maker and freeze according to manufacturer's directions. When ice cream is at the soft-serve stage, add pecans and continue to freeze until thoroughly incorporated, 1 to 2 minutes. Transfer to a covered container and freeze up to 3 days.

YIELDS ABOUT 1½ QUARTS

SPICED ALMOND POWDER

(GARY DANKO)

Gary Danko uses this "magic dust" to flavor the rich custard base of his homemade ice cream. You can also stir it into softened purchased vanilla ice cream (about ¼ cup of almond powder per pint of ice cream) and refreeze it. Poof: it takes on a wonderfully subtle sweet almond flavor. And once you have a batch of this powder on hand, you can sprinkle it just about anywhere regular granulated sugar or cinnamon sugar would go: on buttered toast, oatmeal, muffins, cookies, coffee cakes, even grits or soft polenta (made without the cheese, of course).

¼ CUP ALMONDS

⅓ CUP SUGAR

½ TEASPOON GRATED LEMON ZEST

½ TEASPOON GROUND CARDAMOM

⅛ TEASPOON SALT

PREHEAT oven to 350°. Spread almonds on a baking sheet or in a shallow pan. Bake, stirring once or twice, until lightly browned and fragrant, 10 to 12 minutes. Let cool.

IN a food processor, combine almonds, sugar, lemon zest, cardamom, and salt. Process, pulsing machine on and off, until almonds are chopped from coarse to very fine, depending on your preference. Use at once, or store in an airtight container.

YIELDS ABOUT ¾ CUP

TOASTED PECAN ICE CREAM *with* LAVENDER, HONEY, *and* FIGS

(MARK FRANZ)

1¼ CUPS PECANS

1 VANILLA BEAN

1⅔ CUPS MILK

1⅔ CUPS WHIPPING CREAM

¾ CUP SUGAR

6 EGG YOLKS

½ CUP HONEY

½ TEASPOON FRESH LAVENDER BLOSSOMS, PLUS EXTRA FOR GARNISH

8 FIRM-RIPE BLACK MISSION FIGS

To make this remarkable custard-based ice cream, Mark Franz steeps toasted pecans in whipping cream and then strains the nuts out before freezing. The result is a rich, delicately nutty ice cream with a smooth, satiny texture. His striking presentation involves slicing figs thinly to surround each serving of ice cream. The ice cream alone is well worth making, and you can simply serve it with quartered fresh figs. You can also substitute store-bought lavender honey for the home-made honey-lavender infusion given here.

PREHEAT oven to 350°. Spread pecans on a baking sheet or in a shallow pan. Bake, stirring once or twice, until lightly browned and fragrant, 7 to 10 minutes. Let cool slightly, then coarsely chop. Reserve ¼ cup for garnish.

WITH the pointed tip of a sharp knife, split vanilla bean in half lengthwise and scrape the tiny black seeds into a heavy medium saucepan. Add vanilla bean pod, the chopped pecans, milk, and cream. Cook over medium heat until bubbles appear around edges of pan; do not let mixture boil. Remove pan from heat and let stand 30 minutes to develop flavors.

STIR sugar into pecan-cream mixture. Cook over medium heat until sugar dissolves and bubbles again appear around edges of pan; do not let mixture boil.

IN a medium bowl, whisk egg yolks, then gradually whisk in about 1 cup of the warm pecan cream. Return egg mixture to saucepan; reduce heat to medium-low and cook, stirring, until custard thickens enough to coat the back of a spoon (160° on a thermometer), 5 to 10 minutes. Do not let mixture get too hot or the egg yolks will

curdle. Let cool slightly; refrigerate, covered, until very cold, at least 4 hours or overnight.

STRAIN custard into a bowl, pressing through as many of the vanilla seeds as you can. Discard the pecans and vanilla pod. Pour custard into the canister of an ice cream maker and freeze according to manufacturer's directions. Transfer to a covered container and freeze until firm, at least 3 hours.

IF using purchased lavender honey, omit this step: In a small saucepan, heat the honey over low heat until just warm. (Or heat in a microwave oven.) Remove pan from heat and stir in lavender blossoms. Let stand at least 15 minutes to develop flavors.

FOR each serving, slice 2 figs lengthwise as thinly as possible. Arrange slices around the perimeter of a serving plate or bowl. Place a scoop of ice cream in the center of the fig circle. Drizzle each with about 2 tablespoons of the lavender-infused honey, then sprinkle with lavender blossoms and the remaining toasted pecans. Serve at once.

YIELDS ABOUT 1 QUART

ANY OLD ICE CREAM *with* CHOCOLATE-COVERED WALNUTS

The next best thing to making your own ice cream is doctoring the store-bought kind by folding in something special—homemade chocolate-covered walnuts, for example. The addition of corn syrup helps keep the chocolate coating soft and chewy. You can use any toasted nut—or a combination—in this recipe; we think walnuts and pecans are especially good. You can also simply sprinkle the coated nuts on top of ice cream or use them as a garnish for pies and cakes.

½ CUP WALNUTS

2 OUNCES BITTERSWEET OR SEMISWEET CHOCOLATE, CHOPPED

2 TEASPOONS DARK CORN SYRUP

1 TEASPOON UNSALTED BUTTER

1 PINT PREMIUM VANILLA *(or other flavor)* ICE CREAM OR FROZEN YOGURT

PREHEAT oven to 350°. Spread walnuts on a baking sheet or in a shallow pan. Bake, stirring once or twice, until lightly browned and fragrant, 10 to 12 minutes. Let cool.

IN the top of a double broiler or in a heatproof bowl fitted snugly over a saucepan with 2 inches of hot water, melt chocolate, corn syrup, and butter, stirring until smooth. Add walnuts, stirring to coat well. With a fork or wooden skewer, remove walnuts one at a time; place on a parchment-lined baking sheet or pan. Freeze until chocolate is cold and firm, 10 to 15 minutes.

REMOVE ice cream from freezer and let sit at room temperature 10 to 15 minutes, until softened but not melted. Stir in cold walnuts. Serve at once, or return to the freezer in an airtight container.

YIELDS ABOUT 1 PINT ICE CREAM

COOKIES & CAKES

Here we come

gathering nuts in May

Nuts in May

Nuts in May

Here we come

gathering nuts in May

On a cold and

frosty morning

CHILDREN'S SONG

WALNUTTY CHOCOLATE CHIP
COOKIES

2 CUPS WALNUTS

2½ CUPS FLOUR

1 TEASPOON BAKING SODA

1 TEASPOON SALT

1 CUP UNSALTED BUTTER,
AT ROOM TEMPERATURE

1⅓ CUPS GRANULATED SUGAR

⅔ CUP PACKED LIGHT OR
DARK BROWN SUGAR

2 TEASPOONS VANILLA EXTRACT

2 EGGS

2 CUPS *(12 ounces)* SEMISWEET
CHOCOLATE CHIPS

Chocolate chip is the most popular cookie variety in the United States, and we think our version captures everything good, pure, and, well, American about this national treasure: a slightly chewy center, crisp, golden edges, and the classic crunch of toasted walnuts.

PREHEAT oven to 350°. Spread walnuts on a baking sheet or in a shallow pan. Bake, stirring once or twice, until lightly browned and fragrant, 10 to 12 minutes. Let cool slightly, then chop coarsely. Leave oven set at 350°. Line 2 large baking sheets with parchment paper or coat with vegetable oil spray.

IN a medium bowl, whisk together flour, baking soda, and salt.

IN a large bowl, combine butter, granulated sugar, brown sugar, and vanilla. Beat with an electric mixer on medium-high speed until light and fluffy, about 2 minutes. Add eggs, one at a time, beating well after each addition. Stir in flour mixture until well blended. Stir in walnuts and chocolate chips.

DROP heaping tablespoons of dough 2 inches apart onto baking sheets (or use a 2-ounce ice cream scoop). Bake until cookies are golden brown at the edges and no longer look wet on top, about 12 minutes. Let cool on baking sheets 2 minutes, then transfer to wire racks to cool completely. Store airtight at room temperature up to 1 week.

YIELDS ABOUT 48 COOKIES

Here's the Scoop

Want to make perfectly uniform cookies that look like the work of a professional baker? Try using an ice cream scoop to portion the dough. You can find these handy tools in most cookware shops. Look for the dome-shaped kind with a lever on the side that connects to an internal scraper; the 2-ounce size is perfect for most cookies. Pack the dough into the scoop and remove any excess against the side of the bowl, then release the dough, flat side down, onto a parchment-lined baking sheet. When you make the dough, portion it all this way, and bake as many cookies as you like. Freeze the unbaked balls on a baking sheet, then transfer to resealable plastic bags. Frozen dough balls can go directly from the freezer to the oven; just allow a few extra minutes of baking time.

MACADAMIA—WHITE CHOCOLATE CHUNK COOKIES

The ultimate non–chocolate chip cookie. A word to the wise: white chocolate bars and chips vary tremendously in quality from brand to brand, and it's worth buying the best you can find. Check the ingredients on the package, and look for as short a list as possible, one ingredient of which should be real cocoa butter. For a professional finishing touch, reserve half the white chocolate chunks or chips and press them into the balls of dough just before baking; your finished cookies will look beautiful enough to photograph.

PREHEAT oven to 350°. Spread macadamias on a baking sheet or in a shallow pan. Bake, stirring once or twice, until lightly browned and fragrant, 5 to 7 minutes. Let cool. Increase oven temperature to 350°. Line 2 large baking sheets with parchment paper or coat with vegetable oil spray.

IN a medium bowl, whisk together flour, baking soda, and salt.

IN a large bowl, combine butter, granulated sugar, brown sugar, and vanilla. Beat with an electric mixer on medium–high speed until light and fluffy, about 2 minutes. Beat in the egg. Stir in flour mixture until well blended. Stir in macadamias and white chocolate.

DROP heaping tablespoons of dough 2 inches apart onto baking sheets (or use a 2-ounce ice cream scoop). Bake until cookies are golden brown at edges and no longer look wet on top, about 10 minutes. (Watch carefully during the last few minutes; these cookies can burn easily.) Let cool on baking sheets 2 minutes, then transfer to wire racks to cool completely. Store airtight at room temperature up to 1 week.

YIELDS ABOUT 40 COOKIES

2 CUPS CHOPPED MACADAMIAS

2 CUPS FLOUR

1 TEASPOON BAKING SODA

½ TEASPOON SALT

1 CUP UNSALTED BUTTER, AT ROOM TEMPERATURE

½ CUP GRANULATED SUGAR

¾ CUP PACKED LIGHT BROWN SUGAR

2 TEASPOONS VANILLA EXTRACT

1 EGG

2 CUPS CHOPPED WHITE CHOCOLATE OR WHITE CHOCOLATE CHIPS

HAZELNUT TASSIES

½ CUP UNSALTED BUTTER,
AT ROOM TEMPERATURE

3 OUNCES CREAM CHEESE,
AT ROOM TEMPERATURE

¼ TEASPOON SALT

⅛ TEASPOON GRANULATED
SUGAR

1 CUP FLOUR

1 CUP CHOPPED HAZELNUTS

¾ CUP PACKED LIGHT
BROWN SUGAR

1 EGG

1 TEASPOON VANILLA
EXTRACT

*T*assie is a Scottish word meaning "little cup" (not to be confused with Lassie, meaning big dog). The next time you're feeling nostalgic for an old-fashioned homemade confection, bake a batch of these wee hazelnut tartlets for auld lang syne. They're actually quite simple to make, and they're a nice addition to a tray or tin of holiday cookies. For a slightly smoother filling, chop the hazelnuts a bit more finely after you toast them.

IN a medium bowl or in a food processor, blend together butter, cream cheese, ⅛ teaspoon of the salt, and granulated sugar. Mix in flour just until well blended. Wrap dough in plastic wrap and refrigerate at least 1 hour or up to 3 days; freeze for longer storage.

PREHEAT oven to 350°. Spread hazelnuts on a baking sheet or in a shallow pan. Bake, stirring once or twice, until lightly browned and fragrant, 8 to 10 minutes. Let cool. Reduce oven temperature to 325°.

COAT the insides of 24 small (1¾-inch) muffin cups with vegetable oil spray. Divide dough in half, then form each half into twelve 1-inch balls. Place 1 ball of dough in each muffin cup. Press dough evenly into each cup to line the bottom and sides.

IN a medium bowl, combine the remaining ⅛ teaspoon salt, the brown sugar, egg, and vanilla. Whisk until smooth. Stir in toasted hazelnuts. Divide mixture evenly among the unbaked pastry shells, filling each completely. Bake until filling is set and pastry is just beginning to brown at the edges, about 25 minutes. Working carefully, place a wire rack directly on top of a muffin tin and invert to release tarts; use tongs to turn tarts right side up. Repeat with remaining muffin tin. Let cool completely. Serve at once, or store airtight at room temperature up to 3 days; freeze for longer storage.

YIELDS ABOUT 24 TASSIES

BUTTERY THUMBPRINT COOKIES

1 CUP FLOUR

¼ CUP GROUND WALNUTS

¼ TEASPOON SALT

½ CUP UNSALTED BUTTER,
AT ROOM TEMPERATURE

½ CUP SUGAR

1 EGG, SEPARATED

½ TEASPOON VANILLA EXTRACT

2 CUPS WALNUTS, FINELY
CHOPPED

¼ CUP JAM, ANY FLAVOR,
PREFERABLY SEEDLESS

Another easy classic: almond-coated butter cookies with a pretty jam topping. To create an instant assortment, bake a batch using a few different flavors of jam. Apricot and raspberry are particularly good choices.

PREHEAT oven to 350°. In a small bowl, whisk together flour, ground walnuts, and salt.

IN a large bowl, beat butter and sugar with an electric mixer on medium-high speed until smooth and creamy, about 2 minutes. Add egg yolk and vanilla; beat until light and fluffy, 1 to 2 minutes. Gradually add flour mixture, mixing just until well blended. Divide dough in half, then form each half into twelve 1-inch balls. If dough is too soft to form into balls, cover and refrigerate 1 hour.

LINE a baking sheet with parchment paper or coat with vegetable oil spray.

IN a small bowl, whisk egg white until foamy. Dip each ball of dough into the egg white; roll in chopped walnuts. Arrange at least 1 inch apart on baking sheet. With your thumb, a floured thimble, or the handle of a wooden spoon, make a deep indentation in the center of each cookie. (If dough cracks, press it back together.) With a small spoon, fill each indentation with jam. Bake until cookies are lightly colored on top and golden brown on the bottom, 12 to 15 minutes. Transfer to wire racks to cool completely. Store airtight at room temperature up to 5 days.

YIELDS ABOUT 24 COOKIES

*Opposite Top left: Buttery Thumbprint Cookies
Bottom right: Royal Pecan Shortbread*

ROYAL PECAN SHORTBREAD

¾ CUP CHOPPED PECANS

10 TABLESPOONS UNSALTED
BUTTER, AT ROOM TEMPERATURE

½ CUP POWDERED SUGAR

2 TEASPOONS VANILLA EXTRACT

¼ TEASPOON SALT

1¼ CUPS FLOUR

16 PECAN HALVES

Elegant, nutty shortbread, crowned with pecan halves, is baked the traditional Scottish way in a round pan, then cut into wedges. They're perfect for a tea party—even if it's just you, the cat, and a mug of Earl Grey (see page 169 for shortbread photograph).

PREHEAT oven to 350°. Spread chopped pecans on a baking sheet or in a shallow pan. Bake, stirring once or twice, until lightly browned and fragrant, 5 to 10 minutes. Let cool. Leave oven set at 350°.

IN a large bowl, beat butter with an electric mixer on medium-high speed until light and fluffy, about 2 minutes. Beat in powdered sugar, vanilla, and salt. Add flour, mixing well. Stir in chopped pecans.

PRESS dough evenly onto the bottom of a 9-inch-diameter tart pan with a removable bottom. With a fork, prick dough all over at ½-inch intervals. With a table knife, score the surface about ¼ inch deep into 16 wedges. Press a pecan half into each wedge. Bake until shortbread is lightly browned, 30 to 35 minutes.

LET shortbread cool in the pan about 15 minutes, then cut along scoring into wedges. Carefully remove sides from tart pan; transfer wedges to a wire rack; cool completely. Store airtight at room temperature up to 5 days.

YIELDS 16 WEDGES

RASPBERRY-WALNUT SHORTBREAD BARS

If you like making (and eating) lemon bars, give these walnut bars a try. Instead of lemon on top, their buttery crust is spread with a layer of raspberry jam and a crumbly walnut topping—a bit like a linzertorte.

PREHEAT oven to 350°. Spread walnuts on a baking sheet or in a shallow pan. Bake, stirring once or twice, until lightly browned and fragrant, 8 to 10 minutes. Let cool. Leave oven set at 350°. Coat an 8-inch-square baking pan with vegetable oil spray; set aside.

TO make the crust: In a medium bowl, whisk together 1 cup of the flour, the granulated sugar, and salt. With your fingertips or a pastry blender, cut butter into dry ingredients until mixture resembles coarse meal. Press evenly onto bottom of pan. Bake until crust is lightly browned at the edges, about 25 minutes. Let cool 5 minutes, then spread evenly with raspberry jam.

TO make the topping and bake the bars: In a medium bowl, combine the remaining 2 tablespoons flour, brown sugar, and baking soda. Whisk gently to blend. Whisk in eggs and vanilla until smooth. Stir in walnuts.

SPOON mixture over jam, spreading to the edges with the back of a spoon. Return to oven and bake until topping is set, about 25 minutes. Transfer to a wire rack. Cool completely in the pan before cutting into 2-inch squares. Dust lightly with powdered sugar. Store airtight at room temperature up to 5 days.

YIELDS 16 BARS

1 CUP CHOPPED WALNUTS

1 CUP PLUS 2 TABLESPOONS FLOUR

⅓ CUP GRANULATED SUGAR

¼ TEASPOON SALT

6 TABLESPOONS CHILLED UNSALTED BUTTER, CUT INTO ½-INCH PIECES

⅔ CUP RASPBERRY JAM, PREFERABLY SEEDLESS

⅓ CUP PACKED LIGHT BROWN SUGAR

¼ TEASPOON BAKING SODA

2 EGGS

1 TEASPOON VANILLA EXTRACT

POWDERED SUGAR FOR DUSTING

PINE NUT PORCUPINE COOKIES

1 CUP CHOPPED HAZELNUTS

1 CUP SLIVERED ALMONDS

3¼ CUPS SUGAR

6 EGG WHITES

1 CUP WHOLE ALMONDS

¼ CUP UNSWEETENED COCOA POWDER

3 TABLESPOONS UNSALTED BUTTER, AT ROOM TEMPERATURE

1 TEASPOON HONEY

½ TEASPOON ALMOND EXTRACT

4½ CUPS PINE NUTS

POWDERED SUGAR

Ever eat a porcupine? These tiny, crispy, chewy-inside pine nut–studded cookies are a good reason to start. They're a bit like amaretti, only nuttier and crunchier because they're made with both toasted and untoasted nuts as well as a splash of almond extract.

PREHEAT oven to 350°. Spread hazelnuts on a baking sheet or in a shallow pan. Bake, stirring once or twice, until lightly browned and fragrant, 8 to 10 minutes. Let cool.

IN a food processor, process slivered almonds and ¼ cup of the sugar, pulsing machine on and off, until almonds are finely ground. Add 1¼ cups of the sugar and 3 of the egg whites; process until mixture is well blended. Scrape into a large bowl.

IN the same food processor bowl, combine hazelnuts, almonds, and ¼ cup of the sugar. Process, pulsing machine on and off, until nuts are finely ground. Add the remaining 1½ cups sugar, the remaining 3 egg whites, cocoa, butter, honey, and almond extract. Process until mixture comes together and forms a paste.

SCRAPE into bowl with almond mixture; stir until well blended. If dough is too soft to form into balls, cover and refrigerate 1 hour.

LINE 2 or 3 baking sheets with parchment paper or coat with vegetable oil spray.

SPREAD pine nuts on a plate or in a shallow pan. Working with 1 heaping tablespoon of dough at a time, form into balls; roll balls in pine nuts. Place 1½ inches apart on baking sheets; flatten each ball slightly with the palm of your hand. Let stand, uncovered, overnight at room temperature.

PREHEAT oven to 375°. Sift powdered sugar generously over cookies. Bake until bottoms of cookies are set and tops are puffed and light golden brown, 16 to 18 minutes. Let cool 2 minutes on baking sheets, then transfer to wire racks to cool completely. Store airtight at room temperature up to 5 days.

YIELDS ABOUT 60 COOKIES

HAZELNUT-CRANBERRY RUGALACH

(TODD ENGLISH)

Dough

1 CUP UNSALTED BUTTER,
AT ROOM TEMPERATURE

8 OUNCES CREAM CHEESE,
AT ROOM TEMPERATURE

½ TEASPOON COARSE-GRAINED
SALT

2¼ CUPS FLOUR

Filling

1 CUP CHOPPED HAZELNUTS

7 TABLESPOONS UNSALTED
BUTTER

¾ CUP SWEETENED DRIED
CRANBERRIES, CHOPPED

½ CUP GRANULATED SUGAR

¼ CUP PACKED LIGHT BROWN
SUGAR

¼ TEASPOON COARSE-GRAINED
SALT

¼ TEASPOON GROUND
CINNAMON

EXTRA GRANULATED SUGAR
FOR ROLLING

Rugalach are probably the most famous Eastern European Jewish cookie—tender little butter pastry crescents traditionally filled with nuts and raisins. In America, cream cheese was added to the pastry, making it even richer and flakier. Boston-based chef Todd English gives them his own New England spin, substituting dried cranberries for the raisins.

TO make the dough: In a large bowl, combine butter and cream cheese. Beat with an electric mixer until well blended. Gradually beat in the salt and flour until just combined. (Dough will be soft and sticky.) Divide dough into 4 equal portions; place each on a piece of plastic wrap, press into a disk, and cover tightly. Refrigerate overnight.

TO make the filling: Preheat oven to 350°. Spread hazelnuts on a baking sheet or in a shallow pan. Bake, stirring once or twice, until lightly browned and fragrant, 8 to 10 minutes. Let cool slightly, then chop finely. Reduce oven temperature to 325°. Line a baking sheet with parchment paper.

MELT butter in a small saucepan or in the microwave; let cool slightly. In a large bowl, combine hazelnuts, cranberries, granulated sugar, brown sugar, salt, and cinnamon; toss to mix well. Add melted butter, stirring to moisten ingredients. Divide mixture into 4 equal portions.

TO assemble and bake the rugalach: Sprinkle a thin layer of granulated sugar over a clean work surface. Remove 1 disk of dough from the refrigerator and place on the sugared surface; roll into a 7- to 8-inch-diameter circle. Spread 1 portion of filling evenly over the top. With a large knife or a pizza wheel, cut dough into 8 wedges. Starting at the outside edge, gently roll up each wedge toward the point. (If needed, use a thin metal spatula to loosen the wedges from the work surface. Don't work the dough too much or it will become too soft to roll. If this happens, refrigerate about 5 minutes until firm enough to roll. As each piece is formed, place seam side down and at least 1 inch apart on the baking sheet; bend ends of dough toward the center to form a crescent shape. Repeat with remaining dough and filling, adding sugar to the work surface as needed.

BAKE until rugalach are golden brown on the bottom and no longer look wet on top, 25 to 30 minutes. Let cool on the baking sheets. Store airtight at room temperature up to 2 days.

YIELDS 32 RUGALACH

WALNUT *and* DRIED CRANBERRY BISCOTTI

In Italian, *biscotti* means "twice cooked," and, indeed, these cookies are first baked in a "log" and then sliced into individual bars and baked again until they're crisp and golden. Their sweet-tangy accent comes from the addition of dried cranberries. Be sure to give the logs plenty of space to expand on the baking sheet. It's easiest to cut them when they're still warm; a sharp serrated bread knife is the best tool for the task.

PREHEAT oven to 350°. Spread sliced and ground walnuts separately on a baking sheet or in a shallow pan. Bake, stirring once or twice, until lightly browned and fragrant, 5 to 10 minutes. Let cool. Increase oven temperature to 375°. Line a baking sheet with parchment paper or coat with vegetable oil spray.

IN a large bowl, whisk together ground walnuts, flour, baking powder, and salt. Stir in sliced walnuts and dried cranberries.

IN another large bowl, beat sugar, eggs, and orange zest with an electric mixer on medium-high speed until light and fluffy, about 2 minutes. Beat in melted butter. Stir in flour mixture until well blended. Form dough into 2 logs, each about 16 inches long. Place logs lengthwise at least 3 inches apart on baking sheet; flatten gently with the palm of your hand. Bake until logs are lightly browned and just spring back when touched in the center, about 30 minutes. Reduce oven temperature to 325°.

TRANSFER logs to a clean work surface; cut diagonally into ½-inch slices. Arrange slices, cut sides down, on baking sheets. Bake until crisp and golden brown, about 15 minutes. Remove to wire racks and cool completely. Store airtight at room temperature up to 10 days.

YIELDS ABOUT 60 BISCOTTI

1⅓ CUPS SLICED WALNUTS

⅔ CUP GROUND WALNUTS

3 CUPS FLOUR

2 TEASPOONS BAKING POWDER

¼ TEASPOON SALT

⅔ CUP SWEETENED DRIED CRANBERRIES

1¼ CUPS SUGAR

3 EGGS

1 TEASPOON GRATED ORANGE ZEST

½ CUP UNSALTED BUTTER, MELTED

BROWN SUGAR–ALMOND REFRIGERATOR COOKIES

1½ CUPS SLICED ALMONDS

2¼ CUPS FLOUR

½ TEASPOON BAKING SODA

½ TEASPOON SALT

1 CUP UNSALTED BUTTER,
AT ROOM TEMPERATURE

¾ CUP POWDERED SUGAR

½ CUP PACKED DARK
BROWN SUGAR

1 EGG

2 TEASPOONS VANILLA EXTRACT

¼ TEASPOON ALMOND EXTRACT

Store-bought rolls of refrigerator cookie dough are certainly convenient, but let's face it, they don't always taste that good. Solution: make your own. This buttery brown sugar–almond dough (and our easy chocolate variation) keeps well in the fridge or freezer, so you can slice, bake, and munch in a matter of minutes.

PREHEAT oven to 350°. Spread almonds on a baking sheet or in a shallow pan. Bake, stirring once or twice, until lightly browned and fragrant, 5 to 10 minutes. Let cool.

IN a small bowl, whisk together flour, baking soda, and salt.

IN a large bowl, combine butter, powdered sugar, and brown sugar. Beat with an electric mixer on medium-high speed until smooth and creamy, about 2 minutes. Add egg, vanilla, and almond extract; beat until light and fluffy, 1 to 2 minutes. Stir in flour mixture just until well blended. Stir in almonds. Scrape dough onto a sheet of plastic wrap at least 18 inches long. Form dough into a cylinder 12 to 14 inches long; wrap tightly in plastic wrap, twisting ends to seal. Refrigerate until firm, at least 4 hours or up to 2 days; freeze for longer storage.

PREHEAT oven to 350°. Line 2 baking sheets with parchment paper or coat with vegetable oil spray. With a thin, sharp knife, cut cylinder crosswise into ¼-inch slices. (To maintain cylinder's round shape, give it a quarter-turn after every 6 slices.) Arrange at least 1 inch apart on baking sheets. Bake until cookies are set and edges just begin to brown, 10 to 12 minutes. Let cool on baking sheets 2 minutes, then transfer to wire racks to cool completely. Store airtight at room temperature up to 5 days.

YIELDS ABOUT 48 COOKIES

Variation

CHOCOLATE-ALMOND
REFRIGERATOR COOKIES

REPLACE ½ cup of the flour with ½ cup unsweetened cocoa powder.

CLASSIC WALNUT BROWNIES

2 CUPS WALNUTS

1 CUP UNSALTED BUTTER,
CUT INTO PIECES

8 OUNCES UNSWEETENED
CHOCOLATE, COARSELY
CHOPPED

2½ CUPS SUGAR

2 TEASPOONS VANILLA EXTRACT

4 EGGS, AT ROOM TEMPERATURE

¾ CUP FLOUR

½ TEASPOON SALT

For every baker, there's a favorite style of brownie. If your taste runs to dense, chewy, moist, and candylike, this recipe is for you. These will slice more easily and cleanly if you chill them in the refrigerator or freezer. Bring them back to room temperature before serving.

PREHEAT oven to 350°. Spread walnuts on a baking sheet or in a shallow pan. Bake, stirring once or twice, until lightly browned and fragrant, 10 to 12 minutes. Let cool slightly, then chop finely. Leave oven set at 350°. Generously butter a 9- by 13-inch baking pan. Dust with flour, tapping out excess.

IN the top of a double boiler or in a medium, heatproof bowl fitted snugly over a saucepan with 2 inches of hot water, melt butter and chocolate, stirring until smooth. (Alternatively, in a large microwave-safe bowl, heat chocolate and butter on high, stirring after each minute, until melted and smooth, 1 to 3 minutes total.) Remove from heat. Let mixture cool to luke-warm, 5 to 10 minutes. Mix in sugar and vanilla; beat in eggs. Add flour and salt, stirring until smooth. Stir in walnuts.

SCRAPE batter into the pan, spreading evenly. Bake until the top no longer looks wet and a toothpick inserted slightly off center is still covered with moist chocolate, 30 to 35 minutes. Transfer to a wire rack; let cool completely. Cover with plastic wrap and refrigerate 1 hour (or freeze 30 minutes) before cutting into 2-inch squares. Store airtight at room temperature up to 5 days.

YIELDS 24 BROWNIES

PERFECT PECAN BROWNIES

Brownies, yes, but you could get away with calling these intense, rich chocolate-coffee-pecan confections something entirely different, like a torte or even petits fours. They bake up quite tall, so if you cut them into 1½-inch squares each piece is almost a cube. To serve this as an ice cream cake, just invert it from the pan and split it horizontally with a long serrated knife. On one half, spread 1 pint of slightly softened vanilla ice cream; cover with the other half. Wrap the cake in plastic wrap and place it in the freezer. Before serving, frost it with the glaze for Queen of Nuts Torte (page 184). Add a few candles, and you've got the perfect cake and ice cream finale for a birthday party.

12 CUPS PECANS

1 CUP UNSALTED BUTTER, CUT INTO PIECES

8 OUNCES UNSWEETENED CHOCOLATE, COARSELY CHOPPED

3½ CUPS SUGAR

5 EGGS

1 TABLESPOON VANILLA EXTRACT

¼ CUP BREWED ESPRESSO OR OTHER COFFEE, AT ROOM TEMPERATURE

1½ CUPS FLOUR

¼ TEASPOON SALT

PREHEAT oven to 350°. Spread pecans on a baking sheet or in a shallow pan. Bake, stirring once or twice, until lightly browned and fragrant, 7 to 10 minutes. Let cool. Increase oven temperature to 375°. Generously butter a 9- by 13-inch baking pan. Dust with flour, tapping out excess.

IN the top of a double boiler or in a medium heatproof bowl fitted snugly over a saucepan with 2 inches of hot water, melt butter and chocolate, stirring until smooth. (Alternatively, in a large microwave-safe bowl, heat chocolate and butter on high, stirring after each minute, until melted and smooth, 1 to 3 minutes total.) Remove from heat. Let mixture cool to lukewarm, 5 to 10 minutes.

IN a large bowl, combine sugar, eggs, and vanilla. Beat with an electric mixer on medium-high speed until light and fluffy, about 2 minutes. Mix in chocolate mixture until well blended. Stir in espresso. Add flour and salt, stirring until smooth. Stir in pecans.

SCRAPE batter into pan, spreading evenly. Bake until the top no longer looks wet and a toothpick inserted slightly off center is still covered with moist chocolate, 35 to 40 minutes. Transfer to a wire rack; let cool completely. Cover with plastic wrap and let sit overnight at room temperature before cutting into 2-inch squares. Alternatively, refrigerate cooled brownies 1 hour (or freeze 30 minutes) before cutting. Serve at room temperature. Store airtight at room temperature up to 5 days.

YIELDS 24 BROWNIES

CHEWY WALNUT SQUARES

1 CUP CHOPPED WALNUTS

½ CUP FLOUR

¼ TEASPOON BAKING SODA

¼ TEASPOON SALT

1 CUP PACKED LIGHT OR
DARK BROWN SUGAR

1 TEASPOON VANILLA EXTRACT

1 EGG

This has been one of the most treasured and frequently requested recipes in the Diamond files for as long as anyone can remember. Somewhere between a cookie and a "blondie," these walnut squares are easy enough for kids to make and even easier for adults to enjoy. Don't be alarmed if they seem underdone when baked; once they cool, they become firmer—crisp and crunchy on the top and bottom, and chewy in the center. Serve them with a cup of good strong coffee.

PREHEAT oven to 350°. Spread walnuts on a baking sheet or in a shallow pan. Bake, stirring once or twice, until lightly browned and fragrant, 8 to 10 minutes. Let cool. Leave oven set at 350°.

LINE an 8-inch-square baking pan with a 16-inch sheet of aluminum foil; press foil firmly to make a snug fit, and let excess foil drape over edges. Coat foil generously with vegetable oil spray.

IN a small bowl, whisk together flour, baking soda, and salt.

IN a medium bowl, beat brown sugar, vanilla, and egg until smooth. Gradually stir in flour mixture until well blended. Stir in walnuts; batter will be quite stiff. Scrape into pan, spreading evenly.

BAKE until lightly browned at the edges and the top no longer looks wet, 20 to 22 minutes. (The center will appear soft and underbaked but will firm as it cools.) Transfer to a wire rack and cool completely.

GRASP the overhanging foil and lift from pan in one piece; place on a work surface. With a long, sharp knife, cut into 2-inch squares. Peel squares from the foil and serve at room temperature. Store airtight at room temperature up to 5 days.

YIELDS 16 SQUARES

BLACK WALNUT BUNDT CAKE

Black walnuts are the original native walnut variety of the Americas, and these days they're something of a rare delicacy, having been replaced, for the most part, by the English (Persian) kind. Black walnuts add a sweet, slightly perfumed flavor to this moist pound cake with an easy powdered-sugar glaze. If you can't find them, use English walnuts, pecans, or sliced almonds instead. You can also bake this in a standard 5- by 9- by 3-inch loaf pan.

1½ CUPS PLUS 2 TABLESPOONS BLACK WALNUTS

1½ CUPS FLOUR

½ TEASPOON BAKING POWDER

½ TEASPOON SALT

¾ CUP UNSALTED BUTTER, AT ROOM TEMPERATURE

1½ CUPS GRANULATED SUGAR

3 EGGS

1 TABLESPOON VANILLA EXTRACT

¾ CUP BUTTERMILK

1 CUP POWDERED SUGAR

1½ TABLESPOONS WATER

PREHEAT oven to 350°. Spread walnuts on a baking sheet or in a shallow pan. Bake, stirring once or twice, until lightly browned and fragrant, 10 to 12 minutes. Let cool slightly, then chop coarsely. Leave oven set at 350°.

BUTTER bottom and sides of a 12-cup Bundt pan or a 10-inch-diameter tube pan, or spray with vegetable oil spray. (If using a baking pan with a dark finish, reduce oven temperature to 325°.)

IN a small bowl, whisk together flour, baking powder, and salt.

IN a large bowl, beat butter and granulated sugar with an electric mixer on medium-high speed until light and fluffy, about 2 minutes. Add eggs, one at a time, beating well after each addition; beat in vanilla.

WITH mixer on low speed, add flour mixture in 3 portions, alternating with buttermilk. Stir in 1½ cups of the toasted walnuts. Scrape batter into pan, smoothing the top. Bake until a skewer or knife inserted into the center comes out clean, about 30 minutes. Transfer to a wire rack to cool completely in the pan. Invert onto a serving plate.

IN a medium bowl, combine powdered sugar and water; whisk until smooth. Drizzle mixture over cake and sprinkle with the remaining 2 tablespoons walnuts.

SERVES 8 TO 10

TRIPLE-ALMOND TEA CAKE

½ CUP PLUS 3 TABLESPOONS
SLICED ALMONDS

½ CUP SLIVERED ALMONDS

¾ CUP SUGAR

1 CUP FLOUR

1 TEASPOON BAKING POWDER

½ TEASPOON SALT

¾ CUP UNSALTED BUTTER,
AT ROOM TEMPERATURE

1 PACKAGE *(7 ounces)* ALMOND
PASTE, CUT INTO ½-INCH PIECES

1 TEASPOON VANILLA
EXTRACT

4 EGGS

Ground almonds and almond paste make this dependable little cake moist, and sliced almonds give it a delicate crunch. The cake tastes even better if baked two days ahead. Serve it with a fresh fruit compote or a simple sauce of fresh or frozen raspberries, puréed and strained, and a dusting of powdered sugar.

PREHEAT oven to 350°. Spread ½ cup of the sliced almonds on a baking sheet or in a shallow pan. Bake, stirring once or twice, until lightly browned and fragrant, 5 to 10 minutes. Let cool. Leave oven set at 350°.

BUTTER 8 individual shallow loaf pans, 4 by 2 by ¾ inch, or a 9-inch-diameter cake pan, or coat with vegetable oil spray; line the bottom of pans with parchment or waxed paper. Butter the paper, dust with flour, and tap out the excess.

IN a food processor, whirl the slivered almonds with 2 tablespoons of the sugar, pulsing the machine on and off until almonds are finely ground. In a medium bowl, whisk together flour, baking powder, and salt. Whisk in the ground almond mixture and set aside.

ADD to processor bowl the remaining 10 tablespoons sugar, the butter, almond paste, and vanilla; process until well blended. Beat in eggs, one at a time, processing well after each addition, then add ground almond mixture. Remove blade from processor and scrape mixture into a medium bowl. With a rubber spatula, fold in toasted sliced almonds just until blended. Spoon into prepared pans. Sprinkle with remaining 3 tablespoons sliced almonds.

BAKE until the top is golden brown and a toothpick inserted into the center comes out clean, 20 to 25 minutes for individual loaf pans, 35 to 40 minutes for a cake pan. Cool in the pan 10 minutes, then transfer to a wire rack to cool completely. Store airtight at room temperature up to 5 days.

SERVES 8

QUEEN *of* NUTS TORTE

½ CUP ALMONDS

½ CUP PECANS

½ CUP WALNUTS

3 TABLESPOONS GROUND WALNUTS

8 OUNCES BITTERSWEET OR SEMISWEET CHOCOLATE, CHOPPED

½ CUP SUGAR

1 TABLESPOON GRATED ORANGE ZEST

6 EGGS, SEPARATED

1 TEASPOON VANILLA EXTRACT

⅛ TEASPOON SALT

Chocolate-Walnut Glaze

6 OUNCES BITTERSWEET OR SEMISWEET CHOCOLATE, CHOPPED

2 TABLESPOONS WALNUT OIL

Here's a chocolate cake for nut lovers, made with almonds, pecans, walnuts, chocolate, eggs, and not a whole lot else. You can glaze the cake whole, slice it in thin wedges and dress them up with a drizzle of the melted chocolate glaze, or simply pool the glaze on the plate and top the torte with a dollop of whipped cream and a few curls of orange zest. Refrigerate any leftover glaze, then reheat over hot water.

TO make the torte: Preheat oven to 350°. Spread almonds, pecans, and walnuts on a baking sheet or in a shallow pan. Bake, stirring once or twice, until lightly browned and fragrant, 7 to 12 minutes. Let cool. Set aside ½ cup nuts and chop coarsely. Leave oven set at 350°.

BUTTER a 9-inch-diameter cake pan or coat with vegetable oil spray; line the bottom of the pan with a circle of parchment paper or waxed paper. Butter the paper and sprinkle evenly with ground walnuts.

IN a food processor, process toasted almonds, pecans, walnuts, chocolate, ¼ cup of the sugar, and the orange zest, pulsing machine on and off, until finely ground. Add egg yolks, vanilla, and salt. Process until well blended.

IN a large bowl, beat egg whites with an electric mixer until foamy and about quadrupled in volume. Gradually beat in the remaining ¼ cup sugar. Continue beating until the whites form soft, billowy peaks that droop slightly when the beater is lifted. Scoop about one-fourth of the beaten whites into the chocolate mixture and process, pulsing on and off, just until blended.

SCRAPE chocolate mixture over the remaining egg whites; fold together until no streaks of white are visible. Scrape batter into pan. Bake until the top of the cake is firm to the touch and a toothpick inserted into the center comes out clean, about 30 minutes. Transfer to a wire rack to cool in the pan 15 minutes; unmold onto wire rack, peel off parchment paper, and cool completely.

TO make the glaze: In the top of a double boiler or in a heatproof bowl fitted snugly over a saucepan with 2 inches of hot water, melt chocolate, stirring until smooth. Remove from heat; let cool until the consistency of heavy cream. Gently stir in walnut oil to blend.

GENEROUSLY drizzle glaze over cake. Sprinkle with the reserved ½ cup nuts. Or pour all the glaze onto the top of the torte and, with a metal spatula, quickly ease the glaze over the edges of the torte, covering it completely.

SERVES 8 TO 10

Nut-stitution

As a rule of thumb, in cooking, walnuts are a good staple to have on hand. You can, however, usually substitute one kind of nut for another. Pecans and walnuts, for example, with their similar texture, are almost always interchangeable, as are almonds, hazelnuts, and macadamias. When it comes to the recipes in this book, a little experimentation and substitution can produce all kinds of creative variations that you might actually prefer to the original. In other words, go nuts.

Nuts with a Suntan?

Walnut meats come in two shades, which can be used interchangeably. The light golden brown walnuts, especially walnut halves, are naturally attractive and can make any dish look beautiful. But the darker walnuts—the result of a little extra California sunshine—are every bit as nutritious and tasty. They usually come chopped or sliced and are ideal for recipes like brownies, cakes, and cookies, in which they're less visible but can still provide lots of rich flavor.

CHOCOLATE-PECAN EARTHQUAKE CAKE

1 CUP PECANS

1¼ CUPS GRANULATED SUGAR

¾ CUP UNSWEETENED
COCOA POWDER

5 EGGS, SEPARATED, AT ROOM
TEMPERATURE

½ CUP COFFEE LIQUEUR,
SUCH AS KAHLÚA, OR OTHER
LIQUEUR OF CHOICE

⅓ CUP UNSALTED BUTTER,
MELTED

2 TEASPOONS VANILLA EXTRACT

½ TEASPOON SALT

UNSWEETENED COCOA POWDER
OR POWDERED SUGAR FOR
DUSTING

Some people might call this delectable flourless chocolate-Kahlúa torte a fallen soufflé. Being from California, we like "earthquake cake," a reference to the fissures and fault lines that form on its surface as it cools. Whatever you call it, it's bound to register a 7.0 on your Richter richness scale.

PREHEAT oven to 350°. Spread pecans on a baking sheet or in a shallow pan. Bake, stirring once or twice, until lightly browned and fragrant, 7 to 10 minutes. Butter an 8-inch-diameter springform pan or coat with vegetable oil spray. Dust with flour, tapping out excess.

IN a food processor, whirl pecans and 1 cup of the granulated sugar, pulsing machine on and off until pecans are finely ground. Sift cocoa powder into processor; pulse machine on and off to blend. Add egg yolks, liqueur, butter, vanilla, and salt. Process until well blended, stopping once or twice to scrape down the sides of bowl.

IN a large bowl, beat egg whites with an electric mixer until foamy and about quadrupled in volume. Gradually beat in the remaining ¼ cup sugar. Continue beating until the whites form soft, billowy peaks that droop slightly when the beater is lifted. Scoop about one-fourth of the beaten whites into the cocoa mixture and process, pulsing on and off, just until blended.

SCRAPE cocoa mixture over the remaining egg whites; fold together until no streaks of white are visible. Scrape batter into pan, smoothing top with a spatula. Bake until the top is puffed and cracked, 40 to 50 minutes. The center will still jiggle slightly when pan is gently shaken; cake will fall slightly and center will firm as it cools.

TRANSFER to a wire rack to cool completely, then remove the sides of the pan. Before serving, dust with cocoa powder.

SERVES 6 TO 8

HAZELNUT-CHOCOLATE TORTE
with SOUR CHERRIES

1 CUP HAZELNUTS

1 JAR *(24 ounces)* PITTED TART
RED CHERRIES PACKED IN
WATER OR JUICE

11 TABLESPOONS SUGAR

6 OUNCES BITTERSWEET OR
SEMISWEET CHOCOLATE,
CHOPPED

¾ CUP UNSALTED BUTTER,
AT ROOM TEMPERATURE

3 EGGS

2 TEASPOONS VANILLA EXTRACT

1 CUP FLOUR

Remember the fun of biting into a chocolate-covered cherry? Here's our homage to that unforgettable combination: a dense, sophisticated chocolate cake with a layer of tart cherries baked in the center. Our favorite way to serve it is slightly warm, topped with whipped cream and a sprinkling of chopped toasted hazelnuts.

PREHEAT oven to 350°. Spread hazelnuts on a baking sheet or in a shallow pan. Bake, shaking once or twice, until lightly browned and fragrant, 10 to 12 minutes. Wrap warm nuts in a clean dish towel and let cool 10 minutes. With the towel, rub off as much of the papery skins as possible. Let cool completely. Leave oven set at 350°.

BUTTER a 9-inch-diameter springform pan or coat with vegetable oil spray. Dust with flour; tap out excess. Drain cherries, discarding liquid. Pat dry on paper towels.

IN the top of a double boiler or in a heatproof bowl fitted snugly over a saucepan with 2 inches of barely simmering water, melt chocolate, stirring until smooth. Remove from heat.

IN a food processor, whirl toasted hazelnuts and 2 tablespoons of the sugar, pulsing machine on and off until hazelnuts are finely ground.

IN a large bowl, beat remaining 9 tablespoons sugar and the butter with an electric mixer until light and fluffy, 1 to 2 minutes. Add eggs, one at a time, beating well after each addition; beat in vanilla. On low speed, beat in melted chocolate until well blended, then beat in the ground hazelnut mixture. Mix in flour just until well blended.

SPREAD half the batter in the pan, smoothing the top with a spatula. Arrange cherries in a single layer over the top. Spread remaining batter on top, smoothing with the spatula. Bake until the top no longer looks wet and a toothpick inserted into the center comes out clean, about 50 minutes. Transfer to a wire rack; let cool in pan 15 minutes. Remove sides of pan and let cake cool on rack at least 30 minutes longer. Serve slightly warm or at room temperature.

SERVES 8 TO 10

CARROT CAKE *with*
MAPLE–CREAM CHEESE FROSTING

Served right out of the pan, carrot cake is a guaranteed hit at parties, potlucks, and bake sales everywhere. This recipe makes a particularly moist and tasty version, thanks to the addition of raisins and crushed pineapple. The maple–cream cheese frosting is less one-dimensionally sweet than the standard cream cheese variety, and it benefits beautifully from the final sprinkling of chopped toasted walnuts.

TO make the cake: Preheat oven to 350°. Spread walnuts on a baking sheet or in a shallow pan. Bake, stirring once or twice, until lightly browned and fragrant, 10 to 12 minutes. Let cool slightly; chop finely. Leave oven set at 350°. Butter a 9- by 13-inch baking pan.

IN a medium bowl, whisk together flour, granulated sugar, baking powder, baking soda, salt, cinnamon, nutmeg, and cloves.

IN large bowl, combine carrots, raisins, pineapple, the 2 tablespoons reserved juice, and lemon juice. Toss gently to mix. Stir in oil and eggs. Add 2 cups of the walnuts and the flour mixture; stir until well blended.

SPREAD batter evenly in baking pan. Bake until a toothpick inserted into the center of the cake comes out clean, 30 to 35 minutes. Transfer pan to a wire rack to cool completely before frosting.

TO make the frosting: In a medium bowl, combine cream cheese, maple syrup, and vanilla; beat until creamy. Gradually beat in powdered sugar until smooth.

SPREAD frosting on cooled cake. Sprinkle with remaining ½ cup walnuts.

SERVES 12 TO 16

2½ CUPS WALNUTS

2 CUPS FLOUR

1¼ CUPS GRANULATED SUGAR

1 TEASPOON BAKING POWDER

1 TEASPOON BAKING SODA

1 TEASPOON SALT

1 TEASPOON GROUND CINNAMON

⅛ TEASPOON FRESHLY GRATED NUTMEG

⅛ TEASPOON GROUND CLOVES

2 CUPS FINELY GRATED RAW CARROTS

1 CUP RAISINS

1 CAN *(8 ounces)* CRUSHED PINEAPPLE IN ITS OWN JUICE, DRAINED, RESERVING 2 TABLESPOONS JUICE

2 TABLESPOONS FRESH LEMON JUICE

¾ CUP WALNUT OIL

3 EGGS, LIGHTLY BEATEN

Maple–Cream Cheese Frosting

6 OUNCES CREAM CHEESE, AT ROOM TEMPERATURE

¼ CUP PURE MAPLE SYRUP

1 TEASPOON VANILLA EXTRACT

3 CUPS POWDERED SUGAR

WALNUTTY ROULADE
with COCOA WHIPPED CREAM

(GARY DANKO)

1½ CUPS GROUND WALNUTS

8 EGGS, SEPARATED

¾ CUP GRANULATED SUGAR

1 TEASPOON VANILLA EXTRACT

⅛ TEASPOON SALT

1 TEASPOON BAKING POWDER

POWDERED SUGAR FOR
SPRINKLING

Cocoa Whipped Cream

¾ CUP UNSWEETENED
COCOA POWDER

¾ CUP GRANULATED SUGAR

2 CUPS WHIPPING CREAM

UNSWEETENED COCOA POWDER
FOR DUSTING

If you've never made a roulade or a jelly roll, this elegant dessert—a sheet of airy walnut sponge cake rolled around a simple chocolate-flavored whipped cream filling—would be a great place to start. The ground walnuts give the cake extra body and flavor, making it easy to work with, and the proportions of sugar and cocoa in the whipped cream make it quite stable and spreadable. In fact, you can prepare it up to a day ahead and store it, well covered, in the refrigerator. The ends of a roulade like this are sometimes a bit firmer than the rest of the cake, and don't always get completely filled, so you may want to add an elegant finishing touch by trimming the ends off at a slight angle, and then dusting the top with cocoa powder. Cut slices on the diagonal.

TO make the cake: Preheat oven to 350°. Spread walnuts on a baking sheet or in a shallow pan. Bake, stirring once or twice, until lightly browned and fragrant, 5 to 10 minutes. Let cool. Leave oven set at 350°. Line a heavy 11- by 17-inch jelly-roll pan with parchment paper, then brush with walnut oil or coat with vegetable oil spray.

IN a large bowl, combine egg yolks, granulated sugar, vanilla, and salt. Beat with an electric mixer until mixture is pale yellow and forms thick ribbons, about 3 minutes. Add the ground walnuts and baking powder; mix well.

IN a separate bowl with clean beaters, beat egg whites until soft peaks form. Fold into the walnut mixture until no white streaks are visible. Spread batter evenly into pan, and smooth top with a spatula. Bake just until cake springs back when touched in the center, 20 to 25 minutes. Let cool 5 minutes in the pan. Loosen edges with a metal spatula or blunt knife, then immediately invert cake onto a clean dish towel sprinkled with powdered sugar.

CAREFULLY peel parchment off cake and sprinkle with more powdered sugar. Grasp a long edge of the towel and gently roll up the cake, with the towel rolled inside. Keep cake rolled up until cooled completely. (If making in advance, wrap airtight and refrigerate up to 2 days.)

TO make the whipped cream: Sift cocoa and granulated sugar through a sieve into a large bowl. Stir in cream. Cover and refrigerate at least 30 minutes to dissolve sugar and cocoa. With an electric mixer, beat until soft peaks form. (This mixture whips up very quickly, so be careful to not overbeat.) Refrigerate, covered, until ready to use.

TO assemble the roulade: Unroll cake and remove towel. Spread cake with about 1 cup of cocoa whipped cream. Gently reroll cake from a long side, jelly-roll fashion, into a tight cylinder. Dust with cocoa powder, or use remaining cocoa whipped cream to frost the outside. To serve, cut roulade crosswise into slices about ¾ inch thick. Serve with any remaining whipped cream.

SERVES 6 TO 8

Worth Two in the Bûche

For the holidays, you can turn this roulade into a dramatic Yule log, or bûche de Noël (or, if you prefer, a Hanukkah bûche). Prepare 3 times the recipe of cocoa whipped cream, and then frost the entire outside with the remaining whipped cream. Slice both ends off the roll on the diagonal, and reattach the cut sides of the ends to the body of the "log" with a bit of the whipped cream. Run a fork along the surface of the cream to make a barklike texture. Dust with powdered-sugar "snow," and decorate with sprigs of ivy or winter greenery.

BREADS & QUICK BREADS

*Walnuts and pears
you plant for your heirs.*

MID-SEVENTEENTH-CENTURY

PROVERB

GOOD OLD BANANA-NUT BREAD

1½ CUPS PECANS OR WALNUTS

2½ CUPS FLOUR

2 TEASPOONS BAKING SODA

1 TEASPOON SALT

2 CUPS SUGAR

1 CUP UNSALTED BUTTER,
AT ROOM TEMPERATURE

2 TEASPOONS VANILLA EXTRACT

4 EGGS

2 TO 3 CUPS PACKED
MASHED RIPE BANANAS
(4 to 6 medium bananas)

Whoa. Don't throw away that overripe brown banana lurking at the bottom of the fruit bowl. Peel, mash, and freeze it, and, when you've got 2 to 3 cups' worth, make this moist, rich quick bread.

PREHEAT oven to 350°. Spread nuts on a baking sheet or in a shallow pan. Bake, stirring once or twice, until lightly browned and fragrant, 7 to 10 minutes for pecans and 10 to 12 minutes for walnuts. Let cool slightly, then chop coarsely. Leave oven set at 350°. Butter two 4½- by 8½-inch loaf pans, or coat with vegetable oil spray. Dust with flour, tapping out excess.

IN a medium bowl, whisk together flour, baking soda, and salt.

IN a large bowl, combine sugar, butter, and vanilla. Beat until well blended; mixture will be stiff and appear somewhat gritty. Add eggs, one at a time, beating well after each addition. Mix in the mashed bananas. Stir in nuts. Stir in flour mixture just until well blended. Divide batter equally between pans. Bake until a long skewer or knife inserted into the center of a loaf comes out clean, 50 to 60 minutes. Cool in pans 15 minutes, then transfer to a wire rack to cool completely before slicing.

YIELDS 2 LOAVES

DOUBLE-WALNUT APRICOT QUICK BREAD

Ground walnuts give this simple quick bread an irresistibly delicate texture. The bread is also loaded with chopped walnuts and moist, chewy dried apricots. Here's a tip: when chopping dried apricots, use a large knife, and oil it lightly with vegetable oil or vegetable oil spray to keep the fruit from sticking to the blade.

PREHEAT oven to 350°. Spread chopped walnuts on a baking sheet or in a shallow pan. Bake, stirring once or twice, until lightly browned and fragrant, 8 to 10 minutes. Let cool. Leave oven set at 350°. Butter two 4½- by 8½-inch loaf pans, or coat with vegetable oil spray. Dust with flour, tapping out excess.

SOAK apricots in lemon juice and boiling water until softened, 1 to 2 hours. In a large bowl, whisk together flour, ground walnuts, baking powder, and salt.

IN another large bowl, whisk together milk, sugar, butter, eggs, and vanilla. Stir in chopped walnuts, apricots, and lemon soaking liquid. Stir in flour mixture just until well blended. Divide batter equally between pans. Bake until a long skewer or knife inserted into the center of a loaf comes out clean, or with just a few crumbs clinging to it, 55 to 65 minutes. Cool in pans 10 minutes, then transfer to a wire rack to cool completely before slicing.

YIELDS 2 LOAVES

2 CUPS CHOPPED WALNUTS

2 CUPS CHOPPED DRIED APRICOTS

½ CUP FRESH LEMON JUICE

½ CUP BOILING WATER

3½ CUPS FLOUR

1 CUP GROUND WALNUTS

4 TEASPOONS BAKING POWDER

1 TEASPOON SALT

2 CUPS MILK

1¼ CUPS PACKED LIGHT OR DARK BROWN SUGAR

½ CUP UNSALTED BUTTER, MELTED

2 EGGS

1 TABLESPOON VANILLA EXTRACT

SOUR CREAM—WALNUT COFFEE CAKE

(BETH HENSPERGER)

3½ CUPS WALNUTS

3 CUPS FLOUR

1 TEASPOON BAKING POWDER

½ TEASPOON BAKING SODA

½ TEASPOON SALT

1 TO 2 TABLESPOONS FINELY
GRATED ORANGE ZEST, OR
1¼ TEASPOONS ORANGE OIL

1 CUP UNSALTED BUTTER,
AT ROOM TEMPERATURE

1½ CUPS GRANULATED SUGAR

½ CUP PACKED LIGHT BROWN
SUGAR

6 EGGS

2 TEASPOONS VANILLA EXTRACT

1 CUP SOUR CREAM

¼ CUP BUTTERMILK

POWDERED SUGAR
FOR DUSTING

STRIPS OF ORANGE ZEST
FOR GARNISH

GRATED ORANGE ZEST
FOR GARNISH

TOASTED CHOPPED NUTS
FOR GARNISH

"This elegant, not-too-sweet cake is dense with nuts and bakes into a tall cake, easily serving a crowd," says Beth Hensperger, one of America's favorite baking authorities. She suggests baking it in a tube pan or Bundt pan. It is exceptionally attractive when displayed sliced. Serve it within a day or two of baking as part of a brunch buffet or lightly toasted with sweet butter and orange marmalade at teatime.

PREHEAT oven to 350°. Spread walnuts on a baking sheet or in a shallow pan. Bake, stirring once or twice, until lightly browned and fragrant, 10 to 12 minutes. Let cool slightly, then chop coarsely. Leave oven at 350°.

BUTTER the bottom and sides of a 10-inch-diameter tube pan or a 12-cup Bundt pan. (If using a baking pan with a dark finish, reduce oven temperature to 325°.) Dust with flour, tapping out excess.

IN a medium bowl, whisk together flour, baking powder, baking soda, salt, and orange zest. (If using orange oil, add it with the vanilla.)

IN a large bowl, combine butter, granulated sugar, and brown sugar. Beat with an electric mixer on medium-high speed until fluffy, about 2 minutes. Add eggs, one at a time, beating well after each addition; beat in vanilla (and orange oil, if using). On low speed, add flour mixture in 3 portions, alternating with the sour cream and buttermilk. Increase mixer speed to medium-high

and beat until batter is thick, smooth, and fluffy, 1 to 2 minutes. With a large spatula, fold in walnuts until evenly distributed. Scrape batter into pan, smoothing top with spatula.

BAKE until sides of cake are golden brown and separate slightly from sides of pan, and a cake tester inserted into the top crack comes out clean, 70 to 75 minutes. Place pan on a wire rack to cool at least 30 minutes or up to overnight. With a thin metal spatula or knife, loosen cake from sides and center tube. Carefully unmold cake onto wire rack and let cool completely. (If making in advance, wrap tightly in plastic wrap and store at room temperature up to 3 days.)

TO serve, dust with powdered sugar, and decorate with strips of orange zest, grated orange zest, and chopped nuts. Or, arrange slices on a serving plate.

SERVES 12 TO 16

How to Squeeze Oil from an Orange

Pure citrus oils are now available at many gourmet stores, specialty baking shops, and catalogs specializing in baking supplies. These intensely flavored all-natural essences are nothing like the orange or lemon extracts we all grew up with. They're derived solely from the oils contained in the zest of fresh citrus fruit—no other oil is added—which explains their somewhat steep price. To give you a little perspective, it takes more than 40 oranges to fill a single one-ounce bottle. You'll find a drop or two goes a very long way toward adding bright, real-fruit flavor. —B.H.

BUTTERMILK-PECAN-CRANBERRY SCONES

1 CUP PECANS

3 CUPS FLOUR

2 TEASPOONS BAKING POWDER

1 TEASPOON BAKING SODA

1 TEASPOON SALT

⅓ CUP PLUS 2 TABLESPOONS
SUGAR

¾ CUP CHILLED UNSALTED
BUTTER, CUT INTO PIECES

1 TABLESPOON FINELY GRATED
ORANGE ZEST

½ CUP SWEETENED
DRIED CRANBERRIES

1 CUP BUTTERMILK

1 TO 2 TABLESPOONS
WHIPPING CREAM

The definitive scone should be flaky, buttery, and wedge-shaped. These scones are all of the above, with a tangy hint of buttermilk and orange and plenty of cranberries and pecans in every bite. For an easy variation, substitute raisins or currants for the cranberries, and lemon zest for the orange zest. This recipe makes a large batch, but don't worry: baked scones freeze beautifully. For a sensational summer dessert, use them to make strawberry shortcake: just slice them open, then fill and top with whipped cream and sugared sliced strawberries.

PREHEAT oven to 350°. Spread pecans on a baking sheet or in a shallow pan. Bake, stirring once or twice, until lightly browned and fragrant, 7 to 10 minutes. Let cool. Chop coarsely. Increase oven temperature to 425°.

IN a large bowl, whisk together flour, baking powder, baking soda, salt, and ⅓ cup of the sugar. Add butter and orange zest. With your fingertips, 2 knives, or a pastry blender, cut butter into flour mixture until it resembles coarse meal. Add pecans, cranberries, and buttermilk; stir with a fork just until the dry ingredients are moistened and dough holds together in a rough mass.

SCRAPE dough onto a generously floured work surface and knead gently about 10 times, until smooth. Divide dough into 2 equal portions; lightly pat each into a 6- to 7-inch-diameter circle 1½ inches thick. Brush with cream, then sprinkle with the remaining 2 tablespoons sugar. Cut each round into 8 wedges. Transfer wedges to a large baking sheet, placing them ¼ to ⅓ inch apart. Bake until scones are firm to the touch and golden, 16 to 18 minutes. Serve warm.

YIELDS 16 SCONES

Secrets to Light, Airy Scones

The two big secrets to making light scones are, first, to avoid overmixing, and second, to use chilled butter. Stir the wet ingredients into the dry ones just until everything comes together, then knead briefly and with a light touch. The chilled butter remains in clumps, ready to melt during baking to form air pockets.

BERRY-WALNUT MUFFINS

½ CUP PLUS 2 TABLESPOONS
SLICED WALNUTS

2 CUPS FLOUR

1½ TEASPOONS BAKING POWDER

1 TEASPOON BAKING SODA

½ TEASPOON SALT

¾ CUP BUTTERMILK

¾ CUP PACKED LIGHT
BROWN SUGAR

½ CUP UNSALTED BUTTER,
MELTED

2 EGGS

1 TEASPOON VANILLA EXTRACT

1 CUP FRESH OR UNSWEETENED
FROZEN RASPBERRIES,
BLACKBERRIES, OR BLUEBERRIES

You can use this versatile basic muffin recipe to make all kinds of variations—just substitute your favorite nuts and fresh or dried fruits or frozen berries. It works well for baking mini muffins, too—just keep an eye on the pans and the timer, because minis take less time to bake.

PREHEAT oven to to 350°. Spread walnuts on a baking sheet or in a shallow pan. Bake, stirring once or twice, until lightly browned and fragrant, 5 to 10 minutes. Let cool. Leave oven set at 350°. Line 14 to 16 (2¼-inch) muffin cups with paper baking cups, or coat with vegetable oil spray.

IN a large bowl, whisk together flour, baking powder, baking soda, and salt.

IN another large bowl, whisk together buttermilk, brown sugar, butter, eggs, and vanilla. Stir in ½ cup of the walnuts and the raspberries, then stir in flour mixture just until dry ingredients are moistened (do not overmix). Spoon batter into muffin cups, filling each about three-fourths full. Sprinkle with remaining 2 tablespoons walnuts. Bake until a toothpick inserted into the center of a muffin comes out clean, 20 to

25 minutes. Cool 5 minutes in the pans, then transfer to a wire rack. Serve slightly warm or at room temperature.

YIELDS 14 TO 16 MUFFINS

Variation

APRICOT-ALMOND MUFFINS

INSTEAD of walnuts and berries, substitute ½ cup toasted sliced almonds, 1 cup finely chopped dried apricots, and ¼ cup diced candied ginger. Instead of vanilla, use ½ teaspoon almond extract. Sprinkle tops with extra sliced almonds.

PEAR-PECAN MUFFINS

INSTEAD of walnuts and berries, substitute ½ cup toasted chopped pecans and 1 cup finely chopped dried pears.

PUMPKIN-WALNUT MUFFINS

Crumb Topping

1 CUP FLOUR

½ CUP GRANULATED SUGAR

½ CUP PACKED LIGHT OR
DARK BROWN SUGAR

½ TEASPOON GROUND
CINNAMON

¼ TEASPOON GROUND ALLSPICE

⅛ TEASPOON SALT

¼ CUP UNSALTED BUTTER,
CUT INTO PIECES

½ CUP SLICED WALNUTS

2 CUPS GRANULATED SUGAR

1½ CUPS FLOUR

¾ CUP GROUND WALNUTS

1 TABLESPOON GROUND
CINNAMON

1 TABLESPOON GROUND GINGER

¼ TEASPOON GROUND ALLSPICE

1½ TEASPOONS BAKING SODA

1 TEASPOON SALT

1 CAN (about 15 ounces)
SOLID-PACK UNSWEETENED
PUMPKIN

4 EGGS

½ CUP UNSALTED BUTTER,
MELTED

½ CUP WALNUT OIL

A spiced crumb topping gives these dark, dense muffins an extra-special finishing touch. Serve them warm with sweet butter or whipped honey on the side.

TO make the topping: In a medium bowl, whisk together flour, granulated sugar, brown sugar, cinnamon, allspice, and salt. Add butter. With your fingertips, lightly rub butter and flour mixture together until mixture resembles very coarse meal. Set aside.

TO make the muffins: Preheat oven to 350°. Spread sliced walnuts on a baking sheet or in a shallow pan. Bake, stirring once or twice, until lightly browned and fragrant, 5 to 10 minutes. Let cool. Leave oven set at 350°. Line 24 (2¼-inch) muffin cups with paper baking cups, or coat with vegetable oil spray.

IN a medium bowl, combine sugar, flour, ground walnuts, cinnamon, ginger, allspice, baking soda, and salt. Whisk gently to blend.

IN a large bowl, whisk together pumpkin, eggs, butter, and oil until well blended. Stir in the toasted sliced walnuts. Stir in flour mixture just until dry ingredients are moistened (do not overmix). Spoon batter into muffin cups, filling each about three-fourths full. Sprinkle evenly with crumb topping. Bake until a toothpick inserted into the center of a muffin comes out clean, 15 to 20 minutes. Cool 5 minutes in the pans, then transfer to a wire rack. Serve slightly warm or at room temperature.

YIELDS 24 MUFFINS

LOW-FAT APPLE-HAZELNUT MUFFINS

Applesauce stands in for some of the fat in these easy muffins, but they're so moist and tender, you'll never know what you're missing. Instead of the raisins, you can add cubed fresh tart apple to the batter. These muffins taste just as good after a day or two.

PREHEAT oven to 350°. Spread hazelnuts on a baking sheet or in a shallow pan. Bake, stirring once or twice, until lightly browned and fragrant, 8 to 10 minutes. Let cool. Leave oven set at 350°. Line 16 (2¼-inch) muffin cups with paper baking cups, or coat with vegetable oil spray.

IN a large bowl, whisk together flour, bran, cocoa, baking powder, baking soda, salt, cinnamon, and nutmeg. In another large bowl, whisk together applesauce, ½ cup of the sugar, eggs, and oil. Stir in hazelnuts and raisins. Stir in flour mixture just until dry ingredients are moistened (do not overmix). Spoon batter into muffin cups, filling each about three-fourths full. Sprinkle remaining 2 tablespoons sugar on muffins. Bake until puffed and golden brown and a toothpick inserted into the center of a muffin comes out clean, about 25 minutes. Cool 5 minutes in the pans, then transfer to a wire rack. Serve slightly warm or at room temperature.

YIELDS 16 MUFFINS

1 CUP CHOPPED HAZELNUTS

2½ CUPS FLOUR

½ CUP BRAN

1 TABLESPOON UNSWEETENED COCOA POWDER

1½ TEASPOONS BAKING POWDER

1 TEASPOON BAKING SODA

1 TEASPOON SALT

2 TEASPOONS GROUND CINNAMON

⅛ TEASPOON FRESHLY GRATED NUTMEG

2 CUPS UNSWEETENED APPLESAUCE

½ CUP PLUS 2 TABLESPOONS DARK BROWN SUGAR

2 EGGS

¼ CUP WALNUT OIL

1 CUP RAISINS

PECAN STICKY BUNS

1¼ CUPS WARM MILK
(110° to 115°)

¼ CUP WARM WATER
(110° to 115°)

6¾ TEASPOONS *(¾ ounce)*
ACTIVE DRY YEAST

½ CUP GRANULATED SUGAR

1 TABLESPOON VANILLA
EXTRACT

2 TEASPOONS SALT

½ CUP UNSALTED BUTTER,
CUT INTO PIECES, AT ROOM
TEMPERATURE

2 EGGS

5 TO 5½ CUPS FLOUR

Glaze

3 CUPS PECANS

3 CUPS PACKED DARK
BROWN SUGAR

1 CUP UNSALTED BUTTER

½ CUP LIGHT CORN SYRUP

1½ TEASPOONS GROUND
CINNAMON

2 TEASPOONS VANILLA EXTRACT

The real thing: old-fashioned extra-gooey sticky buns, baked upside down and then flipped out of the pan to reveal a topping of pecans with a cinnamon-caramel glaze.

IN a large bowl, combine milk, water, and yeast. Stir to blend. Let stand until yeast is foamy, 5 to 10 minutes. Stir in granulated sugar, vanilla, and salt. Whisk in butter pieces and eggs until eggs are well blended (any remaining lumps of butter will disappear with further mixing).

BEAT in 2½ cups of the flour. Beat in enough of the remaining flour, about 2½ cups, to make a manageable dough that holds together in a rough mass. Turn out onto a floured work surface and knead 2 minutes. Let dough rest 10 minutes. Resume kneading, adding more flour if dough is sticky, until dough is smooth and elastic. Place in an oiled bowl, cover with a towel, and let rise in a draft-free place until dough is doubled in bulk, about 1 hour.

MEANWHILE, make the glaze: Preheat oven to 350°. Spread pecans on a baking sheet or in a shallow pan. Bake, stirring once or twice, until lightly browned and fragrant, 7 to 10 minutes. Let cool slightly, then chop coarsely.

IN a large saucepan, combine brown sugar, butter, corn syrup, and cinnamon. Cook over medium heat, stirring, until mixture is smooth and bubbles begin to appear around edges of pan. Stir in vanilla.

BUTTER two 8-inch-square baking pans. Spread 1 cup glaze in each pan; top each with 1 cup toasted pecans. Stir the remaining cup pecans into glaze in saucepan. Set aside.

PUNCH down dough. Turn onto a lightly floured work surface; divide into 2 equal portions. Roll or pat 1 portion into a 9- by 14-inch rectangle. Spread dough with half the remaining glaze. Roll up jelly-roll fashion, beginning with the long edge; pinch seam to seal. With a serrated knife, gently cut roll into 9 slices, each about 1½ inches thick. Place slices, cut side down, in one of the prepared pans. Repeat with remaining dough and glaze.

LET rise, uncovered, until dough is not quite doubled, 40 to 60 minutes.

PREHEAT oven to 375°. Place a foil-covered baking sheet on a rack just beneath the sticky buns to catch any glaze that might drip. Bake until buns are puffed and golden and glaze is hot and bubbly, 40 to 50 minutes. Let cool in pan up to 5 minutes. Invert each pan onto a large, heatproof serving platter; wait a few seconds, then carefully lift off hot pans. Serve warm.

YIELDS 18 BUNS

TOASTED WALNUT *and* OLIVE YEAST BREAD

2 CUPS WALNUTS

2 CUPS WARM WATER
(110° to 115°)

½ CUP NONFAT DRY MILK

½ CUP EXTRA VIRGIN
OLIVE OIL

2 TABLESPOONS SUGAR

1 TABLESPOON CHOPPED
FRESH THYME, OR 1 TEASPOON
DRIED

2 TEASPOONS SALT

4½ TEASPOONS *(½ ounce)*
ACTIVE DRY YEAST

2 CUPS WHOLE-WHEAT FLOUR

3½ TO 4 CUPS ALL-PURPOSE
FLOUR

½ CUP GROUND WALNUTS

¾ CUP SLICED PITTED
KALAMATA OLIVES

Salty, tangy kalamata olives (sold in jars or in bulk in upscale supermarkets and delis) are a perfect match for the flavor of walnuts. This recipe makes two beautiful round loaves of country-style crusty bread—just the thing to serve with a big bowl of soup and a spinach salad made with red onions, tomatoes, and feta or goat cheese.

PREHEAT oven to 350°. Spread walnuts on a baking sheet or in a shallow pan. Bake, stirring once or twice, until lightly browned and fragrant, 10 to 12 minutes. Let cool slightly, then chop coarsely, if desired.

IN a large bowl, combine water, milk, olive oil, sugar, thyme, salt, and yeast. Stir to blend. Let stand until yeast is foamy, 5 to 10 minutes. Add whole-wheat flour and 1 cup of the all-purpose flour; beat until smooth. Beat in toasted walnuts, ground walnuts, and olives until well blended. Stir in enough of the remaining all-purpose flour, about 2½ cups, to make a manageable dough that holds together in a rough mass. Turn dough out onto a floured work surface and knead 2 minutes. Let dough rest 10 minutes.

RESUME kneading, adding more flour if dough is sticky, until dough is smooth and elastic. Place in an oiled bowl, cover with a towel, and let rise in a draft-free place until dough is doubled in bulk, about 1¼ hours.

PUNCH down risen dough. Turn onto a lightly floured work surface; divide into 2 equal portions. Stretch and pat each piece of dough to form a smooth, round loaf about 5 inches in diameter. Place loaves at least 3 inches apart on a large parchment-lined baking sheet. Cover loosely with a towel and let rise in a warm place until puffed but not quite doubled in bulk, about 45 minutes.

PREHEAT oven to 400°. With a sharp knife, slash a ½-inch-deep X on the top of each risen loaf; spray or brush loaves with cold water. Bake, brushing or spraying with water twice more during the first 20 minutes of baking, until the crusts are browned and firm, about 50 minutes total. Transfer to a wire rack to cool. Serve slightly warm or at room temperature.

YIELDS 2 LOAVES, EACH ABOUT
7 INCHES IN DIAMETER

NUTS, NOTES & BASIC RECIPES

All of the ingredients included in this book have been purchased at local stores, and all of the recipes have been tested in home kitchens. But if you are unable to find exact ingredients, feel free to experiment with other seasonably available produce, meat, or fish. Just as one nut can be substituted for another, so too can one protein, vegetable, or fruit. Some examples are kale or mustard greens for spinach or red snapper for sea bass.

BUTTER
The salt content in butter varies from brand to brand. Most recipes in this book call for unsalted butter, sometimes known as sweet butter. If you have only salted butter on hand, reduce the amount of salt called for in the recipe.

EGGS
All recipes were tested using Grade AA large eggs.

FLOUR
All recipes were tested using unbleached all-purpose flour.

HERBS
We recommend using fresh herbs. If they are not available, use dried herbs, but because their flavor is more concentrated, use about one-third the amount.

NUTS AND MEASURES
In all of the recipes in this book, we've given measures for nuts (for example, ½ cup) rather than weights. While some nuts are denser than others, and weights vary slightly, for home cooking, you can generally use this rule of thumb: 1 cup shelled nuts weighs about 4 ounces.

NUT BUTTER
Homemade nut butter tastes fresher and toastier than store-bought butters. One of our favorites is pine nut butter spread lightly on bruschetta and topped with a few sliced green olives. Try experimenting with your favorite nut or combination of nuts.

PREHEAT oven to 350°. Spread nuts on a baking sheet or in a shallow pan. Bake, stirring once or twice, until lightly browned, 5 to 12 minutes. Immediately add to bowl of food processor and whirl until completely ground. Scrape down the sides and continue processing until a smooth butter forms, 4 to 6 minutes (almonds sometimes need 1 to 2 tablespoons of additional oil to form a smooth paste). Season with salt or sugar. For a crunchy texture, stir in additional chopped toasted nuts.

NUT MILK

Nut milks, made from ground nuts and water, are a popular drink in many parts of the world and are often used as bases for sauces, soups, and desserts (think coconut milk).

IN a medium saucepan, combine 2 cups toasted sliced nuts and 4 cups water.

BRING to a boil and boil for 2 minutes. Remove from heat and let stand for 1 to 2 hours to develop the flavor. Pour into a blender and process until the nuts are finely chopped. Pour through a fine sieve.

OIL

Unless extra-virgin olive oil is specified, use a mild olive oil in recipes that call for olive oil. When a recipe calls for vegetable oil, we recommend using canola, safflower, or corn oil.

PEPPER

"Pepper" in these recipes refers to freshly ground black pepper.

SALT

When a recipe calls for coarse-grained salt, we recommend kosher salt.

TEMPERATURES

All oven temperatures are in degrees Fahrenheit.

WHIPPING CREAM

Whipping cream and unsweetened heavy cream are interchangeable in these recipes; we recommend avoiding ultrapasteurized cream if possible, which tastes less fresh and doesn't whip as well.

BASIC POULTRY STOCK

When a recipe calls for chicken or turkey stock, we recommend unsalted homemade stock, which is easily made using the following recipe. If you substitute store-bought broth, use the low-sodium variety, and taste before adding salt to a recipe that uses purchased broth.

3 POUNDS CHICKEN AND/OR TURKEY PARTS, INCLUDING BACKS, NECKS, WINGS, AND GIBLETS (NOT LIVERS)

1 LARGE ONION, UNPEELED, CUT IN HALF AND EACH HALF STUCK WITH 1 WHOLE CLOVE

3 STALKS CELERY WITH LEAVES, CUT IN HALF CROSSWISE

2 MEDIUM CARROTS, THICKLY SLICED

2 LARGE CLOVES GARLIC, UNPEELED, SMASHED WITH THE FLAT SIDE OF A KNIFE

8 SPRIGS FLAT-LEAF PARSLEY

2 SPRIGS THYME, OR ½ TEASPOON DRIED

½ TEASPOON WHOLE PEPPERCORNS

1 BAY LEAF

RINSE poultry parts under cold running water. Place them in a large stock pot and add cold water to cover by 1 inch. Bring to a boil over high heat, skimming off and discarding the foam as it rises to the top.

ADD remaining ingredients, reduce heat to medium-low, and simmer, partially covered, 2 hours.

STRAIN stock through a fine sieve and discard the solids. Let stock cool to room temperature, then refrigerate until well chilled, at least 6 hours or as long as 3 days. Remove the congealed fat from top of stock and discard. Use at once, or freeze in airtight containers.

YIELDS ABOUT 2½ QUARTS

BASIC VEGETABLE STOCK

4 TOMATOES, CUT IN HALF CROSSWISE

2 LARGE ONIONS, UNPEELED, CUT INTO QUARTERS

2 SMALL RED OR WHITE POTATOES, CUT IN HALF

2 CARROTS, CUT INTO 2-INCH PIECES

2 STALKS CELERY, CUT INTO 2-INCH PIECES

¼ POUND MUSHROOMS

8 CLOVES GARLIC, UNPEELED, SMASHED WITH THE FLAT SIDE OF A KNIFE

4 SPRIGS FLAT-LEAF PARSLEY

1 SPRIG THYME, OR ½ TEASPOON DRIED

½ TEASPOON WHOLE PEPPERCORNS

1 BAY LEAF

½ TEASPOON SALT

COMBINE all ingredients in a large stock pot and add cold water to cover by 1 inch. Bring to a boil over high heat, skimming off and discarding the foam as it rises to the top. Reduce heat to medium-low and simmer, uncovered, until liquid has reduced to about 6 cups, about 1 hour.

STRAIN stock through a fine sieve and discard the solids. Use at once, or cover and refrigerate up to 2 days. For longer storage, freeze in air-tight containers.

YIELDS ABOUT 1½ QUARTS

INSTRUCTIONS FOR FOLDING PUFF PASTRY FOR TART ON PAGE 128

1. Roll chilled dough into a 10-inch square, about ¼ inch thick. Fold dough in half diagonally to form a triangle. With a long sharp knife, cut a 1-inch strip along the two overlapping sides, stopping about 1 inch from the point of the triangle so the point remains uncut.

2. Open out the triangle to form a square again; brush lightly with beaten egg.

3. Lift one strip of dough and carefully pull across the square diagonally, aligning the edges. Press gently to seal.

4. Repeat with remaining strip, forming a square with raised sides and decorative loops at 2 opposite corners. Brush edges again with beaten egg. Prick base all over with the tines of a fork.

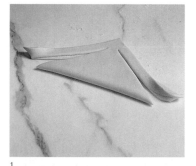

1

2

3

4

DIAMOND OF CALIFORNIA

At Diamond of California, we're proud to be the leading global marketer of culinary nuts. From our earliest days as a grower association in 1912 right through to the 21st century, our goal has always been to bring products to market—products processed and packed to give consumers convenient, flavorful, and nutritious options for home cooking, baking, and snacking.

In-the-shell nuts: Diamond pioneered the growing, processing, and harvesting techniques for nuts offered to consumers in the shell. Our logo stamped on the shell is a guarantee of our commitment to the highest standards of quality, integrity, and flavor.

Shelled nuts: From walnuts and almonds to hazelnuts, pecans, pine nuts, macadamias, and Brazil nuts, we offer an extensive line of slivered, sliced, chopped, and ground products, packaged in a variety of convenient sizes—all designed to make your life a little easier.

New products for new times: As we look ahead, we're constantly working to develop new products that bring value and variety to the consumer. Our Glazed Walnuts—outstanding as a salad ingredient, garnish and snack—are the latest in a long line of popular Diamond product innovations.

Diamond of California
1050 South Diamond St.
Stockton, California 95205
(209) 467-6000
www.diamondnuts.com

1912   A small group of walnut growers incorporate as California Walnut Growers Association in Los Angeles.

1926   Diamond begins branding individual walnuts with its logo.

1956   Operations centralized in Stockton, California

New identity: Diamond Walnut Growers, Inc.

1980   Cogeneration facility turns walnut shells into power for the Stockton plant and the community.

1989   Implements new laser sorting technology to ensure superior quality.

1997   Launches full line of culinary nuts in recipe-ready sizes.

1999   Global expansion continues as exports to more than 45 counties reach 40% of total sales.

New name: Diamond of California.

2000   Takes the lead as the world's #1 marketer of in-the-shell nuts.

21st Century   Diamond named exclusive nut supplier to 2000, 2002, and 2004 U.S. Olympic Teams and 2002 Olympic Winter Games.

Introduces Glazed Walnuts and Premium Walnut Halves.

Launches consumer website with information on health, recipes, and Diamond products.

INDEX

CONTRIBUTORS

BETTY FUSSELL, a native Californian who now resides in Manhattan, is a food historian with a doctorate in English Literature. She has lectured and written widely on the history of American foods, but is probably best known for *I Hear America Cooking* and *The Story of Corn*. Her most recent work, a memoir titled *My Kitchen Wars*, has been adapted for stage performance and has played in both Hollywood and New York.

GENE A. SPILLER, Ph.D., CNS, director of the Health Research and Studies Center and Sphera Foundation in Los Altos, California, is an acclaimed clinical researcher, writer, and editor in the fields of nutrition and disease prevention. He has studied the role of fats in the diet and their effect on blood cholesterol; the interaction of fiber and fats; the effect of whole, unrefined foods on health; and the importance of lesser-known nutrients, such as phenolic compounds and other antioxidants. As head of Nutritional Physiology at Syntex Research in Palo Alto, California, in the 1970s, he conducted pioneering human clinical nutrition studies on dietary fiber, which resulted in publications in several medical journals. In 1975, he edited the first U.S. book on fiber and nutrition. Since the 1980s, he has served as a consultant to the food, vitamin, and pharmaceuticals industries. In recent years, he has been principal investigator on several studies involving blood cholesterol, fiber, fats, phytochemicals, and nuts. He is the author of eight popular books on nutrition: *The Last Puff, The Superpyramid Eating Program, Nutrition Secrets of the Ancients, Eat Your Way to*

Better Health, The Cancer Survivor's Nutrition & Health Guide, Healthy Nuts, Calcium, and Diagnosis: Heart Disease.

GARY DANKO is widely recognized as one of America's most talented and respected chefs. He combines classical training with focuses on French, Mediterranean and regional American cooking, adding seasonings and techniques from Southeast Asia and India. Raised in upstate New York, Danko trained at the Culinary Institute of America and later with renowned author and cooking teacher Madeleine Kamman, who became a major influence in the development of his personal cooking style. He first attracted national acclaim as executive chef at Chateau Souverain in California's Sonoma County, and four years later was opening chef of The Dining Room at the Ritz-Carlton, San Francisco, which rapidly rose to prominence as one of the country's finest restaurants. In 1995, he won the James Beard Award for Best Chef: California. The following year, Danko left the Ritz-Carlton to launch Viognier in San Mateo, California, which *Esquire* named Best New Restaurant. In 1999, Danko and former Ritz-Carlton colleague and maître d', Nick Peyton, launched a new operation, Gary Danko, in San Francisco, which has quickly established itself as one of the country's most exciting restaurants. It won the James Beard Foundation's Best New Restaurant Award for 2000.

TODD ENGLISH began cooking at age 15 and graduated from the Culinary Institute of America in 1982. After a stint at New York's La Côte Basque, he apprenticed at two restaurants in Italy, where he developed a unique approach to cooking that draws on his Italian heritage. At age 25, he opened Michela's in Cambridge, Massachusetts. He is currently chef-owner of Olives in Charlestown, Massachusetts, as well as other Olives locations in New York, Las Vegas, Washington, D.C., and Aspen. He has also opened Miramar in Westport, Connecticut, and Greg Norman's Australian Grille in Myrtle Beach, South Carolina, with golf great Greg Norman. His four Figs restaurants in the greater Boston area and a newly opened LaGuardia location specialize in pizzas and handmade pastas. English opened KingFish Hall, a seafood restaurant in Boston's Faneuil Hall, and Bonfire in that city's Park Plaza Hotel. He was named National Rising Star Chef in 1991 and Best Chef: Northeast in 1994 by the James Beard Foundation. His television credits include a public television series, "Cooking In with Todd English," as well as numerous national appearances. He is the author of the critically acclaimed cookbooks *The Olives Table, The Figs Table,* and *The Olives Dessert Table.*

MARK FRANZ is executive chef and co-owner of San Francisco's Farallon restaurant, where he creates a constantly evolving, sophisticated, ingredient-driven coastal cuisine menu. A Bay Area native, Franz spent more than a decade as executive chef at Jeremiah Tower's Stars and was a shaping force in Tower's restaurants. Before working at Stars, the California Culinary Academy graduate worked with Tower at Balboa Café in San Francisco and Santa Fe Bar and Grill in Berkeley. Farallon was nominated by the James Beard Foundation as one of the best restaurants in the United States and has been named one of the best newcomers in the country by such publications as *Esquire, Bon Appétit,* and *Food & Wine.*

JOYCE GOLDSTEIN is a consultant to the restaurant and food industries, specializing in menu design, recipe development, staff training, and kitchen planning. For 12 years, she was chef-owner of the groundbreaking Mediterranean restaurant, Square One, in San Francisco, which presented the foods of Italy, Spain, France, Greece, Turkey, the Middle East, and North Africa. She was named Best Chef: California by the James Beard Foundation in 1993. Before opening Square One, she was chef of the Café at Chez Panisse in Berkeley for three years. She taught cooking for 18 years and founded San Francisco's first international cooking school, the California Street Cooking School. She has served as visiting executive chef of the Wine Spectator Restaurant at the Culinary Institute of America at Greystone in the Napa Valley, where she continues to teach. A prolific writer, she

has authored 16 cookbooks, including *The Mediterranean Kitchen* and *Back to Square One: Old World Food in a New World Kitchen,* winner of both the Julia Child and James Beard awards for Best General Cookbook of 1992. Her writing has appeared in *Gourmet, Restaurant Hospitality, Wine & Spirits, Food & Wine,* and the *San Francisco Chronicle.*

BETH HENSPERGER, an acknowledged Jersey girl transplanted to California in her teens, is a passionate professional and home baker. Her style is a cross-cultural approach to adapting old-fashioned traditional and professional recipes for today's bakers—a bridge between the simple and more complicated levels of technique, yet creative and innovative. Her writing and recipes have been published in more than a dozen of America's most prominent food and lifestyle magazines. Hensperger learned the basic skills of baking by working as a restaurant and hotel pastry chef for 10 years, having her own custom wedding cake business, and attending classes given by some of the top bakers in America. She is the best-selling author of 12 cookbooks on the art of baking, the most recent of which are *Bread for Breakfast* and *The Bread Lover's Bread Machine Cookbook. The Bread Bible* was the recipient of the James Beard Foundation Award for Baking in 2000. Hensperger writes a monthly food column called *Baking by the Seasons* for the *San Jose Mercury News* and does private catering in Silicon Valley.

GERALD HIRIGOYEN was born in the Basque region of France and, by the age of 13, had already begun to practice the art of pastry making in his hometown, Biarritz. Three years later, he moved to Paris to apprentice under master pâtissiers Jean Millet and Dennis Ruffel. In 1980, he moved to San Francisco, where he worked at Le Castel and Lafayette and was executive chef at Le St. Tropez. In 1991, he opened Fringale, a San Francisco bistro that soon garnered national acclaim. The menu features straightforward, bright flavors inspired by Hirigoyen's Basque background. In 1996, he opened a second San Francisco restaurant, Pastis, serving what he calls "West Coast Basque" fare. He is the author of two cookbooks, *Bistro* and *The Basque Kitchen,* which topped the Bay Area cookbook best-seller list and won the Versailles Award for best regional cookbook.

KIMBALL JONES joined Wente Vineyards in Northern California's Livermore Valley as executive chef in 1989. In this capacity, he has overseen the Vineyard's restaurant kitchen, catering operations, wine-maker dinners, and special events. He has enhanced the perception of American food through Wente-sponsored American Food and Wine Festivals throughout the world. By combining California style with ingredients available in each location, he leaves a California heritage with the resident chefs he works with at the festivals. A graduate of the California Culinary Academy, Kimball spent 2½ years as sous chef to Bradley Ogden at San Francisco's Campton Place Hotel.

It was there that he developed his passion for simple dishes made extraordinary with the use of local and seasonal ingredients. He also served as executive chef for Paula LeDuc Catering, a premier Bay Area catering company. He is the co-author of a cookbook, *Sharing the Vineyard Table: A Celebration of Wine and Food from the Wente Vineyards Restaurant*.

MOLLIE KATZEN, writer, illustrator, and chef, enjoys a coveted position on the *New York Times* list of the 10 best-selling cookbook authors of all time, having sold close to 4 million books. A charter member of the Harvard School of Public Health Nutrition Roundtable and selected by *Health* magazine as one of the "Five Women Who Changed the Way We Eat," she is widely credited with helping move healthful cooking from the fringes of American society squarely onto mainstream dinner tables. Her classic *Moosewood Cookbook* has been enthusiastically embraced by several generations. *The Enchanted Broccoli Forest* and *Still Life with Menu* have also become perennial best-sellers, as has *Mollie Katzen's Vegetable Heaven*, chosen by the International Cookbook Revue as the best vegetarian cookbook published worldwide in 1997. Katzen also illustrated and co-authored two best-selling children's cookbooks, *Pretend Soup* and *Honest Pretzels*, and is currently at work on a book about breakfast, *Mollie Katzen's Sunlight Café*. All of her books are vibrantly illustrated with her original artwork in the form of pen-and-ink drawings, watercolor paintings, and luminous pastel compositions. Since its debut in 1995, the acclaimed "Mollie Katzen's Cooking Show" has ranked as one of the top public television cooking shows nationwide.

HUBERT KELLER was born in France and trained at the École Hôtelière in Strasbourg. He apprenticed at the Auberge de L'Ill in Illhaeusern and went on to train with Paul Bocuse near Lyons and later with Gaston Lenôtre in Paris. But it was his meeting with the grand master of French haute cuisine, Roger Vergé at the Moulin de Mougins, that would be the decisive turning point in his career. Vergé appointed Keller chef saucier and later recruited him to run his restaurant, La Cuisine du Soleil in São Paulo, Brazil. After two years, he moved to San Francisco to manage the kitchen of Sutter 500, also under the aegis of Vergé. In 1986, he became co-owner of Fleur de Lys in San Francisco, where, faithful to the example of his mentor, he offers traditional French cooking with a Mediterranean accent. He has been named one of the 10 Best Chefs in America by *Food & Wine* and Best Chef: California by the James Beard Foundation. He is the author of *The Cuisine of Hubert Keller*.

HEIDI INSALATA KRAHLING was executive chef at Smith Ranch Homes in San Rafael, California, and Butler's in Mill Valley before opening her own restaurant, Insalata's, in San Anselmo in 1996. After receiving formal training in professional cooking and pastry under Mary Risley at San Francisco's respected Tante Marie's Cooking School, she worked at Taste Catering and served as head line cook at Square One in San Francisco. She was named the Bay Area's Rising Star Chef in 1988 by *San Francisco Focus*, and one of *USA Today*'s best women chefs in the same year. Today, Insalata's is on critics' lists as one of the Bay Area's top restaurants. Krahling teaches at

several Bay Area cooking schools and plays an active role in the organization of many special events for community and charitable organizations. At home and at the restaurant, she sums up her philosophy of cooking as follows: "Food lovingly prepared, savored, and enjoyed in the company of family and good friends can make the simplest of meals a memorable feast."

EMILY LUCHETTI is executive pastry chef at Farallon in San Francisco, where she joins forces with her friend and colleague of more than a decade, Mark Franz. Luchetti believes that desserts should taste wonderful and be emotionally fulfilling yet straightforwardly satisfying, requiring no deciphering of complex presentations. She is a sociology graduate of Denison University in Granville, Ohio, and the New York Restaurant School. In addition to working with Franz at Stars, where she spent 11 years, 7 of them as pastry chef, Luchetti opened and ran StarBake, a wholesale and retail bakery. She is the author of two books, *Stars Desserts* and *Four Star Desserts*, which was nominated as one of the best dessert cookbooks of 1996 by the James Beard Foundation. The foundation also twice nominated her as one of the best pastry chefs in the country.

NICK MALGIERI is the author of five cookbooks, including *How to Bake, Chocolate,* and, most recently, *Cookies Unlimited.* The recipient of a James Beard Foundation cookbook award, Malgieri is one of America's premier authorities on baking. He was named one of the 10 best pastry chefs in the United States by *Chocolatier* and *Pastry Art and Design.* Malgieri directs the baking program at Peter Kump's Cooking School in New York, and his recipes and articles have been published in numerous periodicals, including the *New York Times* and *Gourmet.*

PATRICK O'CONNELL began his culinary career at age 15, working in a neighborhood restaurant after school. In the late 1970s, the self-taught chef bought a farm in the rural Shenandoah Valley, about 70 miles west of Washington, D.C., and began a catering business with partner Reinhardt Lynch, which evolved into the luxurious country inn and destination restaurant, the Inn at Little Washington. The Inn was the first to receive two Five Star Awards from the *Mobil Travel Guide*—for both its restaurant and its accommodations—as well as two AAA Five Diamond Awards. The James Beard Foundation named O'Connell Best Chef: Mid-Atlantic Region and awarded the Inn Best Restaurant of the Year in 1993, Best Service in 1997, and Best Wine List in 1998. O'Connell is the author of the best-selling cookbook, *The Inn at Little Washington: A Consuming Passion.*

BRADLEY OGDEN is chef and co-owner of five San Francisco area restaurants, including the renowned Lark Creek Inn in Larkspur and One Market in San Francisco. A native of Michigan, he graduated from the Culinary Institute of America in 1977, and went on to achieve international acclaim for his distinctively contemporary interpretations of traditional American food. He was named Best Chef: California by the James Beard Foundation. His cookbook, *Breakfast, Lunch & Dinner,* won the prestigious International Association of Culinary Professionals (IACP) Award.

ROLAND PASSOT began his culinary career at age 15 in France's gastronomic capital, Lyons, where he worked under such renowned chefs as Paul Lacombe and Pierre Orsi. At 20, he came to Chicago to work under Jean Banchet at Le Français, and four years later moved to San Francisco to work at Le Castel. In 1981, Banchet appointed him opening chef of the French Room in Dallas, where he rose to national prominence. Returning to San Francisco, he was chef at Chez Michel and, in 1988, opened La Folie, an intimate restaurant whose small size has allowed him to develop his signature cuisine based on classical French technique married with innovative flavor combinations and fresh local ingredients. He received the Rising Star Chef Award from the James Beard Foundation in 1990. In 1994, he opened a two-hundred-seat brasserie, Left Bank, in the Marin County town of Larkspur, featuring his version of French home-style cooking. Four years later, a Silicon Valley outpost of Left Bank followed in Menlo Park.

JACQUES PÉPIN, celebrated host of award-winning cooking shows on national public television, master chef, food columnist, cooking teacher, and author of 19 cookbooks, was born in Bourg-en-Bresse, near Lyons. His first exposure to cooking was at his family's restaurant, Le Pelican. At age 13, he began his apprenticeship at the Grand Hotel de l'Europe in his hometown. He subsequently worked in Paris under Lucien Diat at the Plaza Athenée. From 1956 to 1958, he was the personal chef to three French heads of state, including Charles de Gaulle. Moving to the United States in 1959, he worked at New York's Le Pavillon, then served for 10 years as director of research and new development for the Howard Johnson Company, while concurrently earning an M.A. in French literature from Columbia University. His recent ventures include a new public television series and a companion book, *Jacques Pépin Celebrates.* He is also featured, along with Julia Child, in the public television series, "Julia and Jacques Cooking at Home". He serves as dean of special programs at the French Culinary Institute in New York City and teaches at Boston University.

CHARLIE TROTTER started cooking professionally in 1982, after graduating with a degree in political science from the University of Wisconsin. At that time, he embarked on an intense four-year period of work, study, and travel, including stints with Norman Van Aken, Bradley Ogden, and Gordon Sinclair. He lived in Chicago, San Francisco, Florida, and Europe, "reading every cookbook I could get my hands on, working like a maniac, and eating out incessantly." In 1987, he opened Charlie Trotter's in Chicago, now recognized as one of the world's finest restaurants. Trotter's cuisine originates from the finest foodstuffs available. A network of more than 90 purveyors provides the fresh, healthful ingredients that inspire him to create flavorful masterpieces. The restaurant has been honored by a variety of prestigious national and international institutions, including Relais & Chateaux (Relais Gourmand), Mobil Travel Guide: Five Stars, AAA (Five Diamonds), and the James Beard Foundation. Trotter is also the author of several cookbooks, including *Charlie Trotter's, Charlie Trotter's Vegetables, Charlie Trotter's Seafood, Charlie Trotter's Desserts, The Kitchen Sessions with Charlie Trotter* (the companion book to his cooking show of the same name), and *Charlie Trotter Cooks at Home.*

NORMAN VAN AKEN is owner of the award-winning restaurant Norman's, in the historic Coral Gables section of Miami. He is the recipient of a James Beard Award, a Robert Mondavi Award, and a *Food Arts* "Silver Spoon." Recognized as the "father of New World Cuisine," he describes his culinary approach as "creating a marriage of the sensual and rustic with the classic and intellectual in a celebration of the various places we live." He is the author of three cookbooks, including *Norman's New World Cuisine,* nominated for Julia Child and IACP awards. A prominent figure in print and broadcast media, he has cooked, consulted, written, and lectured on New World Cuisine internationally.

JOANNE WEIR is a San Francisco–based, award-winning cookbook author, cooking teacher, chef, and television personality. She is host of the public television series "Weir Cooking in the Wine Country." She was awarded the inaugural IACP Cooking Teacher Award of Excellence. Her cookbooks include two companion volumes to her television series, as well as *You Say Tomato* and *From Tapas to Meze,* both of which were nominated for James Beard Cookbook Awards. Her four-part series, *Seasonal Celebrations: From Tapas to Meze,* was also selected by Julia Child as one of her 12 favorite cookbooks published in 1994. Weir's professional experience includes five years of cooking at Chez Panisse in Berkeley, California. She trained under Madeleine Kamman in New England and France and was awarded a Master Chef diploma. She spends seven to eight months each year teaching throughout the United States, Canada, Australia, New Zealand, Italy, and France.

MARTIN YAN, celebrated host of more than fifteen hundred cooking programs, respected food and restaurant consultant, and certified Master Chef, enjoys distinction as both a teacher and an author. His many talents and warmhearted good humor have found expression in 24 cookbooks, including his definitive *Martin Yan's Feast: The Best of Yan Can Cook* and his recent *Martin Yan's Invitation to Chinese Cooking* and *Chinese Cooking for Dummies.* Born in Guangzhou, China, Yan's formal introduction to cooking began at age 13, when he apprenticed in a renowned Hong Kong restaurant. Having earned his diploma from the Overseas Institute of Cookery in Hong Kong, he traveled to Canada and then to the United States. After receiving an M.S. in food science from the University of California, Davis, he began hosting the popular public television show, *Yan Can Cook.* The founder of the Yan Can International Cooking School in the San Francisco Bay Area, Yan is a frequent guest chef-instructor at many professional culinary schools, including the California Culinary Academy, Johnson & Wales University, and the University of San Francisco. He is the recipient of numerous awards, including a 1998 Daytime Emmy and the Best TV Food Journalism Award from the James Beard Foundation.

ACKNOWLEDGMENTS

(TINA SALTER)

Gathering and developing the recipes in this book, I felt a bit like a very fortunate squirrel, with the delightful task of foraging and storing away all kinds of wonderful nutty treasures. Along the way, dozens of people helped with the harvest—both through their creative and artistic contributions and with the moral support they offered so generously during the many months of its making.

Special thanks to Sandra McBride and Michael Mendes at Diamond of California, whose vision set us on the path to create a book with a contemporary mix of recipes that demonstrate the versatility of cooking with nuts. Many thanks also to Diamond's Donna Samelson, whose boundless knowledge and enthusiastic good humor made the project a pleasure.

My heartfelt thanks go also to the chefs who very generously shared their recipes; Steve Siegelman, whose words and wit so deftly convey the history and heart of Diamond of California; Peggy Fallon, who developed and tested recipes, writing them up with characteristic clarity and concision; Ingrid Ulrich, John Carroll, Rhiannon and Ian Salter, Kate Zilavy, and Sharon Doyle, who assisted with further testing; Margaret McKinnon, whose eagle eye kept us on track as she tirelessly checked and rechecked the facts and edited for accuracy, brevity, and clarity; Madeleine Corson, whose artful eye transformed the beauty of the walnut groves into the design of this book; studio photographer Holly Stewart, food stylist Sandra Cook, and prop stylist Sara Slavin, whose enthusiasm and unfailing sense of style and simple elegance produced the exquisite food photographs; location photographer Bob Holmes, who traveled the walnut-growing regions of California to capture on film the beauty of the groves throughout the seasons; Alex Suchan, the Abbey of New Clairvaux, and everyone at Ralph Panella Enterprises, who opened their gates and allowed us into their orchards; Aaron Wehner of Ten Speed Press, whose guidance in the final stages of this project brought it all together; and Rebecca Pepper, for a final round of skillful editing.

Finally, there would no book at all without the hardworking growers who make up Diamond of California, bringing the best of the crop to market each year. This is their book—the happy fruit of their harvest.